THE HERO'S JOURNEY
TOWARD A
SECOND AMERICAN CENTURY

THE HERO'S JOURNEY TOWARD A SECOND AMERICAN CENTURY

MICHAEL E. SALLA

PRAEGER

Westport, Connecticut
London

Library of Congress Cataloging-in-Publication Data

Salla, Michael E.
    The hero's journey toward a second American century / Michael E. Salla.
        p.   cm.
    Includes bibliographical references (p.   ) and index.
    ISBN 0–275–97373–5 (alk. paper)
    1. United States—Foreign relations—Philosophy.   2. United States—Foreign
relations—21st century—Forecasting.   3. National characteristics, American.   4.
Courage—Political aspects—United States—History.   5. Myth—Political aspects—United
States—History.   6. Courage—Political aspects—United States.   7. Myth—Political
aspects—United States.   8. United States—Moral conditions.   I. Title.
E183.7.S25   2002
327.73—dc21   2001021647

British Library Cataloguing in Publication Data is available.

Library of Congress Catalog Card Number: 2001021647
ISBN: 0–275–97373–5

First published in 2002

Praeger Publishers, 88 Post Road West, Westport, CT 06881
An imprint of Greenwood Publishing Group, Inc.
www.praeger.com

Printed in the United States of America

The paper used in this book complies with the
Permanent Paper Standard issued by the National
Information Standards Organization (Z39.48–1984).

10 9 8 7 6 5 4 3 2 1

CONTENTS

List of Figures and Tables   ix

Acknowledgments   xi

Introduction   1

1 The Hero's Journey   9

   The Hero's Journey   9
   Jung's Theory of Archetypes   11
   Step 1 in the Hero's Journey—Call to Adventure   23
   Step 2 in the Hero's Journey—Great Remembering   24
   Step 3 in the Hero's Journey—The Return to Society 26
   Step 4 in the Hero's Journey—The Deep Forgetting   27

2 The Hero's Journey in World Politics   35

   Political Communities and the Hero's Journey   35
   States as Moral Actors   38
   States and the Hero's Journey   45

3   America's First Hero's Journey (1764–1822)—America as
    Beacon of Liberty and Republicanism   57

    America and the Hero's Journey   57
    America's First Hero's Journey (1764–1822)   61

4   America's Second Hero's Journey (1823–1855)—Rule of
    Law and Manifest Destiny   79

    *Call to Adventure (1823–1831)—Promoting International
        Law*   79
    *Great Remembering (1831–1837)—The Issues of
        Relocation of Native Americans, Slavery, and Texas*   82
    *The Return to International Society (1837–1845)—Manifest
        Destiny*   86
    Deep Forgetting (1846–1855)—American Imperialism   89

5   America's Third Hero's Journey (1855–1891)—Civil War
    and the Monroe Doctrine   97

    *Call to Adventure (1855–1861)—Ending Slavery as a Moral
        Imperative*   97
    *Great Remembering (1861–1867)—Fighting to Preserve the
        Union and Emancipation*   99
    *The Return to International Society (1867–1875)—
        Reasserting the Monroe Doctrine*   104
    *Deep Forgetting (1875–1889)—Ignoring the Plight of
        Indians and Emancipated Slaves*   107

6   America's Fourth Hero's Journey (1889–1912)—America's
    Rise to Great Power Status   113

    *Call to Adventure (1889–1895)—Reasserting the Monroe
        Doctrine*   113
    *Great Remembering (1895–1898)—Supporting Cuban
        Independence*   115
    *The Return to International Society (1898–1903)—
        Commitment to Self-Determination*   118
    Deep Forgetting (1903–1912)—Imperial America   121

7   America's Fifth Hero's Journey (1913–1933)—Making the
    World Safe for Democracy   129

    *Call to Adventure (1913–1914)—Supporting Democracy in
        the Western Hemisphere*   129
    *Great Remembering (1914–1917)—Supporting European
        Democracies*   132

The Return to International Society (1917–1919)—Fighting for Self-Determination, Democracy, and a New World Order   134

Deep Forgetting (1919–1933)—Isolationism Triumphant   137

8   America's Sixth Hero's Journey (1933–1974)—The Democratic Struggle against Fascism and Communism   143

Call to Adventure (1933–1939)—Opposing International Aggression and Supporting Self-Determination   143

Great Remembering (1939–1941)—From Neutrality to Nonbelligerency   147

The Return to International Society (1941–1956)—World War II and the Cold War   149

Deep Forgetting (1956–1974)—Ignoring Self-Determination in the Crusade against Communism   153

9   America's Seventh Hero's Journey (1974–   )—Human Rights, Humanitarian Intervention, and a New World Order   163

Call to Adventure (1974–1981)—Human Rights Diplomacy   163

Great Remembering (1981–1993)—Human Rights and New World Order   166

The Return to International Society (1993–   )— Humanitarian Intervention and New World Order   170

America's Seventh Hero's Journey   175

10 Renewing America's Seventh Hero's Journey for the Second American Century   179

Domestic Policy Imperatives   180

Foreign Policy Imperatives   191

Conclusion—America's Seventh Hero's Journey and the Second American Century   203

Selected Bibliography   211

Index   219

List of Figures and Tables

FIGURES

1.1	Jungian Archetypes of the Unconscious	13
1.2	The Hero's Journey	30

TABLES

3.1	America's First Hero's Journey—Establishing the American Republic as a Beacon of Liberty and Democracy (1764–1822)	76
4.1	America's Second Hero's Journey—Rule of Law and Manifest Destiny (1823–1855)	93
5.1	America's Third Hero's Journey—Civil War and the Monroe Doctrine (1855–1891)	110
6.1	America's Fourth Hero's Journey—America's Rise to Great Power Status (1889–1913)	126
7.1	America's Fifth Hero's Journey—Making the World Safe for Democracy (1913–1933)	141

8.1   America's Sixth Hero's Journey—The Democratic Struggle
      against Fascism and Communism (1933–1974)   160

9.1   America's Seventh Hero's Journey—Human Rights,
      Humanitarian Intervention, and a New World Order
      (1974–   )   176

10.1 Grand Syntheses of Power and Morality in American
      History   181

ACKNOWLEDGMENTS

I first wish to thank Dr. James Sabin and Greenwood Press for their encouragement and assistance in publishing this book. I also thank Eileen Cope from Lowenstein Associates Literary Agency who gave me much encouragement in seeking publication of the ideas expressed in this book. My thanks also go to Elizabeth Dahl and Kelly Andrews who helped me with the stylistic editing and proofreading of this manuscript. In particular Kelly made many helpful suggestions in clarifying some of the more complex points and ideas. I also thank Jillian Frumkin for agreeing to do the indispensable task of indexing this book. I am grateful to David Palmer and the production team at Greenwood Publishing for their numerous suggestions and assistance in getting this book into a presentable format. I thank the School of International Service, American University for its support in providing a teaching and research environment in which I could pursue this project. Finally, my heartfelt gratitude goes to Barbara Saver and the Millennium Group for the inspiration and support they gave me during the writing of this book. I dedicate this book to Sri Chinmoy and the supreme love and wisdom he so wonderfully expresses.

INTRODUCTION

Two powerful processes with global significance coincide at the dawn of the twenty-first century. The first is the continuing role of the United States of America as the preeminent nation in influencing how humans can best organize themselves politically, economically, and culturally on the planet. Just as many have described the twentieth century as the "American century," so too the twenty-first century can be predicted to be the "second American century." Never in human history has a nation occupied the position America now has of influencing all humanity in terms of the core principles at the heart of its own national identity. How Americans identify themselves as a people and nation therefore has global implications. This leads to the second process of global significance, which is America's "seventh hero's journey."

The hero's journey is a process of (re)discovery of the principles that make up national identity. For the seventh time in its history, America has discovered a grand synthesis of power and morality in projecting its resources and principles into the global arena. This makes possible a more assertive and moral foreign policy course in responding to a range of foreign policy challenges. Of these challenges, the most profound in terms of the scale of human suffering around the planet is that concerning violations of the rights of ethnic minorities. According to Ted Robert Gurr from the University of Maryland, in 1998 there were 275 ethnic minorities in 116 countries that were at risk from central governments that resisted the former's efforts to have their rights recognized.[1] Ethnic conflicts, and the humanitarian crises and massive human rights violations they generate, form a foreign policy challenge that will preoccupy the minds of America's best policymakers for much of the twenty-first century. NATO's intervention in the Kosovo crisis is the high watermark for America's "seventh hero's journey." The intervention sends a decisive signal to all governments that America and its allies will no longer remain inactive in the face of the states attempting to militarily repress the aspirations of its ethnic minorities. This high watermark can be extended well into the next century if policymakers wisely combine the moral principles and foreign policy challenges that make up both the "second American century" and America's "seventh hero's journey."

The hero's journey was described by the mythologist Joseph Campbell in his groundbreaking book, *The Hero with a Thousand Faces*. He argued that the hero's journey was a "monomyth" that could be found in all societies. The hero would go through different stages of a journey of self-empowerment and self-discovery that would change forever both the hero and the society in which he or she lived. Campbell's ideas were so influential that George Lucas used them in writing the script for the original *Star Wars* trilogy. The success of *Star Wars* supports Campbell's belief that the hero's journey resonates deep within the collective unconscious of all societies.

The first stage of the hero's journey, the "call to adventure," begins with the hero feeling discontent with the dominant values of his society. The hero then sets out to find a new set of values by which to live. In the process, the hero detaches himself from the practices and beliefs of his former life. In the second stage, the hero undergoes an arduous series of challenges to prove his self-worth. This is the heart of the hero's journey, because it is here that the hero discovers himself. Two challenges are central in this stage: to overcome a fragmented sense of self that breeds self-doubt, and to discover one's life mission. The sense of déjà vu that is often experienced here makes this more of a recovery of something lost than a discovery of something completely new. This stage of the hero's journey therefore can be described as the "great remembering."

In the third stage, the "return to society," the hero returns to his society with the charismatic energy and moral vision to reform it. The hero becomes a great moral teacher, enlightened political leader, or visionary prophet. The critical component in the return to society is that the hero has achieved a synthesis of moral vision and worldly power that forever alters the society in which he or she lives. King Solomon of ancient Israel, the Persian Emperor Cyrus, the Buddhist King Asoka, the Prophet Muhammad, and even Napoleon early in his career are examples of heroes who achieved such a synthesis.

According to Campbell, the hero's journey is a linear process that ends with the hero's return to society. He overlooked, however, a fourth stage that turns this linear journey into a moral cycle. The "deep forgetting" is when the hero's synthesis of moral vision and worldly power collapses. Due to a range of factors—fear, pursuit of power, or materialism—the hero forgets the lessons learned in his or her great remembering. It is here that the great moral teacher becomes a self-righteous bigot, the enlightened political leader a self-serving tyrant, and the visionary prophet a religious fundamentalist. This sets in place the need for a new hero's journey, making the journey a cycle that can be repeated any number of times.

The hero's journey does not apply exclusively to individuals. It can be applied to states as well. States are the institutional representations of a complex web of relationships between individuals, social groups, and political institutions that combine to infuse moral principles into the foreign policy making process. This web of relationships makes states moral actors that can undertake the hero's journey.

The single most important factor for explaining how states transit from one stage of the hero's journey to the next is the dominant national mood at any one time. Like the tides of the ocean that shift in accord to the magnetic pull of the moon, so too do national moods shift. What accounts for these shifts is still not clear. In *The Cycles of American History*, Arthur Schlesinger Jr., argues that these cyclic shifts are due to generational changes. Others cite economic cycles, a combination of international and domestic factors that bring new policymakers to power, or even the astrological influence of the planets and stars. Despite the controversy over the origin of these mood shifts and their relatively small size quantitatively speaking, their significance may be huge in qualitative terms. In a liberal democracy, for example, a mere shift of 5 percent of a nation's population in any election may result in a landslide for a new government. New policymakers come into power believing that they have the mandate to radically change the course of domestic and foreign policy. States then move forward in their hero's journey.

The first stage of the hero's journey for states, the "call to adventure," means that the national mood shifts into discontentment with the dominant foreign policy principles and practices in place at the time. Political leaders set out to define or establish a new moral vision for the nation. This will involve some degree of withdrawal from the way world politics is practiced. Here the national mood reflects an implicit belief in the moral, economic, or political superiority of one's state, but no consensus exists on how to translate this into an effective foreign policy program that can decisively influence world politics. Nevertheless, the state has begun its hero's journey.

A further shift in the national mood leads to the next stage of the hero's journey, the "great remembering." For states, this has two components. The first is to unify all the heterogeneous elements of the state so that it becomes an economically productive and unified political actor. Domestic policies are crafted that aim at economic renewal and reconciling past divisions in society. In short, unity becomes the buzzword for national renewal. The second component is to define the national mission through a new moral vision. Typically, the moral vision of a state's Founding Fathers is the key to unlocking the secret of the nation's mission. An attempt is made to reinterpret the significance of the Founding Fathers' moral vision for the present set of social and historic conditions in which the state finds itself.

Another shift in the national mood leads to the "return to international society." The state as a unified actor with a clear moral vision sets out to influence the dominant practices and value systems in the international system. The state devotes its energies and national resources to this task. As for the individual hero, so too for the state, the key to this stage of the journey is the synthesis of moral vision and real world power possessed by the state. This grand synthesis of morality and power can be achieved by maintaining and renewing the national unity and moral vision at the heart of the great remembering.

Once more the national mood shifts, this time leading to the breakdown of the grand synthesis. The "return to international society" is over, and the final stage of the hero's journey—the "deep forgetting"—has begun. A range of factors can account for this shift in national mood. Public opinion discerns that the state is really using morality as a cloak for merely aggrandizing itself. A significant set of foreign policy failures may lead to the public questioning the effort to reform world politics. Alternatively, the national economy may strain under the expense of committing resources to foreign policy goals. The state then channels its energies into the domestic arena. The hero's journey is at an end. In time, the need for a new hero's journey begins to be felt. In this way, states can undergo a number of hero's journeys. Rather than these journeys being an endless set of historical cycles that repeat the same principles and responses to domestic and international problems, they represent a gradual upward spiral towards a more profound realization of a state's highest national ideals and global mission. The historian's task then becomes twofold. First, the historian needs to discern the shifts in national mood and state policy that demarcate the different stages of the hero's journey. Second, the historian should be able to discover the gradual historical movement towards a more profound realization of a state's ideals and mission.

The first chapter of this book examines Joseph Campbell's idea of the hero's journey as an individual process of self-discovery. Using Carl Jung's theory of archetypes of the collective unconscious, the chapter focuses on three archetypal encounters that are most important for the hero's journey: "slaying the dragon," the "sacred marriage," and "atonement." It is these archetypal encounters that make possible the discovery of a new set of moral principles that becomes the basis of the hero's new self-identity and the hero's activities in the wider society.

The second chapter explores the relevance of the hero's journey for states. The idea that states are moral actors capable of undertaking the hero's journey must deal with the objection that states are amoral. If the objection were true, then this would make states entirely unsuitable for a hero's journey, which only autonomous moral actors can undertake. Leading critics from two schools of thought, realism and liberalism, that view states as amoral actors are examined. Using insights on the character of states developed by the nineteenth-century German theorist Georg Hegel, I evaluate these criticisms and conclude that states are moral actors capable of undergoing a hero's journey.

The choice of which state to examine in terms of undertaking a hero's journey is made easy by America's leading role in influencing ideas, events, and processes around the globe for generations to come. How Americans define themselves as a people and nation will exercise enormous influence on how other political communities do likewise. A further advantage in choosing America is the relatively easy task of finding a precise historical beginning for how it began to define itself as a political community. Consequently, the third chapter examines America's first hero's journey, which begins with events leading up to the Revolutionary War of Independence (1776–1781) and ends with America's refusal to recognize the independence of Latin American Republics from 1814 to 1822. America's Founding Fathers firmly believed that the successful establishment of America as a Republic was an act of Providence. Providence had lent a hand to the beginning of a great experiment for which liberty, democracy, and rule of law would be the guiding principles of a new society on the North American continent. Ensuring the success of America as a republic and democracy would be no easy task. Never before in history had this form of government been attempted on such a vast scale. Moreover, monarchical forms of government were the norm in Europe, and republicanism was widely seen as an unstable and dangerous experiment that had repeatedly failed in the past. America's hero journey would be to make successful a form of government that ran against the trends of history and denied conventional thinking at the time. During the Napoleonic era, America had successive armed confrontations with France and Britain when both threatened American trade and lives on the high seas. This became the basis of America's first grand synthesis when American power was projected to support the liberty of its sailors and the right of free trade by neutral states.

The fourth chapter examines America's second journey. The second journey began with recognition of the Latin American Republics in 1822 and ended with the war against Mexico. The high watermark of this journey was America's second grand synthesis, where it championed the right of self-determination by settlers in Texas and Oregon to choose the country to which they wished to belong. The low watermark was President Polk's imperialist war against a weak and divided Mexico in order to expand

American territory irrespective of the wishes of the population in California and New Mexico.

America's third hero's journey is discussed in the fifth chapter. This journey began with events in 1855 that lead into the Civil War (1861–1865) and ends in 1889 with America ignoring the plight of Native Americans and the emancipated slaves. The apex of this journey was America's third grand synthesis, in which it was able to assert the Monroe Doctrine and ensure the political independence of Latin American states. The nadir of the third hero's journey was collapse in federal government support for protecting the rights of emancipated slaves and honoring treaties signed with Native Americans.

The sixth chapter explores the years from 1889 to 1912 in which America became a great power as a result of its fourth hero's journey. The apex of the journey was its fourth grand synthesis where America used its power to support the principle of self-determination in the Cuban independence struggle. The low watermark was American imperialism in other captured American territories and elsewhere in the Western hemisphere.

The fifth hero's journey runs from 1913 to 1933 and is discussed in the seventh chapter. Here there was a powerful concern to promote and protect democracy both in the Western hemisphere and in the international system. The fifth grand synthesis was America's entry into World War I in support of self-determination and establishing a New World order as illustrated by Woodrow Wilson's Fourteen Points. The collapse of the fifth grand synthesis occurred with the Senate's refusal to ratify the Treaty of Versailles, thereby rejecting American membership in the League of Nations.

In chapter eight, America's sixth hero's journey is examined. In the years spanning from 1933 (when America began to oppose Japanese militarism and European Fascism) to 1974 (when the fall of South Vietnam led to renewed fears of the domino theory), America underwent its sixth hero's journey. The apex of this journey was America's sixth grand synthesis, when American power was used to support the principles of self-determination and democracy in World War II and the early part of the Cold War. The nadir of this journey was America's anticommunist crusade where it lost sight of these political principles.

America's seventh and current hero's journey is discussed in chapter nine. The seventh journey began in 1974 with Congress initiating legislation that gave greater prominence to human rights. The high watermark of this journey was achieved with America's seventh grand synthesis, based on humanitarian intervention in violent internal conflicts. American leadership in the humanitarian interventions in Bosnia in 1995 and Kosovo in 1999 promise an era where America can play a large role in bringing to an early end murderous conflicts where civilians are killed simply for belonging to one ethnic group or another. Most importantly, America has signaled its intention of playing a stronger role in getting states to better protect minority rights in the first place, thereby preventing the kind of genocidal campaigns that happened in Bosnia, Rwanda, and Kosovo.

The final chapter explores how America can maintain the high watermark of its seventh hero's journey by implementing domestic policies that deepen national unity while promoting a greater awareness of America's national mission in the international arena. Adequately addressing issues of multiculturalism, racial justice, and the plight of the Native American population will help promote national unity. At the same time, by cooperating with other states in multilateral organizations, American policymakers can ensure that foreign policy objectives that focus on humanitarian intervention and protection of minority rights, promotion of democracy, and rule of law are met while maintaining a high degree of national consensus.

The misery, death, and destruction caused by violent ethnic conflicts are sure to be repeated well into the twenty-first century. The remedy is twofold. The first is to prevent armed violence arising from ethnic conflicts occurring in the first place. The international community has the resources in most cases to persuade states to make the necessary concessions for political solutions rather than seek military solutions in disputes with their ethnic minorities. The second policy is to react adequately once widespread armed violence breaks out. A tremendous burden in terms of financial resources and possible casualties from military intervention need to be anticipated. America's preeminent position in the "second American century" makes it the logical starting point for most international efforts to prevent and react appropriately to the foreign policy challenges posed by ethnic conflicts. What is most often lacking in the international community in preventing or responding to violent ethnic conflicts is not the military or economic resources but the political will to intervene. Finding the political will to intervene in what is essentially the internal affairs of a sovereign state requires a powerful moral vision in how Americans identify themselves as a community and nation. The hero's journey is all about finding the will to put into effect one's moral vision. It is therefore critical for the international community that Americans continue to support the grand synthesis of power and morality in America's seventh hero's journey well into the "second American century."

NOTE

1. Ted Robert Gurr, *Peoples versus States: Minorities at Risk in the New Century* (Washington D.C.: U.S. Institute of Peace, 2000), 11.

CHAPTER 1

THE HERO'S JOURNEY

THE HERO'S JOURNEY

Joseph Campbell describes the hero's journey in his groundbreaking work, *The Hero with a Thousand Faces*. He argues that the hero's journey is a "monomyth" that recurs in the mythologies of different cultures:

All these different mythologies give us the same essential quest. You leave the world that you're in and go into a depth or into a distance or up to a height. There you come to what was missing in your consciousness in the world you formerly inhabited. Then comes the problem either of staying with that, and letting the world drop off, or returning with that boon and trying to hold on to it as you move back into your social world again. That's not an easy thing to do.[1]

Campbell connects the hero's journey to the rites of passage that are central for children taking the step into adulthood in which they assume responsibility in their community: "The standard path of the mythological adventure of the hero is a magnification of the formula represented in the rites of passage: *separation—initiation—return*: which might be named the nuclear unit of the monomyth."[2] The hero's journey represents a process whereby the individual develops from a fragmented sense of identity to an integrated identity with a clear sense of life's purpose. Jean Bolen describes this individuation process as repairing psychological damage represented in terms of a continuum ranging from multiple personality disorder to psychological dismemberment:

With the help of the inner self helper in psychotherapy [an archetypal encounter], the many fragmentary personalities become aware of the others, after which they can voluntarily integrate into one personality. To a lesser extent, because the damage done is less . . . [t]he task is not to knit together separate personalities, but to reconnect with cut-off parts of ourselves. Psychological "dis-memberment" takes place in the first half of life. . . . To heal and make whole takes "re-membering." To do this, we must go downward or inward to find the pieces and bring them back to light.[3]

The significance of the need to expand one's sense of self in order to fully develop one's inherent potentials is also explained by Marianne Williamson:

There is within every person a veiled, oceanic awareness that we are all much bigger than the small-minded personas we normally display. The expansion into this larger self, for the individual and the species, is the meaning of human evolution and the dramatic challenge of this historic time.[4]

The Swiss psychologist Carl Jung believed that the ego is merely a fragment of a larger self that includes the unconscious:

[T]he personality as a total phenomenon does not coincide with the ego, that is, with the conscious personality, but forms an entity that has to be distinguished from the ego. . . . I have suggested calling the total personality which though present cannot be fully known, the *self*. The ego is, by definition, subordinate to the self and is related to it like a part to the whole. . . . The ego not only can do nothing against the self, but is sometimes actually assimilated by unconscious components of the personality that are in the process of development and is greatly altered by them.[5]

Jung suggests here that individuals need to integrate their personal consciousness with the unconscious elements of their psyches in order to gain a coherent sense of selfhood. These elements of the unconscious correspond to what Jung called archetypes of the collective unconscious. Archetypes of the collective unconscious therefore take on an important role for the establishment of self-identity. Individuals need to engage with these archetypes in a way that expands their sense of self. As the archetypal psychologist Carol Pearson writes, the hero's journey is "a journey about individuation" in which archetypal encounters "help us define a strong ego, and then expand the boundaries of the ego to allow for the full flowering of the self and its opening up to the experience of oneness with other people and with the natural and spiritual worlds."[6]

The key to establishing an integrated sense of identity and finding one's life mission is to encounter what Jung believed to be the three most significant archetypes: the "shadow," the "Mother," and the "Father." To explain these archetypal encounters, it is worth spending some time exploring Jung's theory of archetypes.

JUNG'S THEORY OF ARCHETYPES

As did Sigmund Freud, Carl Jung argued that the human psyche could be divided into two parts—the conscious and the unconscious. Jung differed from Freud in a major way, however, by arguing that the unconscious had two layers.[7] The first was the personal unconscious in which lay the repressed desires and wishes that form the basis for neurotic complexes that are the principle focus in the initial development of psychoanalysis. Jung's notion of "personal unconscious" therefore corresponds to Freud's notion of the unconscious. Jung then argues the existence of a "collective unconscious" fully present and functional at birth:

My thesis, then, is as follows: In addition to our immediate consciousness, which is of a thoroughly personal nature and which we believe to be the only empirical psyche (even if we tack on the personal unconscious as an appendix), there exists a second psychic system of a collective, universal, and impersonal nature which is identical in all individuals. This collective unconscious does not develop individually but is inherited. It consists of pre-existent forms, the archetypes, which can only become conscious secondarily and which give definite form to contain psychic contents.[8]

It was precisely here that Jung departed from Freud in a major way that ultimately would lead to their estrangement. Jung argued that the "archetypes of the collective unconscious" are ideas similar to Plato's theory of forms or pre-existent universal ideas. The archetypes are powerful psychological drives that correspond closely with instinctual drives: "Archetypes are the unconscious images of the instincts themselves, in other words, that they are patterns of instinctual behavior."[9] Therefore, whereas Jung believed that there are numerous archetypes, Freud limited his theory of psychological (and civilizational) development to only two instinctual drives, life and death instincts (*eros* and *thanatos*).

Jung inferred the existence of "archetypes of the unconscious" through his close study of numerous cultures, religious practices, and mythologies throughout the world.[10] He explained the reason for his controversial inference in the manner of a social scientist convinced that s/he has amassed sufficient empirical evidence to validate a hypothesis:

[T]he concept of the collective unconscious is neither a speculative nor a philosophical but an empirical matter. The question is simply this: are there or are there not unconscious, universal forms of this kind? . . . It is true that the diagnosis of the collective unconscious is not always an easy task. It is not sufficient to point out the often obviously archetypal nature of unconscious products, for these can just as well be derived from acquisitions through language and education. . . . In spite of all these difficulties, there remain enough individual instances, showing the autochthonous revival of mythological motifs to put the matter beyond any reasonable doubt.[11]

The myths handed down from generation to generation by peoples throughout the world provided the raw data for filling out these archetypes, which Jung believed to be "ideas without content." To explain the notion of an idea without content, we can look to Jung's Mother archetype. The idea or archetype of a universal protective Mother recurs in numerous myths, yet the content of this idea varies greatly. We can begin with the benign, humble, and meek demeanor of the Virgin Mary rendered in El Greco's famous painting of her floating in Heaven surrounded by adoring angels while lovingly holding the Christ Child, with a lamb situated immediately beneath her. Her demeanor is meek and benign, and her eyes are downcast—as are all depictions of the Virgin Mary in Christian literature.[12] She is depicted wearing royal blue signifying her role as Queen of Heaven, Mother of the universe. Christian representations of the Virgin Mary as the universal mother could not contrast more with representations of the Goddess Kali in Hindu iconography. Kali is a fearsome figure wearing a garland of human heads as her necklace and a girdle of human arms.[13] She holds a bloody saber in her upper left hand and a severed human head in her other left hand. Her upper right hand is held up in a "fear not" gesture while her lower right hand is extended to signify a bestowal of boons.

The same archetype of the universal protective Mother exists here and in other myths, yet it is expressed in ways distinct to the culture and traditions of a people. Similarly, other archetypes of the collective unconscious can be discerned as representing an essential form or primordial idea but being expressed in ways distinct to different peoples and cultures.

Jung described three archetypes that "from the empirical point of view" have the "most frequent and the most disturbing influence on the ego. These are the *shadow*, the *anima* [Mother] and the *animus* [Father]."[14] (See Figure 1.1 for a diagramatic representation of the Jungian psychoanalytical model to be used.)[15]

The Shadow Archetype—"Slaying the Dragon"

In his 1917 essay, "On the Psychology of the Unconscious," Jung described the "shadow" as a fundamental aspect of one's personality made up of negative qualities that are usually hidden or ignored in developing a sense of identity. He wrote: "By shadow I mean the 'negative' side of the personality, the sum of all those unpleasant qualities we like to hide, together with the insufficiently developed functions and the content of the personal unconscious."[16]

Figure 1.1
Jungian Archetypes of the Unconscious

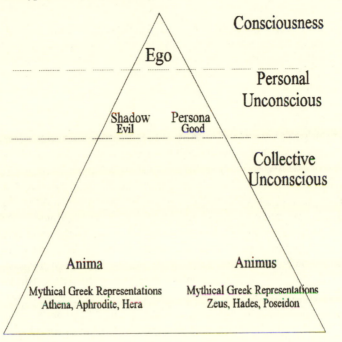

Jung believed that the shadow is the "most accessible" and the "easiest to experience" of all the archetypes because "its nature can in large measure be inferred from the contents of the personal unconscious."[17] This leads to a "moral problem" that results in individuals having to confront their personal shadow in establishing their personal identity:

> The shadow is a moral problem that challenges the whole ego-personality, for no one can become conscious of the shadow without considerable moral effort. To become conscious of it involves recognizing the dark aspects of the personality as present and real. This act is the essential condition for any kind of self-knowledge, and it therefore, as a rule, meets with considerable resistance.[18]

For self-growth to occur, individuals must deal directly with their own negative characteristics; and avoid projection of these onto others. The implication is that undesirable characteristics projected onto others by an individual merely reflect undesirable characteristics that the individual in question personally needs to address directly. As the social psychologist Sam Keen writes: "Depth psychology has presented us with the undeniable wisdom that the enemy is constructed from denied aspects of the self."[19]

The psychoanalyst Erik Erikson explains the role of the shadow in identity formation and its projection of moral categories onto others as follows:

Identity formation normatively has its dark and negative side, which throughout life can remain an unruly part of the total identity. Every person and every group harbors a *negative identity* as the sum of all those identifications and identity fragments which the individual had to submerge in himself as undesirable or irreconcilable or which his group has [been] taught to perceive as the mark of fatal "difference" in sex role or race, in class or religion.[20]

A psychological study on Hindu and Muslim office clerks in Southern India found that each would attribute the friendly behavior of co-religionists to individual personalities and unfriendly behavior to circumstances.[21] This pattern was reversed when it came to the behavior of individuals from different religious backgrounds, thus making possible the projection of negative stereotypes onto whole communities.

Erikson argues that when an individual loses confidence in being able to "contain the negative elements in a positive identity," this leads to an identity crisis in which individuals can be exploited by political elites "who become models of a sudden surrender to total doctrines and dogmas in which the negative identity appears to be the desirable and the dominant one."[22] The role of the shadow in identity formation makes possible the kind of destructive violence that the prominent psychoanalyst Erich Fromm believed was unique to humans and separated them from other species in the animal kingdom who lack the mental ability to project moral categories onto others:

We must distinguish in man *two entirely different kinds of aggression*. The first, which he shares with all animals, is a phylogenetically programmed impulse to attack (or to flee) when vital interests are threatened. This *defensive*, "benign" aggression is in the service of the survival of the individual and the species, is biologically adaptive, and ceases when the threat has ceased to exist. The other type, "malignant" aggression, i.e., destructiveness and cruelty, is specific to the human species and virtually absent in most mammals; it is not phylogenetically programmed and not biologically adaptive; it has no purpose, and its satisfaction is lustful. Most previous discussion of the subject has been vitiated by the failure to distinguish between these two kinds of aggression, each of which has different sources and different qualities.[23]

The role of the shadow in projecting moral categories onto others is exemplified in the dehumanization that takes place in war. The social psychologist Robert Rieber refers to this projection as a critical part of the "enmification process" or creation of enemy images.[24] Once formed, such images or stereotypes are difficult to change and ultimately reinforce one another in conflicts as Janice Gross Stein observes:

Once stereotyped images are in place, they are extraordinarily difficult to change. Because enemy images contain an emotional dimension of strong dislike, there is a strong desire to maintain the existing image and little incentive to seek new information about a foe. Stereotyped images also generate behavior that is hostile and confrontational, increasing the likelihood that an adversary will respond with hostile action. A cycle of reciprocal behavior then reinforces adversary images by providing allegedly confirming evidence of hostile intentions. Enemy images tend to become self-fulfilling and self-reinforcing.[25]

In Jungian psychoanalytical terms, encountering the shadow archetype suggests that individuals deal directly with their own negative characteristics rather than project these onto others. Individuals would then not project dichotomous moral categories of good and evil, right and wrong, normal and abnormal, and the like, onto themselves and to others. In his recent book *Nonviolent Communication*, Marshall Rosenberg argues that dichotomous moral thinking is at the heart of all conflict.[26] The key to resolving conflicts, then, is to restructure the way we communicate in order to identify and respond to what others feel and need, rather than what is right or wrong. Dealing with one's own undesirable characteristics can be represented in allegorical terms as "slaying the dragon." As Jung wrote: "We each must rediscover a deeper source of our own spiritual life. . . . To do this we are obliged to struggle with evil, to confront the shadow. . . . There is no other choice."[27] The archetypal encounter of "slaying the dragon" means that individuals are able to separate the desirable and undesirable characteristics not only for themselves but in others. Demonizing or dehumanizing others in a way that suggests one has nothing to learn from another is unlikely to occur for those who successfully deal with their shadow archetype. In sum, "slaying the dragon" is to communicate and relate with others in a way that avoids projecting one's own undesirable moral categories upon another.

The Mother Archetype—The "Sacred Marriage"

The second archetype that Jung believed to be most important for individual development is that of "the Mother." Jung used the term *anima* to signify the Mother archetype. He argued that it forms an instinctual driving force in the male psyche:

Whenever she [the anima] appears, in dreams, visions, and fantasies, she takes on personified form, thus demonstrating that the factor she embodies possesses all the outstanding characteristics of a feminine being. She is not an invention of the conscious, but a spontaneous product of the unconscious. Nor is she a substitute figure for the [human] mother. On the contrary, there is every likelihood that the numinous qualities which make the mother-imago so dangerously powerful derive from the collective archetype of the anima, which is incarnated anew in every male child.[28]

In contrast to Freud's Oedipus complex in which a male's competitive relationship with his father plays the central role in masculine psychological development, authors such as Michael Gurian suggest that a male's relationship with his mother is more fundamental due to the archetypal relationship with her:

As we grew up in her arms and in her castle, our mother was, in archetypal terms, like a great nurturing Goddess—the Mother-Creator, the Sacred Queen, the wise Crone and the beautiful Maiden all in one. . . . We were attached to our mothers (or other primary caregivers) in a unique way. Our ancestral cultures and their mythologies have symbolized this primal attachment in figures like the Greek goddess Sybil, with her multiple gigantic breasts that feed and nurture the world, or the medieval Christian *vierge ouvrante* in which, when the sculpted cabinet of the Virgin Mary is opened, Jesus is seen within, a small figure wrapped in a much larger chest. What we need in the very early stages of life is profound attachment to Mom, for we live very much by her love and attention. Without her deep attachment to us, especially in the first six months of life, our ability to relate to others is profoundly damaged. Our ability to trust depends on healthy attachment to our mothers during our infancy. If there is abuse, neglect, abandonment during early attachment, we are deeply wounded.[29]

Joseph Campbell suggests that the Mother archetype represents creative universal forces that once were dominant in the fertility cultures of ancient river valley civilizations. In response to a question about the centrality of the Mother Goddess in the ancient world, Joseph Campbell replied:

Well, that was associated primarily with agriculture and the agricultural societies. It has to do with earth. The human woman gives birth just as the earth gives birth to the plants. She gives nourishment, as the plants do. So woman magic and earth magic are the same. They are related. And the personification of the energy that gives birth to forms and nourishes forms is properly female. It is in the agricultural world of ancient Mesopotamia, the Egyptian Nile, and in the earlier planting-culture systems that the Goddess is the dominant mythic form.[30]

These ancient agricultural societies eventually were supplanted by a warrior ethos carried by invading nomadic tribes.[31] He explains how the Babylonian myth of Tiamat and Marduk revealed this profound cultural change by the new male god of Marduk annihilating the previous all powerful goddess, Tiamat:

So the story begins with a great council of the male gods up in the sky, each god a star, and they have heard that the Grandma is coming, old Tiamat, the Abyss, the inexhaustible Source. She arrives in the form of a great fish or dragon—and what god will have the courage to go against Grandma and do her in? ...

So when Tiamat opens her mount, the young god Marduk, of Babylon sends winds into her throat and belly that blow her to pieces, and he then dismembers her and fashions the earth and heavens out of the parts of her body. ...

There was no need for him to cut her up and make the universe out of her, because she was already the universe. But the male-oriented myth takes over, and *he* becomes—apparently—the creator.[32]

The archetypal psychologist Jean Bolen argues that a similar process happened in Europe and is implicit in the myth of one of Zeus's consorts, the goddess Metis, who shrank and was eaten by Zeus:

Metis, as divine feminine wisdom, was indeed swallowed by the patriarchy, and disappeared from the Western world. The myth reflects what happened historically (probably between 4500 B.C and 2400 B.C): successive waves of Indo-European invaders, with their warrior gods and father-based theologies, subjugated the people of old Europe, who for 25,000 years had followed mother-based religions and developed a peaceful, culturally advanced civilization that was unstratified, agricultural, and egalitarian. Because their cities were unfortified and exposed and because they lacked military skills, they were conquered by the horse-riding, sky god-worshiping invaders who imposed their patriarchal culture and religion on the defeated people.

The Goddess (known by many different names) became the subservient consort of the invader gods, and her attributes and powers were absorbed (swallowed) or came under the domination of a male deity.[33]

References to the Mother Goddess also appear in Indian Tantric philosophy where the energy of the Mother Goddess *Kundalini* lies dormant at the base of each individual's spinal column awaiting release in order to integrate all aspects of one's personality. Sri Aurobindo, one of the foremost Indian philosophers in the twentieth century, explains that the Kundalini is "the divine power asleep in the lowest physical center which awakened in the yoga, ascends in light through the opening centers [in the spine] to meet the Divine in the highest center and so connect the manifest and the unmanifested, joining spirit and Matter."[34] The rigorous purification and meditative processes in Tantric philosophy can be likened to a hero's journey in numerous mythologies for which the goal is to awaken the dormant transformative energy of the Mother archetype for the good of the hero and the community:

When in mythology the Goddess is oppressed—by being killed, imprisoned, buried alive, or exiled—the whole community suffers. Often, a Hero's task is to rescue the Goddess, who holds the deed to the community's happiness. Fairy tales, wisdom tales, and medicine tales about men who develop into Warriors and Kings by doing great deeds, including rescuing a princess, are tales about the necessity of men unchaining the Goddess within themselves and in the world, in order to be whole. A primary message men receive in fairy tales is that you cannot have a functioning kingdom without a free feminine.[35]

The hero's journey to liberate the Mother Goddess is represented in what Campbell calls the "sacred marriage" with the Goddess-Mother.[36] In Jungian psychoanalytic terms, the "sacred marriage" suggests a psychological encounter with the Mother archetype that brings about a radical transformation of the individual. James Redfield elaborates on the importance of such an encounter: "[I]f we are to open up to the full potential of transpersonal awareness, we must become conscious of and integrate both the female and male aspects of our higher selves. . . . [I]n order to connect with the divine energy within, we must locate, court, and finally engage the energy of the female nurturer within our own being."[37] Similarly, Corinne McLaughlin and Gordon Davidson write of the importance of finding the feminine dimension within ourselves:

The feminine principle within each person, man or woman, is in tune with the heartbeat of earth—our deepest biological roots as humans. The cause of much of our human pain is our alienation from these deep roots. Many people today are orphaned from the Great Mother, out of touch with nature and their own human nature destroying the earth and the ecological balance. They are often afraid to lose rational control and express their softer, intuitive, feminine side. This overemphasis on the masculine principle has been at great cost to men as well as to women.[38]

A Greek myth that wonderfully illustrates how the feminine dimension has been excluded and marginalized is that of Homer's Iphigenia. Iphigenia was the youngest daughter of King Agamemnon, and when the Greek army could not set sail for Troy due to poor weather caused by the displeasure of the goddess Artemis, it was decided that a sacrifice was needed. Nothing less than the sacrifice of Agamemnon's beloved Iphigenia would placate Artemis, and Agamemnon finally relented. The Greeks then set sail for their long but successful campaign against the Trojans. What the myth illustrates is that in any enterprise involving masculine virtues of courage, leadership, and sacrifice, the feminine dimension must be sacrificed. This can be seen even today in the way business leaders make decisions that drastically affect the lives of others—the feminine dimension of care and nurture is sacrificed to the expedient of making a profit.

The key characteristic of the "sacred marriage" is the integration of all the archetypes of the unconscious, and the power and wisdom to overcome the complexes of the personal unconscious and continue the hero's journey. In terms of the Chinese philosophical categories of Ying and Yang, the integrative function is one of the main characteristics of the feminine Ying energy which must be balanced with the masculine Yang energy.[39] To illustrate both the importance of the "sacred marriage" and the danger that goes with it, we can turn to some themes drawn from Homer's *Iliad*.

In the *Iliad*, the goddess of discord, Eris, is slighted by her companion gods, and in revenge she arranges for a golden apple to be rolled into the hall of Mount Olympus with a message that it was meant for the most beautiful goddess. Eventually the choice comes down to the goddesses Hera (personification of power), Athena (personification of wisdom), and Aphrodite (personification of beauty)—thus representing the three main characteristics of the Mother archetype. The story goes that Paris, a Trojan prince at that time staying with a shepherd family, is given the choice of deciding which of the three goddesses is the most beautiful. Each goddess offers Paris a gift to gain a decision in her favor. Hera offers him political power in the form of an earthly kingdom; Athena offers him wisdom; and Aphrodite offers him the most beautiful woman in the world as a wife. Paris's selection of Aphrodite leads to his death due to the wrath of Hera and Athena.[40] Paris's decision reflects the danger of a partial encounter with the Mother archetype. By choosing only one aspect of the Mother archetype, beauty, Paris did not integrate the other aspects of the Mother archetype. The Trojan War and the conflict between the gods is therefore an allegory for the dangers of a discordant self that has not entered into the "sacred marriage."

In Jungian psychoanalytical terms, the "sacred marriage" with the Mother archetype represents achieving an integrated personality that synthesizes the different archetypes of the collective unconscious. The opposite of such an integration is what the psychologist R. D. Laing refers to as a state of "chaotic non-entity":

The best description of any such condition I have been able to find in literature is in the Prophetic Books of William Blake. In the Greek descriptions of Hell, and in Dante, the shades or ghosts, although estranged from life, still retain their inner cohesiveness. In Blake, this is not so. The figures of his Books undergo division in themselves. These books require prolonged study, not to elucidate Blake's psychopathology, but in order to learn from him what, somehow, he knew about in a most intimate fashion, while remaining the same.[41]

Laing's "chaotic entity" is clearly an extreme version of individual discord. One, however, need only look at mundane examples to realize that there is a degree of discord in otherwise healthy individuals. The person who does not keep New Year resolutions; individuals unable to give up smoking; those unable to change their eating habits; those not able to control emotions like anger; and many such others, are all examples of individual discord.

The "sacred marriage" suggests that to become integrated and whole one must live with the idea of the Mother's unconditional love. This idea must be so strong that nothing can shake it in order for psychological wholeness to come about. This need for wholeness through the mother's love is made startlingly clear in a statement by a patient who suffered from one of the most extreme forms of fragmented identity—schizophrenia:

> Everyone should be able to look back in their memory and be sure he had a mother who loved him, all of him; even his piss and shit. He should be sure his mother loved him just for being himself; not for what he could do. Otherwise he feels he has no right to exist. He feels he should never have been born.
>
> No matter what happens to this person in life, no matter how much he gets hurt, he can always look back to this and feel that he is lovable. He can love himself and he cannot be broken. If he can't fall back on this, he can be broken.
>
> You can only be broken if you're already in pieces. As long as my baby-self has never been loved then I was in pieces. By loving me as a baby, you made me whole.[42]

The psychological qualities unleashed by the "sacred marriage"—the most important of which are the three goddesses of wisdom, power, and beauty who figured in Homer's Trojan War—are necessary for integrating the individual and achieving a coherent sense of identity.

The Father Archetype—Atonement

The third archetype Jung believed to be most important for individual development is that of "the Father." For Freud, development of the super-ego corresponded to the internalization of societal norms that could be directly traced to the competitive relationship between father and son in the Oedipus complex. As mentioned earlier, the Oedipus complex overlooks a more cooperative relationship between father and son, as well. Though Freud's depiction of the father for individual and civilizational development is inadequate, he was correct in identifying its centrality in religious thought. It is therefore to common elements in religious thought I now turn in order to assess the importance of the father archetype.

Rudolph Otto argues that a common element in all religions is that of a "numinous element" that cannot be properly described:

> Accordingly, it is worthwhile, as we have said to find a word to stand for this element in isolation, this 'extra' in the meaning of 'holy' above and beyond the meaning of goodness. . . . I shall speak, then, of a unique 'numinous' category of value and of a definitely 'numinous' state of mind. . . . This mental state is perfectly sui generis and irreducible to any other; and therefore like every absolutely primary and elementary datum, while it admits of being discussed, it cannot be strictly defined.[43]

The idea of the numinous advocated by Otto represents the archetypal experience related by mystics from earliest recorded history. The numinous experience represents Plato's contemplation of the idea of the Good; Buddha's experience of nirvana; Moses' encounter with Yahweh on Mount Sinai; Plotinus's idea of the One; Arjuna's encounter with the universal form of Krishna; and countless other experiences described by mystics all have in common the idea of an ineffable encounter with the numinous.[44] Dante's description of the mystical encounter at the end of the *Divine Comedy* comes close to capturing the essence of such an experience and stands as one of the great pieces of Western literature:

> Shorter henceforward will my language fall
> Of what I yet remember, than an infant's
> Who still his tongue doth moisten at the breast
> Not because more than one unmingled semblance
> Was in the living light on which I looked,
> For it was always what it was before;
> But through the sight, that fortified itself
> In me by looking, one appearance only
> To me was ever changing as I changed.
> Within the deep and luminous subsistence
> Of the High Light appeared to me three circles,
> Of threefold colour and of one dimension
> And by the second seemed the first reflected
> As Iris is by Iris, and the third
> Seemed fire that equally from both is breathed.
> O how all speech is feeble and falls short
> Of my conceit, and this to what I saw
> Is such, 'tis not enough to call it little!
> O Light Eterne, sole in thyself that dwellest,
> Sole knowest thyself, and, known unto thyself
> And knowing, lovest and smilest on thyself!
> That circulation, which being thus conceived
> Appeared in thee as a reflected light,
> When somewhat contemplated by mine eyes,
> Within itself, of its own very colour
> Seemed to me painted with our effigy,
> Wherefore my sight was all absorbed therein.
> As the geometrician, who endeavours
> To square the circle, and discovers not.
> By taking thought, the principle he wants,
> Even such was I at that new apparition;
> I wished to see how the image to the circle
> Conformed itself, and how it there finds place;
> But my own wings were not enough for this,
> Had it not been that then my mind there smote
> A flash of lightning, wherein came its wish.

Here vigour failed the lofty fantasy:
But now was turning my desire and will,
Even as a wheel that equally is moved,
The Love which moves the sun and the other
stars.[45]

Dante's use of metaphor to describe this numinous encounter reveals the extraordinary difficulty in describing a state of consciousness that lies outside the parameters of time and space. Jung divided Otto's idea of the numinous into two elements—anima and animus—Feminine and Masculine components respectively. For Jung, they are powerful psychological driving forces for men and women respectively.

Woman is compensated by a masculine element and therefore her unconscious has, so to speak, a masculine imprint. This results in a considerable psychological difference between men and women, and accordingly I have called the projection-making factor in women the animus, which means mind or spirit. The animus corresponds to the paternal Logos just as the anima corresponds to the maternal Eros.[46]

Jung's distinction between masculine and feminine archetypes as psychological driving forces for women and men respectively needs to be revised. Numerous examples of myths and mystical experiences reveal that the Father archetype plays a powerful psychological role for men. In contrast to Freud's Oedipus complex in which the relationship between father and son is a troubled and competitive relationship, there is in fact a far more cooperative and fulfilling relationship played between father and son, and daughter for that matter. Fulfilling this relationship in terms of encountering the Father archetype is to achieve what Campbell described as *at-one-ment*, where an individual transcends his/her own personal desires and strives to regain a lost kingdom—a self-actualized life.[47] In Virgil's *Aeneid* Aeneas descends into Hades and has his destiny revealed to him by his dead father, Anchises, who prophesies that by establishing a Trojan colony on the river Tiber, Aeneas will lay the foundation for the Roman Republic that will eventually rule the world:

Come, I shall now explain to you your whole destiny. I shall make clear by my words what glory shall in time to come fall to the progeny of Dardanus, and what manner of men will be your descendants of Italian birth, souls of renown now awaiting life who shall succeed to our name. . . . But you, Roman, must remember that you have to guide the nations by your authority, for this is to be your skill, to graft tradition onto peace, to show mercy to the conquered, and to wage war until the haughty are brought low.[48]

More recently, in the animated children's video *The Lion King*, Simba the lion cub returns from exile to combat his nefarious uncle, Scar, to reclaim his dead father's kingdom. This occurs as a result of a vision in which Simba communicates with his dead father's spirit, who reveals that Simba's troubled life in exile stems from having forgotten him, his father Mufasa, and therefore having forgotten who he, Simba, is. Simba can recover his true identity by realizing the will of his dead father and becoming part of the "great circle of life." Simba's decision to confront his uncle and rejoin the great circle of life represents *atonement* with the Father archetype in the sense of finding one's place in a cosmic plan. In Jungian psychoanalytical terms, encountering the Father archetype means that one has discovered his or her mission and calling in life and is committed to achieving that mission.

In sum, the hero is the individual who has successfully encountered the three archetypes: the shadow, the Mother, and the Father. Slaying the dragon, the sacred marriage, and atonement are all archetypal encounters signifying various signposts along the road to an integrated sense of identity where one is confident of one's life mission. I now turn to a closer examination of the three steps in Campbell's hero monomyth—separation, initiation, and return—to make clear the process of self-discovery that is at the heart of the hero's journey.

STEP 1 IN THE HERO'S JOURNEY—CALL TO ADVENTURE

Campbell described the significance of the first step as "a radical transfer of emphasis from the external to the internal world, macro- to microcosms, a retreat from the desperation of the waste land to the peace of the everlasting realm that is within."[49] The hero's withdrawal into an inner world results in him or her discovering their hidden potential with the capacity to become an individual of not only local but world historical moment. Campbell's hero of "world historical" importance corresponds closely with the great German philosopher George Hegel whose own view of the historical hero follows:

The great individuals of world history . . . are those who seize upon . . . [the] higher universal and make it their own end. . . . To this extent they may be called heroes. . . . They are the most far-sighted among their contemporaries; they know best what issues are involved, and whatever they do is right. The others feel that this is so, and therefore have to obey them. Their words and deeds are the best that could be said and done in their time.[50]

There are three phases in the first step of the hero's journey: "Hearing the Call"; "Refusal of the Call"; and "Crossing of the First Threshold."[51]

An illustration of these three phases is the character Odysseus in Homer's *Illiad* and the *Odyssey*. The call to adventure begins when King Agamemnon and his brother King Menelaus arrive in Ithaca to ask Odysseus to join them in the coming war against the Trojans. Odysseus attempts to refuse the call by pretending to be mad and tieing a horse and ox to a plough instead of two oxen. Suspecting Odysseus's trick, Agamemnon arranges for Odyssesus's infant son, Telemachus, to be placed in the path of the plough. In order not to kill his son, Odysseus stops pretending madness. By abandoning his trick, Odysseus has now crossed the first threshold, because to refuse to help his fellow kings would bring him personal dishonor.

Another example is *Episode IV* of the *Star Wars* trilogy. Luke Skywalker is a restless and troubled figure, uncertain of who he is and what his future holds. The call to adventure comes in the form of a robot droid carrying a plea for help for a mysterious figure called Ben Kenobi. Skywalker sets off to find Kenobi and in the process is ambushed by desert creatures. Kenobi arrives on the scene to rescue Skywalker and explain a mysterious "Force" that Skywalker needs to understand in the following way: "The Force is an energy field created by all living things. It surrounds us, it penetrates us, it binds the galaxy together."[52] Skywalker at first refuses to heed the call to adventure due to a strong sense of duty to his foster parents. He, however, crosses the first threshold when he learns that his foster parents have been murdered, thereby cutting down the tree nurturing his former existence.

In Jungian psychoanalytical terms, the call to adventure and refusal of the call signify the human ego recognizing its fragmentation and incompleteness but hesitating to act upon this insight because it would mean abandoning the certainties of rational existence. Then the individual has some life-transforming event that leads to crossing the first threshold into the collective unconscious to begin the journey of self-discovery.

STEP 2 IN THE HERO'S JOURNEY—GREAT REMEMBERING

The second of Campbell's three steps involves initiation and testing in which the hero has to successfully encounter the archetypes of the unconscious. Due to the theme of recovery of something lost or forgotten, this step can be called the "great remembering" rather than Campbell's "initiation and testing." There are three phases in this step, each of which corresponds to one of the three archetypal encounters discussed earlier as the most significant in the self-discovery process: slaying the dragon; the sacred marriage; and atonement.[53]

An illustration of the second step in the hero's journey is Homer's *Odyssey* when Odysseus sets out on his return to Ithaca from the Trojan war.

"Slaying the dragon" represents the many hurdles he must overcome on his journey home: the Scylla and Charybdis; Circe; Cyclops; and so on. All the trials signify an encounter with his personal shadow. After disaster at sea, Odysseus lands shipwrecked on the island of the goddess Calypso. He experiences the "sacred marriage" with her and is offered the boon of immortality if he stays and forgets his wife Penelope and any idea of resuming his journey. This is a boon that ordinarily bestows great fame and honor on the recipient, and could represent the culmination of his many trials and tribulations. Zeus, however, has other ideas and sends Hermes to command Calypso to release Odysseus and allow him to continue his journey. "Atonement" comes with Odysseus continuing his journey and achieving the destiny revealed to him by the prophet Tiresias when Odysseus had earlier journeyed to Hades.[54] Atonement brings with it recovery of the kingdom of Ithaca and reunion with his loyal wife Penelope.

In Jungian terms, the "great remembering" means confronting complexes of the personal unconscious that prevent individual growth and self-actualization. Jung's concept of the shadow is relevant here because it represents in archetypal form the sum of all the obstacles posed by the personal unconscious. Encountering the goddess is an archetypal experience important for elevating and empowering the self—hence the metaphor of Calypso wishing to bestow immortality on Odysseus. The encounter with Calypso suggests an archetypal experience of bliss in which the hero could freely choose to immerse himself/herself—an elevated state of blissful consciousness that contrasts greatly with the struggles of ordinary waking consciousness. This contrasts with the encounter with the nymph Circe who transforms Odysseus's men into swine and would have done the same to Odysseus, thus representing a weakening and sapping of the hero's vital energy.[55]

Odysseus's choice between the boon of immortality offered by Calypso and the resumption of a difficult and dangerous journey represents in mythological terms the same dilemma confronting those who have attained nirvana according to the Buddhist tradition. The dilemma here is whether one should stay immersed in the nirvanic experience—and become boddhisattvas—or to return to the realm of conscious life to relate the archetypal experience—to become buddhas. Those who choose the latter path of eventual return to the external world of consciousness experience atonement—the opportunity to fulfill their revealed destiny. For Odysseus this meant leaving Calypso to fulfill the destiny revealed to him by Tiresias.

Slaying the dragon, the sacred marriage, and atonement are archetypal encounters with the shadow, Mother, and Father archetypes respectively. These experiences are essential for integrating the conscious and unconscious parts of the self, for personal empowerment, and for gaining direction and meaning in life. These three archetypal encounters are the heart of the self-discovery process. If one is not prepared for these archetypal experiences, then one exposes himself/herself to powerful disintegrative forces. Those who have taken hallucinogenic drugs often report terrifying archetypal experiences that can lead to schizophrenia and other personality disorders. Campbell explained this as follows:

What is the difference between a psychotic or LSD experience and a yogic, or a mystical? The plunges are all into the same deep inward sea; of that there can be no doubt. The symbolic figures encountered are in many instances identical. . . . But there *is* an important difference. The difference . . . is equivalent simply to that between a diver who can swim and one who cannot. The mystic [or hero], endowed with native talents for this sort of thing and following, stage by stage, the instruction of a master, enters the water and finds he can swim; whereas the schizophrenic, unprepared, unguided, and ungifted, has fallen or has intentionally plunged, and is drowning.[56]

STEP 3 IN THE HERO'S JOURNEY—THE RETURN TO SOCIETY

The third step in the hero's journey involves a return where the hero shares the fruits of his/her journey in terms of wisdom, compassion, and leadership for one's society and for global humanity. There are three phases in this step: "Refusal of the Return," "Crossing of the Return Threshold," and "Master of the Two Worlds."[57]

An illustration of the three phases in the final step is what is reported to have occurred after Prince Siddhartha (Gautama Buddha) gained enlightenment under the Bodhi Tree. He faced a difficult choice between whether to teach the sublime truth to a critical and uncomprehending public or to remain immersed in the nirvanic experience. Rendered in poetic terms by Sir Edwin Arnold, we gain a sense of the difficulty of the choice for the Buddha:

> But many days the burden or release—
> To be escaped beyond all storms of doubt,
> Safe on Truth's shore—lay, spake he, on that heart
> A golden load; for how shall men—Buddha mused—
> Who love their sins and cleave to cheats of sense,
> And drink of error from a thousand springs—
> Having no mind to see, nor strength to break
> The fleshly snare which binds them—how should such
> Receive the Twelve Nidanas and the Law
> Redeeming all, yet strange to profit by,
> As the caged bird oft shuns its open door?[58]

Siddartha chose to cross the return threshold and therefore became the Buddha. This was the point of no return, because it represented his decision to follow his *calling*—teaching others the truth of his revelation.[59] The Buddha became "Master of the Two Worlds" by being able to re-experience nirvana to both reinvigorate himself and to show the path to his students. He no longer lived a life of attachment, and therefore was free from the cosmic drama of birth and rebirth.

In Jungian terms, "refusal of the return" implies the reluctance to leave the elevated state of consciousness reached in the journey of self-discovery and to reenter the normal waking consciousness. Crossing the return threshold signifies that one is willing to forego remaining immersed in an elevated state of consciousness (the sacred marriage) and to return to ordinary waking consciousness in order to realize one's *calling* (atonement). "Master of the Two Worlds" means that one has integrated the elevated state of consciousness and normal waking consciousness in a grand synthesis that empowers and gives purpose to the self. This is powerfully described by the famous Indian yogi Paramahamsa Yogananda in terms of both living in an elevated state of ecstatic consciousness and fulfilling daily duties:

In the initial states of God-communion (*sabikalpa* samadhi) the devotee's consciousness merges in the Cosmic Spirit; his life force is withdrawn from the body which appears 'dead,' or motionless and rigid. The yogi is fully aware of his bodily condition of suspended animation. As he progresses to higher spiritual states (*nirbikalpa* samadhi), however, he communes with God without bodily fixation; and in his ordinary waking consciousness, even in the midst of exacting world duties.[60]

Becoming "Master of the Two Worlds" means that one has achieved the ultimate boon—the creation of a self-actualized identity where one is in full control of his or her own destiny. Rather than being pulled in different directions by unconscious forces that typically overwhelm the rational self or ego, one has harmonized these powerful forces under the leadership and direction of the self-actualized self. "Master of the Two Worlds" signifies achieving the mythical kingdom of God.

STEP 4 IN THE HERO'S JOURNEY—THE DEEP FORGETTING

The self-actualized identity at the end of Campbell's three-step hero's journey means that individuals go through a linear process of self-discovery. One is simply at various stages on a straight road and one, at worst, is prevented from progressing further at the various hurdles that appear in the self-discovery process. This overlooks a more cyclical process where self-discovery develops in a more circular fashion. Carol Pearson advocates a cyclical process for the hero's journey as follows:

I would illustrate the typical hero's progression as a cone or three-dimensional spiral, in which it is possible to move forward while frequently circling back. Each stage has its own lesson to teach us, and we reencounter situations that throw us back into prior stages so that we may learn and relearn the lessons as new lessons at new levels of intellectual and emotional complexity and subtlety.[61]

In a cyclic process, then, there needs to be a further step in which one temporally falls back or loses what was earlier achieved. This backward step is absent in Campbell's three-step hero's journey of self-discovery. Yet this backward step, in fact, is a common motif in mythology—the "deep forgetting" or the "fall from a state of grace."

In Plato's *Republic* he explains how souls, before coming to Earth, drink from *Lethe*—the river of forgetfulness:

[T]hey camped at eventide by the River of Forgetfullness, whose waters no vessel can contain. They were all required to drink a measure of the water, and those who were not saved by their good sense drank more than the measure, and each one as he drank forgot all things.[62]

Similarly, in Virgil's *Aeneid*, the river of forgetfulness is again mentioned:

And now Aeneas saw at the far end of the valley, apart, a bushy wood loud with a forest's rustling sounds; and saw too Lethe's river, where it flows before the Homes of Peace. About this river, like bees in a meadow on a fine summer day settling on flowers of every kind . . . the souls of countless tribes and nations were flitting. Aeneas was startled by the sudden sight, and in his bewilderment wished to hear his doubts explained, and find what might this river be which he saw before him, and who they were who crowded its banks with this numerous array. His father Anchises gave answer: "They are souls who are destined to live in the body a second time, and at Lethe's wave they are drinking the waters which abolish care and give enduring release from memory."[63]

In Hindu mythology, the theme of forgetting plays an important part in the journey toward self-identity. The famous mythologist Mircia Eliade argues that the theme of forgetfulness is a "pan-Indian motif" that corresponds with "loss of consciousness of the Self."[64]

An allegorical interpretation of the Fall in the book of Genesis is that the expulsion from Eden was a form of forgetfulness. This is well described in Christian Gnostic myths. For example, in the *Hymn of the Pearl* in the *Acts of Thomas*:

A prince comes to Egypt from the East, seeking "the one pearl, which is in the midst of the sea around the loud breathing serpent." In Egypt he was made prisoner by the men of the country. He was given their food to eat and forgot his identity. "I forgot that I was a son of kings, and I served their king; and I forgot the pearl of which my parents had sent me, and because of the burden of their oppressions

I lay in a deep sleep." But his parents learned what had befallen him and sent him a letter. "From thy father, the king of kings, and thy mother, the mistress of the East. . . . Call to mind that thou art a son of kings! See the slavery,—whom thou servest! Remember the pearl, for which thou wast sent to Egypt!" The letter flew in the likeness of an eagle, alighted beside him, and became all speech. "At its voice and the sound of its rustling, I started and rose from my sleep. I took it up and kissed it, and I began and read it; and according to what was traced on my heart were the words of my letter written. I remember that I was a son of royal parents, and my noble birth asserted its nature. I remember the pearl, for which I had been sent to Egypt, and I began to charm him, the terrible loud-breathing serpent. I hushed him to sleep and lulled him into slumber, for my father's name I named over him, and I snatched away the pearl, and turned to go back to my father's house."[65]

In the *Hymn of the Pearl*, the father and mother are allegorical represen-tations of the archetypal experiences of atonement, and the sacred mar-riage; the pearl represents the subsequent mastery of the two worlds that one had earlier achieved. The motif of remembering one's previous identity corresponds to reclaiming a lost kingdom and memory of one's divine an-cestry—the integrated and empowered self, confident of his or her life mis-sion.

Consequently, a fourth step in the hero's journey is a "deep forgetting" or "fall from grace" where one loses all memory of one's previous identity and of integration of self gained through the archetypal encounters of slay-ing the dragon, the sacred marriage, and atonement. Such individuals must begin again the self-discovery process, which now can be more properly understood as a *rediscovery* of a lost identity rather than a *discovery* a new identity. Just as there were three phases in each of the three previous steps of the hero's journey, so too three phases exist in the deep forgetting. One can forget one's self-identity either through fear, lust for power, and/or materialism.

Fear is an important cause of forgetting one's life mission. In *Fear Itself*, Rush Dozier argues that fear is the most basic of human drives:

Through understanding fear we understand ourselves. Fear is something humans have in abundance—more, I believe, than any other species. Science calls human beings Homo sapiens: wise man. A better name might be fearful man. Within the animal kingdom, we humans are the connoisseurs of fear. Our big brains harbor vastly more fears than any other animal.[66]

Fear can lead to the empowered and integrated sense of identity achieved in the "great remembering" falling apart. Fear therefore results in a frag-mented sense of identity where one becomes disempowered. This leads to a desire for power or control, which is the second stage of the deep for-getting.

Figure 1.2
The Hero's Journey

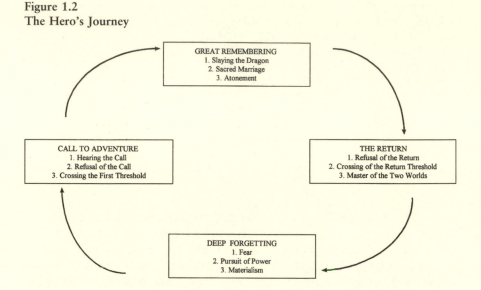

The second phase of forgetting is the quest for personal power. This results in an effort to control one's personal environment in the face of external threats to achieving one's desire. According to James Redfield, there are four strategies for controlling one's environment and achieving personal power.[67] The first is intimidation, where one controls one's environment through threats of erupting into rage and violence. The second is interrogation, where one controls through judging and criticizing others. The third is victimization, where one controls through uses of sympathy and guilt trips. And the fourth is aloofness, where one controls through the use of silence and ambiguity. In the political arena, the quest for power leads to political and military leaders using the resources of their society to devastating effects for both their community and neighboring societies.

The third phase of the deep forgetting is materialism and sensuality, which is a powerful means of forgetting one's identity and is a common theme in many myths. Mircea Eliade describes a famous example from Indian folklore about the great yogi Matsyendranath:

[T]he master, traveling in Ceylon, fell in love with the queen and went to live in her palace, completely forgetting his identity. . . . Gorakhnath realizes that his master is doomed to die. . . . He then goes to Matsyendranath, in Kadali, presenting himself under the form of a dancing girl, and falls to dancing, at the same time singing enigmatic songs. Little by little, Matsyendranath remembers his true identity; he understands that the 'way of the flesh' leads to death, that his 'oblivion' was, basically, forgetfullness of his true and immortal nature, and that the 'charms of Kadali' represent the mirages of profane life.[68]

Similarly, in Homer's *Odyssey*, Odysseus and his men land on the isle of Circe, and while having an affair with Circe, his men degenerate into pigs through their unrestrained gratification of their sensual desires. Odysseus was able to remember his mission and thus remained human, whereas his men had forgotten theirs. Odysseus then left Circe and freed his men.

In conclusion, the hero's journey spans four steps, each of which has three phases. The hero's journey is a cyclic process in which the hero goes through various stages of discovering and forgetting his or her self-identity. The journey can be represented as a cycle, as represented in Figure 1.2, but should be thought of more as an upward spiral in which the hero moves gradually toward a more profound understanding of his or her identity and life mission. The hero's journey involves a conscious decision by the hero to proceed in his or her journey of self-discovery, and face his or her complexes of the personal unconscious and the archetypes of the collective unconscious.

NOTES

1. Joseph Campbell and Bill Moyers, *The Power of Myth* (New York: Doubleday, 1988), 129.

2. Joseph Campbell, *The Hero with a Thousand Faces* (Princeton, N.J.: Princeton University Press, 1968), 30.

3. Jean Bolen, *Gods in Everyman: A New Psychology of Men's Lives and Loves* (San Francisco: Harper and Row, 1989), 291.

4. Marianne Williamson, *The Healing of America* (New York: Simon and Schuster, 1997), 41.

5. Carl Jung, "Aion: Phenomenology of the Self," in *The Portable Jung* (New York: Viking Press, 1971), 142–43.

6. Carol Pearson, *The Hero Within*, xxvi.

7. For Jung's discussion of these classifications, see "Aion: Phenomenology of the Self," in *The Portable Jung*, 139–44.

8. Carl Jung, "The Concept of the Collective Unconscious," in *The Portable Jung* (New York: Penguin Books, 1976), 60.

9. Ibid., 61.

10. Jung traveled extensively. See his autobiographical *Memories, Dreams, Reflections* (Collins Fount Paperbacks, n.d.), 266–319.

11. Jung, "The Concept of the Collective Unconscious," in *The Portable Jung*, p. 62.

12. A recent book challenging this traditional portrayal and arguing a more assertive and radical view of the Virgin Mary led to the excommunication of the author, a Sri Lankan Catholic theologian. See Fr. Tissa Balasuriya, *Mary and Human Liberation: The Story and the Text* (Trinity Press International, 1997).

13. Cf. Joseph Campbell, *The Hero with a Thousand Faces*, 115.

14. Jung, "Aion: Phenomenology of the Self," in *The Portable Jung*, 145.

15. This contrasts with the six archetypes—innocent, orphan, wanderer, martyr,

warrior, magician—Carol Pearson uses in her *The Hero Within* (New York: Harper and Row, 1989).

16. R.F.C. Hull, trans. *The Collected Works of C.G. Jung* (Princeton University Press), vol. 7, p. 66, n.5.

17. Jung, "Aion: Phenomenology of the Self," in *The Portable Jung*, 145.

18. Ibid.

19. Sam Keen, *Faces of the Enemy: Reflections of the Hostile Imagination* (San Francisco: Harper and Row, 1991).

20. Erik Erikson, *Life, History and the Historical Moment* (New York: W.W. Norton and Co., 1975), 20.

21. Psychologists for Social Responsibility, *Dismantling the Mask of Enmity: Educational Resource Manual* (Washington, D.C.: Authors, 1991), 1–15; 62–68.

22. Erikson, *Life, History and the Historical Moment*, 20.

23. Erick Fromm, *The Anatomy of Human Destructiveness* (New York: Holt, Rinehart and Winston, 1973), 4.

24. Robert Rieber, ed., *The Psychology of War and Peace: The Image of the Enemy* (New York: Plenum, 1991).

25. Janet Gross Stein, "Image, Identity, and Conflict Resolution," in *Managing Global Chaos*, ed. Chester Crocker and Fen Hampson (Washington, D.C.: U.S. Institute of Peace, 1996), 98.

26. Marshall Rosenberg, *Nonviolent Communication: A Language of Compassion* (Del Mar, Calif.: Puddle Dancer Press, 1999).

27. Quoted in Jeremiah Abrams, "Shadow and Culture," in *The Shadow in America: Reclaiming the Soul of a Nation*, ed. Jeremiah Abrams (Los Angeles: Nataraj, 1994), 24.

28. Jung, "Aion: Phenomenology of the Self," in *The Portable Jung*, 151.

29. Michael Gurian, *Mothers, Sons & Lovers: How a Man's Relationship with His Mother Affects the Rest of His Life* (London: Shambhala, 1994), 50–51.

30. Campbell and Moyers, *The Power of Myth*, 167.

31. Ibid., 169.

32. Ibid., 170.

33. Bolen, *Gods in Everyman*, 298.

34. Sri Aurobindo, *Letters on Yoga* (Pondicherry, India: Sri Aurobindo Ashram, 1995), Part III, 977.

35. Gurian, *Mothers, Sons & Lovers*, 85.

36. Campbell, *The Hero with a Thousand Faces*, 246.

37. James Redfield, *The Celestine Vision: Living the New Spiritual Awareness* (New York: Warner Books, 1997), 160.

38. Corinne McLaughlin and Gordon Davidson, *Spiritual Politics: Changing the World from the Inside Out* (New York: Ballantine Books, 1994), 60.

39. For description of the respective attributes of the Ying and Yang principles, see McLaughlin and Davidson, *Spiritual Politics*, 61.

40. For description of these events, see Donna Rosenberg, *World Mythology: An Anthology of the Great Myths and Epics*, 2nd ed. (Chicago: NTC Publishing Group, 1996), 45–46.

41. R. D. Laing, *The Divided Self* (New York: Penguin Books, 1979), 162.

42. Ibid., 172.

43. Rudolph Otto, *The Idea of the Holy* (Oxford: Oxford University Press, 1923; reprint 1958), 6–7.

44. For a detached yet sympathetic description of the mystical experience, see William James, *The Varieties of Religious Experience* (New York: Macmillan Pub. Co., 1961), Lectures 16 and 17.

45. Dante, *The Divine Comedy*, English Edition. Henry Wadsworth Longfellow, trans. Canto XXXIII, 106–145. http://www.divinecomedy.org/divine_comedy. html.

46. Jung, "Aion: Phenomenology of the Self," in *The Portable Jung*, p. 152.

47. Campbell, *The Hero with a Thousand Faces*, 246.

48. Virgil, *Aeneid* [Book VI, 752–879], trans. W. F. Jackson Knight (London: Penguin, 1958), 170, 173.

49. Campbell, *The Hero with a Thousand Faces*, 17.

50. Georg Hegel, *Lectures on the Philosophy of World History*, trans. H. B. Nisbet (Cambridge: Cambridge University Press, 1975), 82–84.

51. Campbell includes two other phases, "supernatural aid" and the "passage into the belly of the night," which I omit as they conflate with the archetypal encounters to be discussed later. *The Hero with a Thousand Faces*, 36. I also have renamed his first phase, which he calls the Call to Adventure, "Hearing the Call."

52. Cited in Campbell, *The Power of Myth*, 145.

53. Campbell, *The Hero with a Thousand Faces*, 36. Campbell has an additional three phases: woman as temptress, apotheosis, and the ultimate boon, which I delete because they are not as significant as the first three.

54. Homer, *The Odyssey* [Book XI], trans. E. V. Riev (Baltimore, MD: Penguin, 1946), 173–75.

55. The encounter with Circe corresponds with Campbell's idea of overcoming "woman as temptress." *The Hero with a Thousand Faces*, 36.

56. Joseph Campbell, *Myths to Live By* (New York: Bantam Books, 1988), 215–16.

57. Campbell, *The Hero with a Thousand Faces*, 37. Campbell describes a further three: "freedom to live," "The Magic Flight," and "Rescue from Without." I omit these three phases because they unnecessarily overlap with one another and with the archetypal encounters found in the testing and initiation stage of the hero's journey.

58. Sir Edwin Arnold, *The Light of Asia* (Wheaton, Ill.: The Theosophical Publishing House, 1969). Book VII, 120.

59. If the Buddha and heroes in general had just one *calling* unique to themselves, this would signify no real choice. There consequently must be a number of callings revealed to the hero that he/she can choose among.

60. Paramahamsa Yogananda, *Autobiography of a Yogi* (Los Angeles: Self-Realization Fellowship, 1983), 278.

61. Pearson, *The Hero Within*, 13.

62. Plato, "Republic" [Book 10, 621a–b], in *Plato: The Collected Dialogues*, ed. Edith Hamilton and Huntington Cairns (Princeton: Princeton University Press, 1982).

63. Virgil, *The Aeneid* [Book VI, 688–720], 168.

64. Joseph Campbell, *Myth and Reality* (New York: Harper and Row, 1963), 116.

65. Ibid., 127.

66. Rush Dozier, *Fear Itself: The Origin and Nature of the Powerful Emotion That Shapes Our Lives and Our World* (New York: St. Martin's Press, 1998), 6.

67. Redfield, *The Celestine Vision*.

68. Campbell, *Myth and Reality*, 114–15. This particular myth corresponds closely to Campbell's phase of "woman as temptress" in the second step of the hero's journey—the road of trials. I believe it more accurate to include this phase as an entirely distinct fourth step of the great forgetting.

CHAPTER 2

THE HERO'S JOURNEY IN WORLD POLITICS

POLITICAL COMMUNITIES AND THE HERO'S JOURNEY

The hero's journey is a process of self-discovery. This journey takes the hero from being a restless and troubled individual to a self-actualized being empowered to transform his or her social and political environment. The keys to this transformation in the hero's journey are three archetypal encounters—slaying the dragon, the sacred marriage, and atonement. The archetypal encounters happen in a cyclical pattern due to some critical event that leads to a loss of memory of what has been earlier gained. This makes it necessary to begin once again the hero's journey. The four steps of the hero's journey—call to adventure, great remembering, return to society, and the deep forgetting—are repeated again and again as the hero moves ever closer toward a deeper understanding and expression of the archetypal encounters at the heart of the journey. The challenge in understanding the relevance of the hero's journey for world politics is to explore whether it applies to political communities as well as to individuals.

The central character of the hero's journey is clearly the individual who makes the decisions necessary for transforming his or her self-consciousness as a result of archetypal encounters. The hero is a self-conscious entity capable of making moral choices, and making these choices as a basis for his or her self-identity. For example, as children we repeatedly were told injunctions in the form of "good children do not . . ." This made it possible for us to make a moral choice each time we did something. We therefore were able to develop a sense of self-identity based on what we believed to be right or wrong, good or bad. In world politics, the hero archetype corresponds to political communities that are self-conscious and autonomous. Such communities can make the moral choices they take the basis for establishing their self-identity. Political communities at the international level have similar transformative potential for their self-consciousness as that for the individual hero. If the hero's journey is a process of self-discovery, what sort of political communities can take this journey?

Candidates for a self-discovery process, or hero's journey, at the international level can be any political community ranging in size from a tribal group up to nation state. Such communities have the necessary self-consciousness to make moral choices. These choices then become the basis of their self-identity as symbolized in constitutions, flags, or emblems used by all political communities. All these symbols illustrate the positive qualities of the political community and what it hopes to achieve. Nation states have been the traditional focus in the study of world politics, and still remain central players in the international system due to a combination of military, political, and economic resources at their disposal. States, therefore, are the most important place to begin examining the idea of a political community undergoing a hero's journey.

Some of the main characteristics of nation states now can be described so as to show how the hero's journey applies to them. A well-respected international relations theorist, Hedley Bull, defines states to be "independent political communities, each of which possesses a government and asserts sovereignty in relation to a particular portion of the earth's surface and a particular segment of the human population."[1] He lists four characteristics of states: first, "they are territorially based"; second, they comprise people within that territory; third, "some of the people of a state are designated as its official representatives, as constituting its government"; and fourth, they each refer to themselves as sovereign.[2]

As far as the fourth characteristic is concerned, there is a difference between internal and external sovereignty. Bull argues that internal sovereignty "means supremacy over all other authorities within that territory and population," whereas external sovereignty means "not supremacy but independence of outside authorities."[3] The power of a state to organize its population and use its territorial resources free from external influence is the best indicator of its sovereignty. According to Bull, a "political community which merely claims a right to sovereignty . . . but cannot assert this right in practice, is not a state properly so-called."[4] States such as Lebanon whose institutions do not have complete control due to external interference—that is, Syria—have only a limited degree of sovereignty in both the internal and external senses. In the globalization process a state's power to counter external influence is being eroded especially in the financial sphere. The Asian financial crisis in 1998 prompted the intervention of the International Monetary Fund in many countries that were forced to implement unpopular austerity measures. This brought pressure to bear on all governments responding to the crisis, but nowhere more so than in Indonesia where, in a remarkable development in May, the long-standing leader President Suharto was forced to resign. This is evidence that the sovereignty of the modern state is very much being gradually eroded by global economic processes.

The modern state has a range of political institutions responsible for developing domestic and foreign policy. The policy-making process involves a complex relationship between executive and legislative branches of government, competing bureaucratic departments and other governmental actors, and finally citizen groups.[5] What remains at the center of this complex policy-making process is the concept of national interest.[6] Hans Morgenthau, the most important international relations theorist to promote the idea of national interest, wrote:

Without such a concept [interest defined as power, i.e., the national interest] a theory of politics, international or domestic, would be altogether impossible, for without it we could not distinguish between political and nonpolitical facts, nor could we bring at least a measure of systematic order to the political sphere. . . . The concept of interest defined as power . . . infuses rational order into the subject matter of politics, and thus makes the theoretical understanding of politics possible.[7]

The concept of national interest gives us the key to unlocking the door to national self-consciousness. National self-consciousness reflects a consensus by actors involved in the policy-making process that they wish to promote the national interest of the state. The common aim to promote the national interest is what is shared by all involved in the policy-making process. Political leaders, Morgenthau wrote, "think and act in terms of interest defined as power, and the evidence of history bears that assumption out."[8] One nineteenth-century German author argued that "no state has ever entered a treaty for any other reason than self interest . . . [and adds that] a statesman who has any other motive would deserve to be hung."[9] A British contemporary rejoined, "Where British interests are at stake, I am in favor of advancing these interests even at the cost of war. The only qualification I admit is that the country we desire to annex or take under our protection should be calculated to confer a tangible advantage upon the British Empire."[10]

A primitive organism will seek to satisfy its vital needs and therefore can be seen as a form of consciousness. Even microscopic organisms such as single cells display a level of consciousness. So too the modern state can be said to have a degree of self-consciousness insofar as it is a political community seeking to promote its national interest. According to the great

Indian philosopher, Sri Aurobindo, the recognition and promotion of self-interest is the key to recognizing the self-consciousness of states:

The primal law and purpose of the individual life is to seek its own self-development. Consciously or half-consciously or with an obscure unconscious grop-ing it strives always and rightly strives at self-formulation. . . . In the same way the primal law and purpose of a society, community or nation is to seek its own self-fulfilment; it strives rightly to find itself, to become aware within itself of the law and power of its own being and to fulfil it as perfectly as possible, to realize all its potentialities, to live its own self-revealing life.[11]

For Hans Morgenthau, the recognition and promotion of national inter-est leads to the "struggle for power" becoming a fundamental principle of international relations.[12] Others such as Stephen Walt describe this power struggle as "an innate desire to dominate others."[13] Power politics is therefore nothing other than states pursuing their national interest in a competitive international system where nothing less than national survival is at stake.

STATES AS MORAL ACTORS

The political theorist most famous for developing the notion that states have a degree of self-consciousness that gives them a moral dimension is the early nineteenth-century German philosopher Georg Hegel.[14] He wrote:

The actual state is animated by this spirit [of the people] in all its particular affairs, wards, institutions, etc. This spiritual content is something definite, firm, solid, completely exempt from caprice, the particularities, the whims of individuality, of chance. . . . The state does not exist for the citizens; on the contrary, one could say that the state is the end and they are its means. But the means-end relation is not fitting here. For the state is not the abstract confronting the citizens; they are parts of it, like members of an organic body, where no member is end and none is means.[15]

Hegel is suggesting here that individuals relate to the state in the same way that blood cells relate to a healthy and functioning human. The state is therefore not a lifeless abstraction but a living conscious entity comprised of individuals who share in the spirit or morality of the state. A similar idea was proposed by Sri Aurobindo:

The nation or society, like the individual, has a body, an organic life, a moral and aesthetic temperament, a developing mind and a Soul. . . . [I]t is a group Soul that, once having attained a separate distinctness, must then become more and more self-conscious and find itself more and more fully as it develops its corporate action and mentality and its organic self-expressive life.[16]

The nineteenth-century British theorist T. H. Green also argued that states have a moral dimension:

The doctrine that the rights of government are founded on the consent of the governed is a confused way of stating the truth, that the institutions by which man is moralized, by which he comes to do what he sees that he must, as distinct from what he would like, express a conception of a common good; that through them that conception takes form and reality; and that it is in turn through its presence in the individual that they have a constraining power over him.[17]

Green wrote at a time when many called for state action to deal with social problems caused by the Industrial Revolution. He responded to the dominant view in England that states need to have firm limits on their ability to tax and implement moral social policies on their citizens. Green believed that the best way of addressing social problems is through moral policy-making at the state level rather than individual morality through charity and philanthropy.

Writing in Prussia at a similar time, Hegel found it much easier to argue the case for firm state action to address social problems. In fact, Hegel's view of the state as a self-conscious political community that recognizes its own moral development was embraced enthusiastically by the political leaders of the Prussian state. Prussia was the first to establish a comprehensive social welfare system, and the first to grant universal franchise to all its male citizens. With Prussia providing a solid example, Hegel's view of the moral qualities of the state seemed to have no limit. He wrote:

All the value man has, all spiritual reality, he has only through the state [emphasis added]. For his spiritual reality is the knowing presence to him of his own essence, of rationality, of its objective, immediate actuality present in and for him. Only thus is he truly a consciousness, only thus does he partake in morality, in the legal and moral life of the state. . . . The state is the divine Idea as it exists on earth.[18]

Hegel here argues that individual morality should be subordinated to the morality of the state. This makes possible the mistaken belief that state authorities are correct in establishing a mold of the "ideal citizen" that can be used as a measure for individual behavior and morality. State authorities therefore can use all their resources in forcing conformity to the notion of the citizen that would best serve the interest of the state. This made Hegel the intellectual godfather of the Prussian state that promoted an aristocratic militarist culture that later imposed its model of citizenship on the princely states that joined the unified German Empire.

The attempt to subordinate individual morality to state morality also was attempted by totalitarian states in the twentieth century. This belief led to incredible misery and destruction in different parts of the planet. What

Vladimir Lenin, Joseph Stalin, Adolf Hitler, and Mao Tse Tung all had in common was the idea that individual identity should be cast from a mold created by the state, which could impose the desired moral consciousness on its citizens. For Hitler, the mold was defined in terms of the Aryan ideal:

In this world, human culture and civilization are inseparably bound up with the existence of the Aryan. His dying off or his decline would again lower upon this earth the dark veils of a time without culture. The undermining of the existence of human culture by destroying its supporters [e.g. Aryans] appears as the most execrable crime.[19]

A similar effort had been attempted by Stalin, where there was an effort to create a "new human being" unique to Soviet society. This new human being was described by one Soviet commentator as follows: "[T]he 'Soviet man' [*Sovetskiy chelovek*] will emerge with a 'Soviet', 'international', 'proletarian' supranational consciousness. National differences will disappear, national cultures will survive only as folklore. All Soviet citizens will have . . . 'the Weltanschauung of the Petrograd worker'."[20] Suppressing different cultural and ethnic groups so as to promote one distinct Soviet identity led to a profound instability in the Soviet Union. This made it impossible for the Soviet state to survive the centrifugal forces of nationalism once Mikhail Gorbachev began implementing his reformist policies in 1985 that effectively ended the forced imposition of a collective Soviet identity.[21] Whether the identity mold was a *Sovetskiy chelovek*, the Aryan man or its equivalent in another totalitarian system, the underlying idea of imposing a set of state-determined moral norms on all citizens, and repressing cultural and ethnic differences, was the same.

The fundamental flaw in Hegel's analysis of the state as the proper starting point for developing moral codes for society has led to his views being either ignored or strongly condemned. But this too is a mistake. Hegel exaggerated the role of the state as a superior moral actor to individuals. However, he was correct to point out that the state has a degree of self-consciousness that makes it an autonomous actor that builds its self-identity on the moral policy choices it takes. Put more simply, Hegel is correct in describing the state as an evolving moral actor that is self-conscious of its morality and willing to promote its moral norms both within and outside the state. Such a view is strongly challenged by two sets of thinkers. I examine each of these sets of criticisms in order to determine whether states have the necessary degree of morality to undergo a hero's journey.

Realist Critics of the Idea of the Moral State

Realists are commentators of world politics who argue that states are at their core motivated by the pursuit of power and promoting their national interests. A realist critic of the idea that states are moral actors is Reinhold Niebuhr, who believes that morality should be expected only of individuals and not of states. In his most celebrated work, *Moral Man and Immoral Society*, Niebuhr wrote the following in his introduction:

Individual men may be moral in the sense that they are able to consider interests other than their own in determining problems of conduct, and are capable, on occasion, of preferring the advantages of others to their own. They are endowed by nature with a measure of sympathy and consideration for their kind, the breadth of which may be extended by an astute social pedagogy. Their rational faculty prompts them to a sense of justice which educational discipline may refine and purge of egoistic elements until their own interests are involved, with a fair measure of objectivity. But all these achievements are more difficult, if not impossible, for human societies and social groups. In every human group there is less reason to guide and to check impulse, less capacity for self-transcendence, less ability to comprehend the needs of others and therefore more unrestrained egoism than the individuals, who compose the group, reveal in their personal relationship.[22]

Niebuhr is here suggesting, in agreement with Hegel, that states, like individuals, have a degree of self-consciousness or "egoism." However, he disagrees profoundly that a state's self-consciousness is capable of pursuing moral norms in any way similar to individuals. Essentially, the larger the human group, the less likely can it be expected to behave in a moral way similar to individuals. To illustrate his belief of how states do not behave morally, and, in fact, cynically manipulate morality, Neibhur wrote:

The Italian statesman, Count Sforza, has recently paid a witty and deserved tribute to the British art in politics. They have, he declares, "a precious gift bestowed by divine grace upon the British people: the simultaneous action in those islands, when a great British interest is at stake, of statesmen and diplomats coolly working to obtain some concrete political advantage and on the other side, and without previous base secret understanding, clergymen and writers eloquently busy showing the highest moral reasons for supporting the diplomatic action which is going on in Downing Street. Such was the case in the Belgian Congo. Belgian rule had been in force there for years; but at a certain moment gold was discovered in the Katanga, the Congolese province nearest to the British South African possessions; and the bishops and other pious persons started at once a violent press campaign to stigmatize the Belgian atrocities against the Negroes. What is astonishing and really imperial is that those bishops and other pious persons were inspired by the most perfect Christian good faith, and that nobody was pulling the wires behind them."[23]

Niebuhr here implies that hypocrisy drove Imperial British policy. The implication is that moral concerns merely mask the selfish national interests of states. Other realist writers on world politics such as Hans Morgenthau and Henry Kissinger similarly agree that states are intrinsically driven by power interests. They thereby elevate amoral political calculations into the realm of prudent statecraft, and they criticize moral principles as imprac-tical and naive.[24] Agreeing with this approach, Kenneth Waltz wrote the following in the conclusion to his famous *Man, The State and the State of War: A Theoretical Analysis*:

Each state pursues its own interests, however defined, in ways it judges best. Force is a means of achieving the external ends of states because there exists no consistent, reliable process of reconciling the conflicts of interest that inevitably arise among similar units in a condition of anarchy. **A foreign policy based on this image of international relations is neither moral nor immoral, but embodies merely a rea-soned response to the world about us** [emphasis added].[25]

What critics of the idea of states as moral actors overlook is that morality is not always a mask for deep national interests based on power. Though many holding the levers of the policy-making process operate under shrewdly calculated power principles, others may be more in tune with the moral impulses that tug at the heart strings of the educated population. History is full of debates between statesmen desiring to bring the ship of state closer to their preferred island of national interest or moral rectitude. For every calculating Prince von Metternich, there is the idealist Tsar Al-exander; for every saber-rattling Otto van Bismark, there is a cooperative William Gladstone; for every pragmatic Theodore Roosevelt, there is a vi-sionary Woodrow Wilson.

The nineteenth-century movement against slavery shows how a clear hu-manitarian concern gradually displaced a state practice that was earlier seen as sanctified by God and a permanent testimony to the fallen nature of humanity. Similarly, the Treaty of Versailles that gave self-rule to many former colonial territories was an imperfect compromise between the altru-istic Woodrow Wilson's support for self-determination and the European victors that were more intent on divvying up the spoils of the German, Austro-Hungarian, and Ottoman Empires. Though it would be foolish to say states do not act out of self-interest, it would be similarly foolhardy to say that states cannot rise above their immediate self-interest or "national egoism." States can and often do pursue a policy based on moral principles. A more powerful set of arguments critical of the idea that states are moral is posed by liberal thinkers.

Liberal Critics of the Idea of the Moral State

The growth in liberal thought in seventeenth-century England urged lim-its to the power of the state over its citizens. The underlying idea was that states, in the personage of a monarch, had grown too powerful and would tyrannize their citizens if not curbed. In simple terms, the ability of states to adopt amoral policies at the expense of their citizens had to be curbed.

The political theorist who went further than any other in arguing for firm constraints on the power of states was John Locke. He urged that the state had a duty to protect the natural rights of its citizens. At the same time, however, there needed to be limits to the powers of the state:

But though men when they enter into society give up the equality, liberty and executive power they had in the state of nature into the hands of the society, to be so far disposed of by the legislative as the good of the society shall require; yet it being only with an intention in every one to better preserve himself, his liberty and property (for no rational creature can be supposed to change his condition with an intention to be worse), the power of the society, or legislative constituted by them, can never be supposed to extend farther than the common good, but is obliged to secure every one's property by providing against those three defects above-mentioned that made the state of nature so unsafe and uneasy.[26]

The "natural rights" that are the anchor of Locke's thinking are life, liberty, and property. He argued that these rights were the basis of an imaginary "social contract" between the state and its citizens. When state leaders infringed the "natural rights" of its citizens, revolution was not only justified but obligatory:

This I am sure, whoever, either ruler or subject, by force goes about to invade the rights of either prince or people, and lays the foundation for overturning the constitution and frame of any just government, he is guilty of the greatest crime I think a man is capable of, being to answer for all those mischiefs of blood, rapine, and desolation, which the breaking to pieces of governments brings on a country. And he who does it is justly to be esteemed the common enemy and pest of mankind, and is to be treated accordingly. **Whosoever uses force without rights as everyone does in society who does it without law, puts himself into a state of war with those against whom he so uses it, and in that state all former ties are canceled, all other rights cease, and everyone has a right to defend himself and to resist the aggressor** [emphasis added][27]

Locke's writings have given birth to a powerful distinction between "civil society" and "state." The state's potential for violence, repression, power politics, and subordination of moral considerations leads to the need for firm constraints on the state. On the other hand, civil society—for example, trade unions, professional associations, employer associations, and religious organizations—is the bastion of moral concerns that plays a restraining role on the potential excesses of the state. Put simply, a consequence of Locke's writings is the idea of coexistence between an immoral state and a moral civil society. Civil society needs a strong state in order to protect it, and the state needs a strong civil society in order to curb it.

A number of recent writers have described the different functions of the state and civil society, and how the two ought to interact. Beverly Woodward for example argues that the functions of civil society include: "to create a sphere of autonomous social activity, to campaign and agitate in behalf of political and social objectives, to provide a counterweight to governmental power, and to oppose the illegitimate exercise of governmental power."[28] Authors such as Philip Smith have commented on the "civilizing process" played by civil society in its dealings with the state that would otherwise be tempted to use repression on its own citizens or on other states.[29] The implication is that when a clear separation exists between the state and civil society, the conditions are present for a strong civil society to fulfill its "civilizing process." When state and civil society are combined, it is argued, this poses a dangerous antidemocratic development. For example, in response to the claim that "civil society in power" is where "the good men in power have formed the republic of virtuous men," Woodward objects as follows:

[T]he claim "civil society is in power" obliterates the distinction between society and government; that the identification of government and civil society eliminates, in theory at least, the basis for opposition to governmental power; that the virtue of individuals is equated (wrongly) with governmental power; that this presumption of virtue makes governmental power holders intolerant of opposition and insensitive to the needs and claims of societal interest groups.[30]

Woodward here argues that the exercise of power is a corrupting influence and that civil society should therefore remain clearly separate from the state.

Woodward's, Smith's, and others' preference for a clear separation between state and civil society supports descriptions of the state as a set of amoral political institutions that are power driven. In this view, the state must be necessarily restrained by elements of civil society if moral policies are to be incorporated into the policy-making process. Such a view, however, overlooks that the separation between state and civil society is difficult to prove in practice. Numerous relationships and influences occur between political institutions (the state) and social institutions (civil society). This was the case for Locke's seventeenth-century England and even more so in the twentieth and twenty-first centuries with modern democratic states.

The growth in democracies is an undisputed feature of the twentieth century. Indeed, so rapid has been the growth of democratic states that Francis Fukuyama sees democracy in his famous "End of History" article as the final stop on a historic journey:

What we may be witnessing is not just the end of the Cold War, or the passing of a particular period of postwar history, but the end of history as such: that is, the end point of mankind's ideological evolution and the universalization of Western liberal democracy as the final form of human government. . . . The state that emerges at the end of history is liberal insofar as it recognizes and protects through a system of law man's universal right to freedom, and democratic insofar as it exists only with the consent of the governed.[31]

An important aspect of the democratic form of governance is the wide ranging web of influences, interdependencies, and connections between governmental and nongovernmental sectors of society. In fact, any clear distinction between civil society and the state becomes difficult to sustain in modern democratic states. Forces of globalization are making it even more difficult to maintain the distinction and separation between civil society and state due to the phenomenal growth in the number of transnational corporations. The U.S. Congress, for example, is strongly influenced by powerful lobby groups that represent civil society. These groups influence how Congress formulates and implements legislation by either making direct financial contributions or by threatening a representative's reelection prospects by lobbying against him or her. The difficulty experienced by the Clinton administration over campaign contributions to the 1998 Congressional elections, is one example of the power of lobby groups in the U.S. Congress. In practice then, rather than there being a clear separation between state and civil society, there is an intertwined relationship between them. This makes any distinction between an amoral state and moral civil society, especially in the case of modern democratic states, very difficult if not impossible to establish.

A result of the intertwined relationship between state and civil society means that the state cannot be seen simply as an amoral set of political institutions. The state represents the focal point of the goals, values, and beliefs of civil society. Rather than there being a clear distinction between state and civil society, an organic metaphor is more appropriate. In this metaphor, the state is the head, arms, and feet of the body, while civil society provides the heart and other vital organs. A result of this organic relationship is that the state can be expected to incorporate a moral element as a consistent feature of its policy-making. I can now return to Hegel's insight that states are self-consciousness political entities that are evolving in the moral dimension. One can now conclude that morality can be introduced as an important basis in the motivation and behavior of a state. Consequently, the self-consciousness and morality of states are important for understanding world politics. As a result, states have the necessary degree of self-consciousness, autonomous decision-making, and morality required for embarking on a hero's journey.

STATES AND THE HERO'S JOURNEY

If states can embark on the hero's journey, then the various steps of the hero's journey may be examined in the context of states rather than individuals. These steps were earlier described in terms relevant to individuals. Now, they must be described in terms that make sense when applied to states. To illustrate these steps, it is useful to refer to various events in American history. Indeed, in subsequent chapters, I argue that America forms an exemplary case of a state undergoing a hero's journey, and is currently in its seventh journey.

The Call to Adventure

The first step in the hero's journey is a rejection of the value system promoted by the community. In psychoanalytical terms, this is a recognition of the fragmentary nature of the human ego and the dissatisfaction that results. This leads to the need to discover a new basis of identity. The first step for states, then, is a rejection of the dominant value system found in the international state system due to a dissatisfaction with the morality of these values. Such a rejection for states would make possible the discovery or consolidation of a new set of moral principles not at the time possible for the international system. As explained in chapter 1, there are three phases in the first step of the "Call to Adventure" in the hero's journey: "hearing the call," "refusal of the call," and "crossing the first threshold."

"Hearing the call" for a state means a rejection of the dominant moral values upon which the international system is based. It means the start of a new attempt at establishing moral principles for guiding national policies and for influencing the policies of other states in the international system. In this phase, those controlling the policy-making process would be idealist in orientation and very critical of the dominant way in which in the international system operates. For example, after its independence in 1776, America took a foreign policy approach based on a fundamental difference between the new Republic and European states. The latter practiced power politics at the expense of indigenous populations around the world. There was an implicit belief that as a political community, America was morally superior to the imperialist European states engaged in amoral power politics. America was therefore bound to take a foreign policy approach that would be based firmly on sound moral principles. In this regard Henry Kissinger wrote: "American leaders rejected the European idea that the morality of states should be judged by different criteria than the morality of individuals."[32]

The "refusal of the call to adventure" is the belief that there is no moral difference between one's own state and the international system. In this phase of the journey, policymakers take a more realist perspective that all states mask their national interests in the guise of good moral principles. In this sense, morality should not be used as a basis for organizing national policy. For example, after American independence, there were therefore advocates of America practicing power politics. Supporters of such a view could look to the separation of powers in the American political system and argue that preserving the balance of power in Europe was vital for American interests. John Adams, America's second president, for example, wrote:

There is a Balance of Power in Europe. . . . Nature has formed it. Practice and Habit have confirmed it, and it must exist forever. It may be disturbed for a time, by the accidental Removal of a Weight from one Scale to the other; but there will be a continual Effort to restore the Equilibrium. . . . Congress adopted these Principles and this System in its purity.[33]

Others could point out instead that there was nothing morally superior in America's democratic system, because history showed that republics could also be involved in wars of conquest. As Alexander Hamilton wrote:

Sparta, Athens, Rome, and Carthage were all republics; two of them, Athens and Carthage, of the commercial kind. Yet were they as often engaged in wars, offensive and defensive, as the neighboring monarchies of the same times. . . . In the government of Britain the representatives of the people compose one branch of the national legislature. Commerce has been for ages the predominant pursuit of that country. Few nations, nevertheless, have been more frequently engaged in war.[34]

In sum, "refusal of the call to adventure" represents the belief that America is not all that different from other nations and should not commit its vast resources to ensuring a more moral framework for the conduct of world politics.

"Crossing of the first threshold" represents crossing the Rubicon in which a state commits itself to the moral principles it believes fundamental for the behavior of states. This typically would occur by some tangible policy that cannot be reversed. For example, soon after American independence, this was done by America refusing to compromise its moral principles and engage in the power politics that bedeviled the international system. America subsequently withdrew from the international system and made this a sign that America lived in a very different moral universe. As President Monroe declared, "In the wars of the European powers in matters relating to themselves we have never taken any part, nor does it comport with our policy so to do."[35]

Great Remembering

The second step of the hero's journey, the "great remembering" refers to the encounter with the three archetypes most meaningful for the self-discovery process: the shadow; the Mother; and the Father. In psychoanalytical terms, these encounters lead respectively to recognition of the moral limitations of the individual; integration of all aspects of the individual and self-empowerment; and discovery of a new calling or purpose in life. Similarly, the encounter with these archetypes would enable a political community to achieve three related things. The encounter with the shadow allows a community to adequately deal with its own deficiencies. The key national motif here would be the war against some category of national enemy. The encounter with the Mother archetype leads to the community integrating all elements of its diverse population and to renew its economic vitality. "National unity" and "renewal" would be the key phrases here. Finally, the encounter with the Father archetype leads to (re)discovery of the moral principles at the core of a community's national identity. The key motif here is to be faithful to one's national calling or mission.

As mentioned earlier, encountering the shadow archetype suggests that an individual deals with the negative or dark aspects of the self without projecting these undesirable qualities onto others. In similar terms, states successfully encounter the shadow archetype when they deal with their negative attributes in a way that does not allow them to project these onto other states or political communities. A state then would be unlikely to project dichotomous moral categories of good and evil respectively onto itself and to other states or communities. "Slaying the dragon," for states, is a policy-making process that avoids the creation of enemy images whereby another state or community is dehumanized or depicted as the embodiment of evil. An example of shadow projection for states and how "slaying the dragon" occurred is described by Corinne McLaughlin and Gordon Davidson:

A classic case of shadow projection is found in the recent history of U.S.-Soviet relations. Americans used to believe that it was the former Soviets who were aggressive, expansive, and deceptive—never ourselves. Clearly they were the "bad guys." Conversely, the Soviets believed that we were the "bad guys" and that they did nothing wrong. But, in fact, both countries are mirrors for each other in certain ways. . . . This projection began lessening when President Reagan, who had referred to the Soviet Union as the "evil empire," actually went into "the heart of the beast" at Red Square and embraced his "shadow"—projected onto Gorbachev—thereby helping to transform the collective projection.[36]

"Slaying the dragon," as occurred with Reagan's visit to Moscow and embrace of Mikhail Gorbachev, is a process states undergo when political leaders, business interests, or ordinary citizens begin to humanize the other. This means avoiding dichotomous moral values of good and evil, right and wrong, and the like, in the way different communities understand and communicate with one another. This means moving from a "values based moral system," to a "needs based moral system" where each community's needs are recognized and respected. This is not to suggest, however, that we can live in a world without opponents, because there are always likely to be antagonistic political forces and movements in world politics.[37] The important thing to do is to identify and acknowledge the truths, no matter how distorted we feel them to be, that our political opponents are committed to in order to humanize them. As Sam Keen has thoughtfully recommended, we must strive to humanize our enemies in order to unmask our own deficiencies and to avoid excesses in dealing with the other side.[38]

The encounter with the Mother archetype—the sacred marriage—was described earlier as unleashing psychological qualities that are necessary for empowering the individual and achieving an integrated sense of identity. In similar terms, the "sacred marriage" for states corresponds to states being able to integrate all their citizens and groups into one political community. National unity is therefore an important part of this encounter. For example, the rapid decolonization of states after World War II led to them all emphasizing national unity. Nation building through the creation of a set of political myths for the heroes of the independence struggle was emphasized. However, these top-down approaches to national unity often used coercion and have been failures. This suggests that there is something more than simply emphasizing national unity that is the key to the sacred marriage for states. A deeper form of unity than simply celebrating national symbols is needed. Corinne McLaughlin and Gordon Davidson insightfully write about what this deeper unity may mean for states:

Just as individuals must struggle with the process of personality integration, bringing the physical, emotional, and mental components of their personalities into a coordinated, working whole, so too must a nation become an integrated personality before it can successfully invoke its Soul.[39]

Establishing more integrated and "connected" political communities is increasingly argued to be an important paradigm shift in all disciplines. Robert Bush and Joseph Folger, for example, argue that numerous writings reflect that we are moving from an "individualist worldview" based on individual autonomy and competition, to a "relational" worldview emphasizing mutual connectedness and cooperation:

Carol Gilligan's work on moral theory and development stresses the equal importance of both individuality and connectedness in human consciousness and the resulting capacity for integrating strength of self with concern for other. . . . In the work of contemporary thinkers such as [Gilligan] . . . the shape of the Relational worldview is emerging. Moreover, most of these thinkers are quite explicit about the fact that their ideas are meant to express a new worldview that contrasts with the Individualist outlook. Indeed, almost all of these "relational" writers explicitly criticize the Individualist worldview, usually in quite similar terms. The fact that elements of this worldview are being expressed similarly, across such a range of fields, signals the beginning of another paradigm shift, from the Individualist to the Relational worldview.[40]

Encountering the "sacred marriage" means the establishment of political communities that are more interconnected and integrated. Tangible benefits of the sacred marriage are that states can more effectively use the territory and resources over which they have sovereign control. The state could therefore reap a rich harvest, in the sense of goods and services, necessary for the prosperity and well-being of the entire political community. The productivity of the land and the entrepreneurial efforts of the population thus become benefits attributed to the archetypal encounter of the sacred marriage. These benefits, made possible by the state integrating its citizenry and faithfully using the resources made available to it, lead to the empowerment of the state.

In sum, the sacred marriage signifies a transition within a state's self-consciousness in which a greater degree of interconnectedness and integration occurs between the population. The sacred marriage leads to a very deep sense of national unity that allows the state to enjoy its material prosperity or to continue its hero's journey. The Buddha could choose to immerse himself in nirvana (immersion in the sacred marriage) or become a world teacher (atonement). So too states can immerse themselves in the fruit of their endeavors (materialism) or begin a hero's quest to change the international system.

Encountering the Father archetype suggests a transition in national self-consciousness so that a state identifies its place in history and its calling in the global community. This can be done by turning to those expressions of a national identity—constitutions, emblems, flags, literature, and songs—that illustrate the aspirations of those who founded the state. This step of the hero's journey means discovering the national ideals embodied in the clearest expressions of national identity, and trying to achieve them. The ultimate task of any political community, according to Hegel, was achieving its highest ideals. When this is realized, the state has achieved what he believes to be national self-consciousness. Hegel writes that world history is an unfolding process of the Spirit realizing itself through individuals, peoples, and states, where Spirit achieves higher and higher degrees of self-consciousness:

We have already seen what the final purpose of this process is. The principles of the national spirits progressing through a necessary succession of stages are only moments of the one universal Spirit which through them elevates and completes itself into a self-comprehending totality. . . . This implies that the present stage of Spirit contains all previous stages within itself. These, to be sure, have unfolded themselves successively and separately, but Spirit still is what it has in itself always been. The differentiation of its stages is but the development of what it is in itself.

. . . The moments which Spirit seems to have left behind, it still possesses in the depth of its present.[41]

Hegel here argues that states are self-conscious actors that can become aware of a historical process in which they play a primary role. This self-awareness gives a state a place in world history. For states such as colonial India, Hegel believes that despite India's profound literary and religious output over millennia, "it has no history."[42] He believed that this was due to the absence of a political community in India that achieved self-consciousness. Achieving self-consciousness and recognizing their role in an unfolding historical process is therefore fundamental for a state and its citizenry. The recognition of a historical process and one's relationship to this process, for Hegel, stands as the basis for all morality.

The deeds of great men who are individuals of world history thus appear justified not only in their intrinsic, unconscious significance but also from the point of view of world history. It is irrelevant and inappropriate from that point of view to raise moral claims against world-historical acts and agents. They stand outside of morality.[43]

Atonement corresponds to the discovery that global events and processes are steps in an unfolding historical purpose. The state's awareness of its role in this historical drama is its calling. Fulfilling this calling is how the state achieves atonement with the Father archetype. History is therefore purposive, and states can achieve a degree of self-consciousness that makes them autonomous moral agents in an unfolding historical drama.

In the individual hero's journey, atonement comes about when the individual leaves behind the selfish desires of his or her personal consciousness and adopts a calling that would transform the community in which he or she lived. For a state, atonement comes by leaving behind its limited national-interest. Instead, the state sets out to achieve a set of interests defined in terms of its national calling or national mission as embodied in different expressions of the political community's ideals. The result is a transformation of the international system. In Hegelian terms, "atonement" represents a state recognizing itself as a "self-comprehending *totality*."[44] Atonement for states, then, comes about when the national interest is firmly understood in terms of the global interest (Hegel's "totality"). This broadened self-interest then becomes part of the national self-consciousness and the fundamental basis of the policy-making process.

The Return to International Society

The third step in the hero's journey is a return to one's community with a new identity and value system, and desiring to establish one's values in the community. As explained earlier, there are three phases in the third step of the Return: "refusal of the call," "crossing the return threshold," and "master of the two worlds." In psychoanalytical terms, the Return corresponds to sharing the wisdom achieved through the great remembering with the wider community. The third step for states, then, is a return to the international state system after periods of discovering a new set of moral principles upon which to base foreign policy. The returning state has a mission to promote a set of moral principles that finally has become possible for the behavior of states in the international system.

In psychoanalytical terms, "refusal of the return" means a reluctance to leave the elevated state of consciousness reached in the journey of self-discovery, and to reenter the normal waking consciousness. For states, this would correspond to the belief that one's own value system is superior to that of other states, and that it is almost impossible to change the international system for the present moment. For example, after World War I, many Americans despaired of reforming the international system after the harsh peace imposed on Germany in the Treaty of Versailles. The U.S. Senate refused to ratify the Treaty and to join the League of Nations. The refusal to join the League of Nations corresponded to Campbell's "Refusal of the Return" in which America signaled that despite its formidable resources and clear interest in maintaining peace and order in the European continent, it would not participate in an international system corrupted by principles of power politics. America would not compromise its belief that the international system had to be based on sound moral principles before America would fully commit itself to the cause of international peace and order.

Crossing the return threshold means for individuals that one is willing to give up remaining immersed in an elevated state of consciousness (the sacred marriage), and return to ordinary waking consciousness in order to realize one's *calling* (atonement). For states, this means making an irreversible commitment to reforming the international system. For example, after World War II, America took up the mantle of undisputed leadership among the Western democracies. This was due to the material devastation of continental Europe; economic exhaustion of the imperial powers, Britain and France, and the ensuing task of decolonization; and the threat cast by the Soviet Union. America was ready to take up its national calling and demonstrate its *atonement* with the Father archetype. In doing so, America would cross the threshold of no return and commit itself to fulfilling the Wilsonian vision of a universal peace based on liberty, democratic political institutions, and a global association of nations—the United Nations.

"Master of the Two Worlds" means that an individual has integrated the elevated state of consciousness and normal waking consciousness in a way that empowers and gives purpose to the Self. For states, this achieves a harmony between the moral principles at the base of national identity, and the political, economic, and military resources that a state possesses. In short, being master of the two worlds means fusing power and morality in a grand synthesis. For example, in acting to protect the rights of ethnic minorities through a mix of diplomatic and economic resources at the end of this century, America has become Master of the Two Worlds. America has channeled its vast resources to a set of political principles that represent a higher moral truth—liberty.

The Deep Forgetting

The fourth step of the hero's journey is to forget the sense of identity gained as a result of the archetypal encounters of "slaying the dragon," the "sacred marriage," and "atonement." Just as individuals undergo three types of a "great forgetting," so too do states undergo a national parallel of "fear," "pursuit of power," and "materialism."

The national parallel for "fear" is where the state becomes preoccupied with the security threat, diplomatic consequences, and/or economic costs of pursuing a moral foreign policy. Any benefits from pursuing a moral foreign policy are overshadowed by the dangers of such a policy in the minds of key policymakers and leading political figures in the broader public. The state consequently abandons the grand synthesis achieved earlier in the return to international society.

The national parallel for "pursuit of power" is imperialism, in which states feel free to ignore more legitimate forms of international authority such as the various organs of the United Nations. The transition from mastery of the two worlds to imperialism is a real and slippery one. Confident that they have fused the spheres of morality and politics, states in time come to act as though the views of policy elites are all that matter. This may seriously compromise international public opinion and the moral principles that lie at the heart of America's identity. For example, America has come under strong international criticism for acting in an imperialistic manner by ignoring the will of the international community. On issues such as creating an international criminal court, banning antipersonnel land mines, and ratifying human rights treaties, American policymakers have been out of step with the moral principles and views of the broader international public opinion.

The parallel for "materialism" for states is excessive preoccupation with increases in a state's gross national product with little regard given to distributing this in an equitable manner. For example, at the international level, industrialized states do not do enough to change the iniquitous nature of the international trade system. Europe and America insist on a high wall of tariffs, subsidies, and regulations for imported agricultural products, but they insist that such walls against manufactured and service products must be eliminated. This unfortunately puts at a disadvantage developing countries that rely on agricultural exports to pay for manufactured products and services from developed countries.

In conclusion, states are political communities that have the necessary degree of self-consciousness and moral development necessary for embarking on a hero's journey. The four steps of the hero's journey for individuals parallel the policies states can take at the international level. All four steps are psychosocial events and processes similar to the psychological processes undergone by individuals. Just as an individual achieves self-transformation by undergoing the hero's journey, so too states can undergo a transformative process by experiencing archetypal encounters. To illustrate the hero's journey for states, I now turn to an examination of the United States of America.

NOTES

1. Hedley Bull, *The Anarchical Society: A Study of Order in World Politics* (London: Macmillan, 1977), 8.

2. Alan James, *Sovereign Statehood: The Basis of International Society* (London: Allen and Unwin, 1986), 13–14.

3. Bull, *The Anarchical Society*, 8.

4. Ibid., 8–9

5. For discussion of the foreign policy-making process in the United States see James A. Nathan and James K. Oliver, *Foreign Policy Making and the American Political System*, 2nd ed. (Boston: Little, Brown and Co., 1987), 1–20.

6. Henry Kissinger discusses the development of the forerunner to this concept, the French notion of raison d'état in *Diplomacy* (New York: Simon and Schuster, 1994), 58–59.

7. Hans Morgenthau, *Politics among Nations*, 5th ed., rev. (New York: Knopf, 1978), 5.

8. Ibid.

9. Quoted from Reinhold Niebuhr, *Moral Man & Immoral Society* (New York: Charles Scribner's Sons, 1960), 84.

10. Ibid.

11. Sri Aurobindo, *The Human Cycle, The Ideal of Human Unity, War and Self-Determination* (Pondicherry, India: Sri Aurobindo Trust, 1977), 29.

12. Morgenthau, *Politics among Nations*, 5–8.

13. Stephen Walt, "International Relations: One World, Many Theories," *Foreign Policy* (Spring 1998): 31.

14. Indeed, Hegel goes further than anybody else in elevating the position of the state. Consult James Pfaltzgraff and Robert Dougherty, *Contending Theories of International Relations: A Comprehensive Survey*, 4th ed. (New York: Longman, 1997), 64.

15. Georg Hegel, *Reason in History: A General Introduction to the Philosophy of History* (New York: The Bobbs-Merrill Company, 1953), 52.

16. Sri Aurobindo, *The Human Cycle*, 29.

17. T. H. Green, "Society as Positive Freedom," in *The Development of the Democratic Idea* (New York: Washington Square Press, 1968), 412.

18. Hegel, *Reason in History*, 52–53.

19. Quoted in G. L. Mosse, ed., *Nazi Culture: Intellectual, Cultural, and Social Life in the Third Reich* (New York: Schocken Books, 1966), 6.

20. Alexandre Bennigsen and Marie Broxup, *The Islamic Threat to the Soviet State* (London: Croom Helm, 1983), 26.

21. See Corinne McLaughlin and Gordon Davidson, *Spiritual Politics: Changing the World from the Inside Out* (New York: Ballantine Books, 1994), 282–83.

22. Niebuhr, *Moral Man & Immoral Society*, xi–xii.

23. Ibid., 108–9.

24. Kissinger, *Diplomacy*, 58.

25. Kenneth Waltz, *Man, The State and the State of War: A Theoretical Analysis* (New York: Columbia University Press, 1959), 238.

26. John Locke, "Second Treatise of Civil Government," chapter 9, section 131, quoted in *The Development of the Democratic Idea*, ed. Charles M. Sherover (New York: Washington Square Press, 1968), 162.

27. Ibid., chapter 19, section 230, 232, quoted in *The Development of the Democratic Idea*, 181.

28. Beverly Woodward, "Civil Society in Transition," in *Rethinking Peace*, ed. Robert Elias and Jennifer Turpin (Boulder, Colo.: Lynne Rienner, 1994), 226.

29. Philip Smith, "Civil Society and Violence," in *The Web of Violence*, ed. Jennifer Turpin and Lester Kurtz (Chicago: University of Illinois, 1997), 110–12.

30. Woodward, "Civil Society in Transition," in *Rethinking Peace*, 228.

31. Francis Fukuyama, "The End of History?: The New Shape of World Politics: Contending Paradigms in International Relations," *Foreign Affairs* (1997): 2, 4; originally published in *The National Interest* (Summer 1989).

32. Kissinger, *Diplomacy*, 32.

33. Quoted in Arthur Schlesinger, Jr., *The Cycles of American History* (Boston: Houghton Mifflin Co., 1986), 52.

34. Quoted in Kissinger, *Diplomacy*, 33.

35. Ibid., 36.

36. McLaughlin and Davidson, *Spiritual Politics*, 177.

37. For discussion of antagonistic political forces, see McLaughlin and Davidson, *Spiritual Politics*, 256–63.

38. Sam Keen, *Faces of the Enemy: Reflections of the Hostile Imagination* (San Francisco: Harper and Row, 1991).

39. McLaughlin and Davidson, *Spiritual Politics*, 281.

40. Robert Bush and Joseph Folger, *The Promise of Mediation: Responding to Conflict through Empowerment and Recognition* (San Francisco: Jossey Bass Publishers, 1994), 256.

41. Hegel, *Reason in History*, 95.

42. Ibid., 76.

43. Ibid., 82–83.

44. Ibid., 95.

CHAPTER 3

AMERICA'S FIRST HERO'S JOURNEY (1764–1822)—AMERICA AS BEACON OF LIBERTY AND REPUBLICANISM

AMERICA AND THE HERO'S JOURNEY

America is a remarkable example of how states can embark on a hero's journey in the international system. There are a number of reasons for choosing America as the state to examine for a hero's journey. First, America was dominant in shaping the moral principles that underlay world politics in the twentieth century. As Henry Kissinger points out in the opening paragraph of his popular book *Diplomacy*:

Almost as if according to some natural law, in every century there seems to emerge a country with the power, the will, and the intellectual and moral impetus to shape the entire international system in accordance with its own values. . . . In the twentieth century, no country has influenced international relations as decisively and at the same time as ambivalently as the United States. No society has more firmly insisted on the inadmissibility of intervention in the domestic affairs of other states, or more passionately asserted that its own values were universally applicable. No nation has been more pragmatic in the day-to-day conduct of its diplomacy, or more ideological in the pursuit of its historic moral convictions.[1]

Not only did America dominate the twentieth century, but it looks ready to repeat this for the twenty-first century. In short, we now enter a second American century where America again will be dominant in shaping world affairs in accord to the moral principles at the core of its national identity.

A second reason for choosing America as a state undergoing a hero's journey is that its history as a political community is relatively short. Indeed, the revolutionary war that led to the Declaration of Independence in 1776 forms the starting point of America as a self-conscious political community. This makes it easier to find the key events and processes that distinguish it at various stages of the hero's journey. A final reason is that as a political community, America's national identity is defined in terms of a set of moral principles that are remarkable for their global scope and vision. This makes it relatively easy to examine how well America is fulfilling its national identity by the way it formulates and implements its foreign policy.

Three main moral principles make up America's national mission and form the basis of its hero's journey, and indeed its national identity. The first is the principle of liberty, in which individuals are free from oppressive and despotic rule that denies fundamental rights such as freedom of speech, freedom of assembly, freedom to travel, and freedom to form political organizations. The second is representative democracy, where political institutions are in place that enact, interpret, and enforce laws. The third is rule of law, where all individuals are equal under a body of laws that are enforced without reference to rank or influence. The recognition and pursuit of America's national mission by foreign policy makers and the support of American citizens that makes this possible is a psychosocial process. Such a process is similar to the self-discovery process taken by individuals when experiencing the three archetypal encounters and four steps of the hero's journey already described.

America's hero journey can be recognized through an examination of historical events and policies that reveal an unfolding self-discovery process. The core of this process is the extent to which foreign policy makers base their decisions on moral principles at the heart of American identity as opposed to short-term national interests. The psychosocial process of America becoming conscious of its national identity is exemplified in the hero's journey. America is now in its seventh hero's journey. Each completed journey forms the culmination of an international adventure in pursuit of a distinct set of moral principles that are related to the three core principles at the heart of American identity: liberty, democracy, and rule of law. America has recently entered the most internationally active phase of its seventh hero's journey. This phase will see American power wedded to moral principles in a vigorous attempt to transform world politics.

The idea that American policy-making experiences cycles was explained first by the historian Arthur Schlesinger, Sr., in a controversial essay that appeared in the *Yale Review* in 1939. The "Tides of National Politics" argued that the ebb and flow of American policy-making revolves around a "period of concern for the rights of the few" being followed by a period of "concern for the wrongs of the many."[2] This means that American politics is fairly evenly balanced between supporters of policies that merely want government to protect their basic liberties and those that believe the role of government is to be more active in addressing all forms of injustice.

Taking up the same idea of his father, Arthur Schlesinger, Jr., similarly explained that America's politics changes approximately every thirty years due to a new generation taking the helm of policy-making from periods of private interest to public purpose.[3] Private interest periods focus on America renewing its economic vitality:

A nation's capacity for high-tension political commitment is limited. Nature insists on a respite. People can no longer gird themselves for heroic effort. They yearn to immerse themselves in the privacies of life. Worn out by the constant summons to battle, weary of ceaseless national activity, disillusioned by the results, they seek a new dispensation, an interlude of rest and recuperation.[4]

In contrast to private interest periods, public purpose periods are those where moral principles can once more be vigorously promoted. This is because American citizens feel that their nation's batteries have been recharged and they are confident enough to begin realizing their national identity:

The vacation from public responsibility replenishes the national energies and recharges the national batteries. People begin to seek meaning in life beyond themselves. They ask not what their country can do for them but what they can do for their country. They are ready for a trumpet to sound. A detonating issue—some problem growing in magnitude and menace and beyond the capacity of the market's invisible hand to solve—at last leads to a breakthrough into a new political epoch.[5]

In the foreign policy sphere, this movement from private interest to public purpose periods amounts to cycles of withdrawal and return—two of the four steps of the hero's journey.[6] This approach to explaining foreign policy cycles is most clearly described in a little known book by Frank Klingberg. In *Cyclical Trends in American Foreign Policy Moods: The Unfolding of America's World Role*, Klingberg argues that American policy swung like a pendulum between periods of extroversion and introversion.[7] In a period of extroversion, America is willing "to bring its influence to bear upon other nations, to exert direct positive pressure (especially military or diplomatic) outside its borders."[8] In contrast, introversion meant an "unwillingness to exert much direct pressure on other nations, and a desire to concentrate upon internal problems." This results in pendulum-like swings between periods when America is willing or not to use its energies to support moral principles in foreign policy.

A more recent attempt to describe American history through a cyclic theory based on generational change appears in a 1997 book by William Strauss and Neil Howe.[9] In *The Fourth Turning: An American Prophecy: What the Cycles of History Tell Us about America's Next Rendezvous with Destiny*, they argue that American politics goes through a cycle with four phases. In the "First Turning" (the "high") there is a weakening of individualism and a strengthening of institutional action in addressing problems. A new civic order replaces an older societal value system. In the "Second Turning" (the "awakening") intense spiritual upheaval occurs when the civic order comes under attack from a new value system. In the "Third Turning" (the "unraveling") individualism is strengthened and there is an erosion in trust in public institutions. Again, a new value system erodes the old civic order. Finally, in the "Fourth Turning" (the "crisis") a profound era of secular upheaval leads to the replacement of the old civic order by a new value system. Strauss and Howe argue that soon after the start of the new millennium, America will enter a new crisis period: "The Fourth Turning will trigger a political upheaval beyond anything Americans could today imagine. New civic authority will have to take root, quickly and firmly—which won't be easy if the discredited rules and rituals of the old regime remain fully in place."[10]

The cycle theories described here argue that American politics undergoes periodic changes based on moral considerations. The reason for these periodic changes is the closely balanced sets of political forces that make up at any one time the dominant American mood. Arthur Schlesinger, Sr., trying to answer the question of why these shifts in public mood occur, wrote:

Jefferson hinted at the answer when he observed, "Men, according to their constitutions, and the circumstances in which they are placed, differ honestly in opinion." Some, he said, "fear the people, and wish to transfer all power to the safest depository of power in the last resort; they cherish them therefore, and wish to leave in them all the powers to the exercise of which they are competent." He called these contrasting conceptions Tory and Whig, aristocratic and democratic, Federalist and Republican. Today we would call them conservative and liberal. A Gallup poll taken in 1939, when conservatism was on the upgrade, revealed that the voters were about equally divided between the two schools, 52 percent describing themselves conservatives and 48 as liberals. Probably the balance has always been much the same, a small shift from one side to the other determining the dominant mood.[11]

The idea that public opinion moves in periodic tides is a fundamental insight into the nature of American politics. Such changes come from the willingness to support foreign and domestic policy initiatives that reflect the moral principles at the core of American national identity. America is a rare, if not unique, example of a political community whose national identity is based almost entirely on moral principles. This contrasts with the more common effort to identify national identity in terms of ethnicity (e.g., Greece), religion (e.g., Pakistan), colonial heritage (e.g., Australia and Great Britain), tradition (e.g., Thailand), or ideology (e.g., China). The vigor with which America promotes moral principles will reflect a number of factors, such as the state of the national economy, American power to influence the international system, threats from other states to American interests, international crises, and differing generations coming to political maturity and taking power. Therefore, the change from one part of the cycle to another is due to a broad range of factors. This is an important difference with the cyclic theories, which all focus on one factor—generational change—as the key to understanding shifts in the cycle. This chapter focuses on identifying cyclic changes in American foreign policy using the model of the hero's journey developed earlier. The transition from one phase in the cycle to the next is made possible by a set of events that transforms the national mood. I argue that America is currently in its seventh cycle or hero's journey.

AMERICA'S FIRST HERO'S JOURNEY (1764–1822)

America's first hero's journey begins with the Revolutionary War of independence. Much more than merely a war of independence against colonial rule, America's founding fathers firmly believed that the establishment of America as a Republic was an act of Providence. Providence was lending a hand to the beginning of a great experiment where liberty, democracy, and rule of law would be the guiding principles of a new society on the North American continent. Ensuring the success of America as a republic and democracy would be no easy task. Never before in history had this form of government been attempted on such a vast scale. The democracies of ancient Greece were city-states that were small in terms of territory and population. America covered a vast area, and its population was rapidly growing. Moreover, monarchical forms of government were the norm in Europe, and republicanism was widely seen as an unstable and dangerous experiment that had repeatedly failed in the past. Americans could look back, for example, to seventeenth-century England and the failure of Oliver Cromwell's Christian Commonwealth. This form of republican government proved too unstable, and England eventually reintroduced the monarchy. America's hero journey would be to make successful a form of government that ran against the trends of history and denied conventional thinking at the time.

The Call to Adventure (1764–1776)—Liberty from Unrepresentative Taxation

The beginning of the Revolutionary War of independence lies in the attempt by Britain to raise revenue from taxation of goods imported into the American colonies. For Americans, a practice that had been accepted since the beginning of English colonization had now become odious and repressive. What explains this dramatic change in American public opinion? The most plausible explanation was the growing perception that the American colonies were no longer children that had to listen to and apply the dictates of the mother country. American colonies had grown into adulthood through their sweat and labor and had a right to be heard. If Britain refused to grant the American colonies representation in the British Parliament, then Americans would increasingly chafe and grow restless under the unrepresentative taxation of the mother country. King George's Britain would not grant Americans the right to sit in its Parliament. The colonies began the first step of America's hero's journey by withdrawing from the colonial system that had existed since the founding of English settlements on North America.

Hearing the call

The establishment of English colonies in the Americas was done in a very different way to that of other European states. Whereas Spain, France, and Portugal all established colonies under the direct rule of the state, England used the principle of charters whereby a group of individuals or a company could establish a colony. This arrangement was far less expensive for the English government than the European model. For those in the colonies, it had the advantage that the colonies were essentially self-governing. For example, the Virginia Company was a joint stock company established in 1606 and given a royal charter to establish a colony in Virginia. Stockholders could elect or remove a governor of the colony, and, more importantly, direct how the governor should administer the colony. In an effort to address problems with Virginia's first governors, the new governor, Sir George Yeardly, was instructed "to abolish arbitrary rule, introduce English common law and due process, encourage private property, and summon a representative assembly. This assembly would have power, with the appointed council, to pass local laws, subject to the Company's veto."[12] Rule of law and self-government became the norm for all Britain's American colonies, whether established by royal charter or under direct rule by the Crown. Consequently, up until the revolutionary era beginning with the Revenue Act of 1764, there had developed a compromise between imperial control and colonial self-government. As Samuel Morison wrote: "King and Parliament had undisputed control of foreign affairs, war and peace, and overseas trade. . . . In almost every other respect Americans had acquired home rule."[13]

In 1764, Britain passed the Revenue Act that imposed duties on a number of goods imported into the colonies. This aroused immediate opposition. A petition by the New York Assembly argued that "exemption from burthen of . . . involuntary taxes, must be the grand principle of every free state . . . [without which] there can be no liberty, no happiness, no security."[14] Many American colonists saw the Revenue Act as an attack on their liberty. A boycott of the imported goods covered by the Act began in New Haven by Yale students. In 1765, the Stamp Act was passed from the British Parliament. It was the first time an internal tax, as opposed to a customs duty, had been explicitly levied on the colonists. In condemning the tax, the Virginia assembly declared that it had "the only and sole exclusive right and power to lay taxes . . . upon the inhabitants of this Colony."[15] Middle-class citizens calling themselves the "Sons of Liberty" organized themselves in every seaport and began burning the stamped paper, destroying the property of officials responsible for distributing the paper, and coercing others into resigning. So successful was the opposition that after a couple of months businesses reopened without the stamped paper being used. The Stamp Act was repealed by Parliament in 1766. Nevertheless, the lines of future conflict had been drawn with Parliament's declaration that it had the right to tax the American colonies. The "call to adventure" had begun for the future American Republic. The adventure was to be one of preserving the liberty of Americans to be taxed by assemblies in which they had representation.

Refusal of the call to adventure

Colonial Americans believed that the British Parliament had no right to create internal taxes such as the Stamp Act. However, for many, this was not the case with external taxes such as customs duties that had always been levied against goods entering the colonies. The Townshend Act of 1767, taking note of this distinction, imposed customs duties on a number of imported goods, including tea. There was not the same opposition as shown against the Stamp Act, because many Americans did not question the legitimacy of the Act. For them, the problem was that it placed an unwelcome burden on commerce. For perhaps the majority of colonial Americans, opposition to the Townshend Act came not from embracing the principle of liberty but from reduced profits in hard economic times. Many were satisfied with repeal of the more burdensome parts of the Townshend Act in 1770 with the result that considerable revenue flowed into the British Treasury.[16]

Crossing the first threshold

For the Sons of Liberty the Townshend Act was illegitimate and had to be opposed at all costs. They continued to organize boycotts and nonimportation agreements. Their most audacious act was the Boston Tea Party in December 1773. Valuable tea had been dumped, and the British Parliament demanded compensation. A series of acts Americans called the Coercive Acts included the blockade of Boston. This led to the convening of the First Continental Congress in Philadelphia in 1774 and support for Boston and Massachusetts by the other colonies. A British military force of 700 men was sent to Concord to destroy munitions in April 1775 and were met at Lexington by 70 armed Minutemen. Fighting broke out, and

8 militia men were killed. The British met stronger resistance at Concord with 3 killed. The retreat by the British to Boston was a bloody affair where in total 73 troops were killed and 174 injured. America had crossed the first threshold of its hero's journey by committing itself to an armed struggle with Britain to abolish the unrepresentative taxation imposed upon them.

Great Remembering (1776–1789)—Founding of the American Republic

Why call this stage of America's hero's journey the "great remembering" when it was America's first journey and therefore there was nothing to remember? This statement overlooks that the principles that underscored the birth of the American Republic did not come out of a vacuum. The seeds for the principles of liberty, democracy, and rule of law could all be found in the royal charters permitting English colonies in the New World. Nothing comparable could be found in the colonies established by Spain and France in the New World. The great remembering was therefore an attempt by the American colonies to apply the underlying moral principles that had existed in some form since the establishment of the colonies to the political environment and conflict in which they now found themselves.

Slaying the dragon

Opposition for many Americans to Britain's taxation was divided between the Sons of Liberty, who questioned Britain's right to tax, and those who merely wanted taxes cut due to financial reasons. To find themselves suddenly embroiled in a bloody conflict came as a shock for many Americans. Britain was a great imperial power that had a long and rich tradition, and a King to whom loyalty was almost instinctual. The second Continental Congress met in May 1775, and appointed George Washington as commander in chief. The word "independence" was not mentioned because loyalty to the King was still strong. The war that had begun would be a war of Americans as King George's loyal subjects fighting for their rights against Acts imposed by the King's unrepresentative Parliament. Indeed, after fighting broke out, Washington continued to toast the King in his officers' mess until January 1776.

For many Americans, the struggle was deeply disturbing because it raised the whole question of legitimacy. Was the struggle similar to a child usurping the right of a parent to command? Indeed, in a letter written during the furor of the Townshend Acts, John Dickenson used the parent metaphor to describe the conflict: "Let us behave like dutiful children, who have received unmerited blows from a beloved parent. Let us complain to our parent; but let our complaints speak at the same time the language of affliction and veneration."[17] For those who thought that the struggle was more about money than deep moral principle, legitimacy was a great problem. This problem of the legitimacy of the struggle was the dragon Jefferson attempted to slay in writing the Declaration of Independence.

Jefferson used arguments in the Declaration made first by the great English moral philosopher, John Locke. In Locke's *Second Treatise on Government*, he argued that if a sovereign should violate the natural rights of his subjects—life, liberty, and property—rebellion would not only be justified but would become a moral obligation. As Samuel Morison wrote, Jefferson's Declaration "was a godsend to tender souls among the Patriots who could not get over their duty to honor the king."[18] The Declaration of Independence was the most powerful weapon used in the long revolutionary struggle. For many, it slayed the dragon of residual loyalty to King George and legitimacy of the struggle. The Declaration enabled colonial Americans to remain for the most part united in fighting a long and costly struggle against a revered imperial power.

The sacred marriage

Some principles were needed to unite the thirteen colonies during the long independence struggle. This was critical if they were to eventually succeed. The colonies would have to be united if they wanted to ensure that Britain would not attempt to regain control. There was also the problem with France and Spain that were helping America for the moment, but had their own ambitions on the American continent. There was nowhere in existence a federal model for uniting different political units. One had to be developed. The Articles of Confederation were the first attempt at outlining a federal form of government. They were submitted by the Continental Congress to the different colonies in November 1777. The Articles were slowly ratified by all colonies, with Maryland being the last in March 1781.

The signing of a peace treaty in Paris in 1783 saw the formal end of the Independence War. America had emerged victorious as a Republic with a federal form of government. There was no precedent in history for something so ambitious. No wonder the first generation of independent Americans believed America to be a "Great Experiment." Unity was the key word, and the Great Seal adopted by Congress in 1782 symbolized what would be the key to success in this great experiment, *e pluribus unum*— out of many, one! The sacred marriage symbolized the unity achieved by a federal system of government for the thirteen former colonies, and the economic benefits this would bring.

A revival of commerce for the economically exhausted colonies that made up the new Republic was at first slow to come. Trade was the lifeblood of the American colonies, which had previously traded exclusively with Britain. As an independent state, America had to sign commercial treaties with other European countries with whom direct trade had not previously existed. Trade with Britain also gradually revived. Once again large profits were being made in America, and the years up to 1789 saw the revival of commerce.

Despite the commercial revival, problems soon appeared with the Articles of Confederation. A new attempt would have to be made to develop a federal form of government. The Federal Convention that met in Philadelphia for four months in 1787 drafted the most successful constitution in history. The Constitution was successful in outlining the division of powers between the central and state governments; and the separation of powers between the executive, legislative, and judicial branches of government. Excepting the Civil War period, the Constitution has provided a suitable framework for uniting the vast and diverse population of America. The Constitution made possible "an intimate union," which Washington believed was the key to stability.[19]

Atonement

Victory by colonial rebels against the world's greatest imperial power inspired belief that the hand of Providence sanctioned this "Great Experiment." The principles at the heart of this experiment were liberty, democracy, and rule of law. Victory ensured that these principles could be transmitted like a beacon for the rest of the world to see. The reverse side of the Great Seal exemplified this belief. What appears is the Great Pyramid at Giza with its missing capstone returned and illuminated with the Eye of Horus appearing—the ancient Egyptian symbol for the Eye of God. The Latin inscription *novus ordo seclorum* (New Order of the Ages) appears below the Great Pyramid; and the inscription *Annuit Coeptis* (It [the Eye of Providence] Is Favorable to our Undertakings) appears above it. Here in pictorial terms was the global vision of those who truly fathomed the significance of the American Republic. No wonder Virgil's *Aeneid* inspired the Founding Fathers in designing the Great Seal! America's victory against Britain was evidence that Providence had sanctioned a New Rome to bring peace eventually to the world as Virgil believed had happened two millennia ago with Ancient Rome:

But you, Roman, must remember that you have to guide the nations by your authority, for this is to be your skill, to graft tradition onto peace, to show mercy to the conquered, and to wage war until the haughty are brought low.[20]

The significance of the symbolism in the Great Seal is described by the philosopher, David Spangler:

The United States has particular responsibility to "be about its Father's business," and to honor the spiritual sources and visions that gave it birth. It is a planetary nation, emerging not from a particular race or people, but from the efforts, hopes, and dreams of men and women of all races and nations. It is the site of a great planetary experiment, a human experiment the United States emerged with a destiny to serve humanity in ways no other country has ever done before. [I]t was ordained to be the trustee of hope and service for humanity in this time.[21]

America's victory against Britain was a sign of the legitimacy of the global vision of the Founding Fathers of America's purpose in spreading the principles of liberty and representative government. The Declaration of Independence written by Thomas Jefferson, exemplified these principles:

We hold these truths to be self-evident, that all men are created equal, that they are endowed by their Creator with certain unalienable rights, that among these are life, liberty and the pursuit of happiness. That to secure these rights, governments are instituted among men deriving their just powers from the consent of the governed. That whenever any form of government becomes destructive of these ends, it is the right of the people to alter or to abolish it, and to institute new government, laying its foundation on such principles and organizing its powers in such form, as to them shall seem most likely to effect their safety and happiness.

Atonement would be achieved by America keeping faith with promoting these principles throughout the planet. America's atonement is wonderfully expressed by Marianne Williamson in *The Healing of America*:

A national ideal is not an intellectual exercise. It is a sacred, emotional commitment. The statement that our "Creator . . . created all men equal" and endowed them with "certain inalienable rights, that among these are life, liberty and the pursuit of happiness" is not an early American public relations slogan. It is a bright light shot like a laser through thousands of years of history. . . . These words carry such emotional and philosophical power that should enough Americans truly embrace the principles behind them and try their best to live according to them, not one penny would have to be spent—nor ultimately one bullet have to be fired—to protect our interests and extend our most precious truths around the world.[22]

The Return to International Society (1789–1815)—Liberty and Neutrality Rights

Trade between the new American Republic and the European continent was vital to the growth and well-being of the American republic. America had need of the manufactured goods found in Europe and had the means to pay for these through the primary products it could ship to feed and clothe Europe. All this was threatened in times of war in Europe when belligerents would attack the merchant shipping of their rivals and of neutral nations. Furthermore, merchant seamen could be imprisoned, killed, or forcibly conscripted. It was therefore vital for America to ensure that the right of neutral nations to trade freely with warring protagonists was not violated and that the liberty of merchant seamen was respected. This brought America into conflict with both sides in the Napoleonic Wars that eventually consumed Europe.

Refusal of the return

When the cannon sound of the French Revolution was heard across the Atlantic, Americans were thrilled to learn of the creation of the French Republic. The French Constituent Assembly had adopted the Rights of Man modeled on the American Bill of Rights. The overthrow of absolute monarchical rule heralded the start of a New Order of the Ages on the European continent. Here was ample proof that Providence was on the side of liberty and representative government. America was right in her revolutionary struggle against Britain.

Early in the new year 1793 the French decree of a "war of all peoples against all kings" reached America. Enthusiasm then became almost hysterical. Even Puritan Boston held a civic feast in French style. A procession of "citizens eight deep" escorted a roasted ox labeled "Peace Offering to Liberty and Equality," . . . to a spot rechristened Liberty Square. . . . [I]f anyone had been so tactless as to suggest that all was not well in France, he would probably been ducked in the Frog Pond.[23]

France's attempt to create a society purely on rational principles mirrored the creation of the American Republic. Here surely was a wonderful opportunity to spread the principles of liberty and representative government at core of America's national identity! For Thomas Jefferson and most Americans, the French Revolution was the instrument needed to introduce the New Order of the Ages in Europe. He believed the cause of France to be "the most sacred cause that ever man was engaged in."[24]

The initial delight in news of the French Revolution soon gave way to deep misgivings once the excesses of the revolution became known in 1793. Religious institutions were under attack and property was being confiscated. King Louis XVI, America's firm supporter in the revolutionary struggle, had been executed and many fine men and women were being executed for no other reason than belonging to the aristocracy. All the traditions of the *ancien regime* were being overthrown. Human reason was rewriting a whole society from the ground up! For pious Americans who saw the hand of Providence guiding their own revolution, this was too much. How could reason so arrogantly usurp the legitimacy of all forms of piety and tradition that had guided humanity for millennia! In his farewell speech, Washington tacitly criticized this aspect of French revolutionary thought: "[L]et us with caution indulge the supposition that morality can be maintained without religion. Whatever may be conceded to the influence of refined education on minds of peculiar structure, reason and experience both forbid us to expect that national morality can prevail in exclusion of religious principle."[25] Edmund Burke, another firm supporter of the American struggle, was the most eloquent in expressing misgivings over the French Revolution in his reflections on the French Revolution in 1790.

The very idea of the fabrication of a new government is enough to fill us with disgust and horror. We wished at the period of the [English] Revolution, and do now wish, to derive all we possess as an inheritance from our forefathers. . . . All the reformations we have hitherto made have proceeded upon the principle of reverence to antiquity; and I hope, nay, I am persuaded, that all those which possibly may be made hereafter will be carefully formed upon analogical precedent, authority, and example.[26]

For Burke, the Revolution far exceeded what was needed in reforming French society. Both monarchy and religion still had a role to play as the embodiments of tradition and the inheritance of one's forefathers. For many Americans, monarchy could be dispensed with but not religion!

France's 1793 declaration of "war of all peoples against all kings" also applied to Britain. France and Britain were now at war. If France was the instrument to introduce the New Order of the Ages in Europe, then America was too far away and too divided to give support in her revolutionary struggle against the monarchies of Europe. President Washington declared neutrality in April 1793 and summarized this at his farewell address in 1796:

Europe has a set of primary interests, which to us have none, or a very remote relation. Hence she must be engaged in frequent controversies, the causes of which are essentially foreign to our concerns. . . . Our detached and distant situation invites us to pursue a different course. . . . 'tis our true policy to steer clear of permanent alliances, with any portion of the foreign world. . . . Taking care always to keep ourselves, by suitable establishments, on a respectable defensive posture, we may safely trust to temporary alliances for extraordinary emergencies.[27]

At first, Washington's neutrality policy attracted wide criticism. In the then capital of Philadelphia, according to John Adams who was at the time Washington's vice president, "ten thousand people in the streets of Philadelphia, day after day, threatened to drag Washington out of his house, and effect a revolution in the government, or compel it to declare war in favor of the French revolution and against England."[28] With time, the revolutionary passion for France began to cool and Washington's neutrality policy enjoyed broad support. America would not give tangible support to France in supporting liberty and democratic government in Europe.

The consequence of Washington's neutrality policy was that America would attempt to trade impartially with both sides and their colonies. America stood for the principle "Free ships make free goods." Therefore the right of neutral shipping in times of war would be vigorously supported by America. America's policy on neutral shipping was soon challenged by two British decrees. The first was the Order in Council of June 8, 1793, authorizing the seizure of all neutral (i.e., American) cargoes destined for ports under French control. The second decree was the Order in Council of November 6, 1793, allowing for the detention of all neutral ships carrying goods from or to French ports. The consequence of the British Orders in Council is described by the historian Thomas Bailey:

Hard-boiled British naval officers proceeded to carry out these new orders with ruthlessness and dispatch. They speedily seized about 300 American vessels, mostly in the West Indies, and threw many of their crews into foul jails or forcibly impressed them into the British navy. American shipping, which had experienced a life-giving boom since the beginning of Anglo-French hostilities, was partially paralyzed.[29]

War fever broke out in America as soon as news began circulating of the British actions against American merchant ships. In an effort to prevent war, John Jay, the Chief Justice of the Supreme Court, was selected as a special envoy to negotiate a treaty on all outstanding issues between the two countries, including neutral shipping. His instruction was to sign no pact that would be contrary to America's treaty engagements with France. Although the Jay Treaty (1795) contained British concessions on a number of outstanding issues, it was notorious for its silence on the British practice of seizing American sailors and conscripting them into the Royal Navy. Also seized were goods bound for French ports and detention of ships trading with France or her colonies. In fact, the Treaty backed down on these key provisions as Bailey explains: "[Jay] agreed in effect that American foodstuffs bound for French ports might in certain circumstances, be seized if paid for, and that French property on American ships might be confiscated by the British. In short, 'free ships' do not make 'free goods.' "[30]

The Jay Treaty embodied a compromise between the American policy of supporting the rights of its sailors and neutral shipping and Britain's desire to man her warships and stop all supplies to her enemy France. The Treaty was condemned by the American populace, who were in no mood to compromise the rights of its merchant seamen and neutral ships to trade with both sides in times of war. France too protested vehemently that the Jay Treaty was in practice, if not in word, an alliance with Britain. Nevertheless, the Treaty was reluctantly ratified by the Senate and signed by President Washington. The Jay Treaty was a "refusal of the return" insofar as it compromised America's policy of protecting the rights of its merchant seamen and for neutral ships to trade with belligerents in times of war.

Crossing the return threshold

The Jay Treaty greatly reduced tensions between Britain and America. American losses in trade with France and her colonies were compensated by the rise in trade with Britain and her colonies. As mentioned, France viewed the Jay Treaty as an informal alliance with Britain, and tension between America and France began to rise. In an effort to blockade Britain, France began seizing all ships trading with Britain. Secretary of State Pickering reported that between July 1796 and June 1797, 316 American ships had been captured by France and their crews mistreated. A mission sent to Paris to negotiate an end to French abuses against neutral shipping was advised that a bribe would have to be paid for negotiations to begin. The mission refused, and when news of the French demand reached America, war fever rose. Public opinion now turned against France as it had turned four years earlier against Britain. A popular slogan that captured the public mood was "Millions for defense but not once cent for tribute."[31] Congress in May and July of 1798 authorized the capture of French armed ships. Thus began an undeclared naval war with France.

The undeclared war lasted two and half years and was confined to the sea. America had to outfit a navy to engage with hostile French ships both on the Atlantic and in the Caribbean. President Adams was only just able to keep the formal peace; and in September 1800, signed a convention that ended the undeclared war. The peace agreement with France, however, alienated his supporters and contributed greatly to his unsuccessful campaign for a second term in the election of 1800. The undeclared war with France was the first time independent America had used force outside of its borders in support of a moral principle that coincided with its national interests. The right of neutral shipping to trade in time of war was vital to America's economy and was vital for countries wishing to avoid taking sides in a conflict. America had now crossed the "return threshold" on its first hero's journey. It had established its first grand synthesis of morality and power. America was now firmly on the international stage as an actor with the will and capacity to use force to protect its vital interests and an important moral principle.

Master of the two worlds

It was peculiar that the payment of "tribute" to France to negotiate an end to attacks on American shipping was so odious to Americans in 1797. Since 1789 the Washington and Adams administrations had paid "tribute" to the Barbary pirates from the Muslim states of Algiers, Tunis, and Tripoli. The pirates routinely attacked American merchant ships, enslaved the crews, and stole the ships and goods. The Barbary pirates had made a mockery of the notion of free trade on the high seas. In a humiliating incident, an American warship, the *George Washington*, was forced to haul down the American flag, raise the flag of Algiers, and sail to Constantinople. When the ship's captain protested, the Dey of Algiers replied: "You pay me tribute, by which you become my slaves. I have therefore, a right to order you as I may think proper."[32]

America's initial policy under President Washington of bribing these states to leave American ships alone and to ransom enslaved sailors, proved a dismal failure. Indeed, almost one fifth of the annual federal revenue had been paid to these states by the time Jefferson became president in 1801. Jefferson's solution was to dispatch a naval force in late 1803 to punish the pirates of Tripoli who were the prime culprits. This was finally achieved with the capture of Tripoli and a treaty negotiated with the Prince of Tripoli in early 1805. Despite this "punishment," a $60,000 ransom still had to be paid for enchained American prisoners!

The conflict with the pirates of Tripoli was only a warm-up to the looming conflict with Britain. In order to recruit men for its war against Napoleon, Britain had the policy of impressing British-born sailors from American ships that the British navy inspected. This was a practice Britain had used against its own citizens for over 400 years in order to ensure that its warships were fully manned. Britain insisted that it would impress only British subjects, but Americans who were wrongly impressed would have to prove their birth. This could take years while they were forced to work in British warships. One British naval commander bluntly described his approach to impressment: "It is my duty to keep my Ship manned, and I will do so wherever I find men that speak the same language with me."[33]

To pluck American citizens from their ships on the spurious grounds of their place of birth was too much for a Congress already angry over Britain's refusal to recognize the neutrality of American shipping. Recognition of American neutrality was something the wily Napoleon had done in theory, if not in practice, in 1810. The war for "Free Trade and Sailors' Rights" began in 1812 and ended in 1814 with the Treaty of Ghent. The war did not resolve outstanding territorial issues between America and British North America. It also became redundant with the defeat of Napoleon and the end of the European war. The issues of free trade and impressment of sailors were no longer relevant. Nevertheless, America had shown that it was prepared to use its rapidly growing national resources to support the liberty of its sailors and the principle of free trade.

In the undeclared naval war against France (1798–1800), the Tripoli campaign (1804–1805) and the 1812–1814 war against Britain, America had combined power and morality. The principles of free trade, neutral rights, and safety of sailors had been combined to produce America's first grand synthesis of power and morality. America was master of the two worlds in so far as it projected its military power in pursuit of principles essential for America's national prestige and economic health.

Deep Forgetting (1815–1822)—Ignoring Republicanism in Latin America

America's undeclared naval war with France (1798–1800) and the war against Britain (1812–1814) had been fought over the rights of neutral vessels and the liberty of merchant seamen rather than over the revolutionary principles of liberty, democracy, and rule of law that had swept through both the New and Old World. Liberty and democratic government became dormant principles in continental Europe after the crushing defeat of Napoleon. However, they were very much alive throughout Latin America. Spain found it difficult to restore control over its restless colonies after the Napoleonic wars when they had enjoyed *de facto* independence since 1809–1810. Inspired by revolutionary ideals of liberty and democratic government, the colonies valiantly struggled against Spain's attempt at regaining control. From 1815 to 1822, numerous republics were declared all over Latin America. Throughout this time, President Monroe refused to support formally the revolutionary forces or to extend recognition to America's sister republics. A recognition resolution introduced into the House of Representatives by supporters of the American republics in March was opposed by the Monroe administration. Secretary of State Adams argued that the administration should only recognize the republics when Spain's chances of recovery had become "utterly desperate."[34] Until that time, he proposed that America should withhold recognition. The recognition resolution was defeated by a margin of 45 to 115. This lack of formal government support for independent republics in South America appears surprising today because it was happening in America's backyard rather than in distant Europe. The colonies' struggles against Spain also duplicated America's own revolutionary war. The lack of formal government support for principles at the center of American national identity was the beginning of America's "deep forgetting."

Fear

A major reason for the Monroe administration not extending recognition to the republics declared in South America was fear that this would lead to war with Spain. In that case, Russia, Austria, and France either separately or together might intervene on behalf of Spain. Russia, Austria, and France were all members of the Holy Alliance, which was committed to supporting monarchical governments. The Alliance saw republicanism as a menace that had to be stamped out to maintain order in Europe and arguably even in the New World. An intervention of the Alliance on behalf of Spain could have spelled disaster for America. Though nominally a member of the alliance, Britain had less to fear from republicanism because its constitutional monarchy was a compromise between monarchy and republicanism. However, bad feelings from the war of 1812–1814 meant that Britain could not be counted on to support America in any war against Spain and the Holy Alliance. Though the possibility of the Alliance's intervention on behalf of Spain against America was not that great, it was real enough to deter the Monroe administration's support for republicanism. Instead, the Monroe administration adopted a policy of strict neutrality, the history of which he explained in his second inaugural address in March 1821:

This contest was considered at an early stage by my predecessor a civil war in which the parties were entitled to equal rights in our ports. This decision, the first made by any power, being formed on great consideration of the comparative strength and resources of the parties, the length of time, and successful opposition made by the colonies, and of all other circumstances on which it ought to depend, was in strict accord with the law of nations. . . . Our attitude has therefore been that of neutrality between them, which has been maintained by the government with the strictest impartiality. No aid has been afforded to either, nor has any privilege been enjoyed by the one which has not been equally open to the other party, and every exertion has been made in its power to enforce the execution of the laws prohibiting illegal equipments with equal rigor against both.[35]

Monroe's policy of strict neutrality in the civil war was a deep forgetting of America's national mission in promoting the growth of democratic systems of government based on liberty and rule of law. Fear was the driving force of the Monroe administration's strict neutrality.

Imperialism

A compelling reason for the Monroe administration's refusal to support recognition of the Latin American republics and opposition to the 1818 recognition resolution was that America was negotiating with Spain for the purchase of the Spanish Floridas. Florida was a territory over which Spain could not effectively govern, and it had become a refuge for Indians, runaway slaves, and white renegades that periodically launched attacks into American territory. In 1817 General Andrew Jackson launched a raid into Florida to chastise the Indians and punish those who had participated in or failed to prevent attacks on American territory. In the former case, two British citizens were captured and executed for having incited Indian attacks. In the latter case, Spanish forts were taken over for not having done enough to prevent the raids. During the furor that erupted over the excesses of Jackson during the raid, the Secretary of State penned an ultimatum to the Spanish Crown:

Spain must immediately make her election [choice], either to place a force in Florida adequate at once to the protection of her territory, and to the fulfilment of her engagements, or cede to the United States a province, of which she retains nothing but the nominal possession, but which is, in fact, a derelict, open to the occupancy of every enemy, civilized or savage of the United States, and serving no other earthly purpose than as a post of annoyance to them.[36]

A treaty finally was signed in February 1819 that ceded all of Spanish Florida to America. Spain proceeded painfully slowly to ratify the treaty because it feared that America would then recognize the rebellious South American republics. It was only in February 1821 that the ratification process was finally completed. A factor in the delay in recognition of the Latin American republics was therefore the increased power that would inevitably come to America by acquiring more territory for settlement and trade. America had chosen the pursuit of power or imperialism through territorial expansion over the revolutionary ideals that inspired the sentiments of her citizens. Power and morality were in opposition, and America was indeed undergoing a deep forgetting!

Materialism

An important factor in the lack of support for recognition of Latin American republics, and the defeat of the 1818 recognition resolution, was lack of public support of the revolutionaries. In 1815, when the Napoleonic wars had ended and peace had been reached with Britain, an agreement was reached for limiting the number of warships in the Great Lakes region. This meant America was safe enough to disarm and devote itself to that natural right that has never been far from the sentiments of all Americans. The "pursuit of happiness" in the Declaration of Independence meant the right to engage in commerce and free trade in order to enrich oneself with all the material possessions necessary for eliciting good cheer. The years from 1815 to 1819 have been called by historians the "Era of Good Feeling."[37] Talk of revolutionary principles and the duty to help South American colonies gain their independence from 1815 to 1822 was drowned out by the banter of those enjoying good economic times after a series of wars that had badly affected American trade.

The bank crash of 1819 instantly brought an end to the Era of Good Feeling. Americans experienced unemployment in large numbers. The Philadelphia cotton mills, for example, employed 2,325 in 1816; but by 1819 all but 149 had been sacked.[38] In such harsh economic times, Americans became concerned largely with material concerns rather than with the revolutionary struggles elsewhere in the Western hemisphere.

In summary, a combination of fear of a devastating war with Spain, the increased power that would come to America with the purchase of the Spanish Floridas, and economic conditions immediately after the Napoleonic wars and the 1819 bank crash all shaped the Monroe administration's policy. The natural affinity of Americans for the revolutionary principles of the rebellious Spanish republics found no outlet in official support from the federal government. America for the first time in its short history was experiencing a deep forgetting. Thus ends the first hero's journey of the American Republic, which is summarized in Table 3.1.

Table 3.1
America's First Hero's Journey—Establishing the American Republic as a Beacon of
Liberty and Democracy (1764–1822)

Phase of Hero's Journey	Step of Hero's Journey	Key Events	
CALL TO ADVENTURE Liberty from Unrepresentative Taxation (1764 - 1775)	Hearing the Call	•	Public Opposition to Revenue Act (1764)
		•	Public Opposition to Stamp Act (1765)
	Refusal of the Call	•	Muted Opposition to Townshend Act (1767)
	Crossing the First threshold	•	Boston Tea Party (1773)
		•	First Continental Congress (1774)
		•	Fighting at Lexington and Concord (1775)
GREAT REMEMBERING Founding of the American Republic (1776-1789)	Slaying the Dragon	•	Declaration of Independence (1776)
	Sacred Marriage	•	Articles of Confederation 1777
		•	Great Seal of USA officially adopted (1782)
		•	Constitution adopted (1787)
	Atonement	•	Great Seal of USA officially adopted (1782)
		•	Principles of Liberty, Democracy & Rule of Law enshrined in Constitution (1789)
RETURN TO INTERNATIONAL SOCIETY Liberty & Neutrality Rights (1789 - 1815)	Refusal of the Return	•	Jay Treaty & lack of support for rights of American merchant seamen (1795)
	Cross Return Threshold	•	Undeclared Naval War against France (1798-1800)
	Master of the Two Worlds	•	War against Barbary Pirates (1804-1805)
		•	War against Britain (1812-1814)
		•	**First Grand Synthesis: Liberty of Sailors, Free Trade, & Neutrality Rights**
DEEP FORGETTING Ignoring Republicanism in Latin America	Fear	•	Monroe's Neutrality Policy in Latin American independence Struggles against Spain (1817-1822)
	Imperialism	•	Treaty of Acquisition of Spanish Floridas (1819-1821)
	Materialism	•	Era of Good Feelings (1815-1819)
		•	Bank Crash (1819)

NOTES

1. Henry Kissinger, *Diplomacy* (New York: Simon and Schuster, 1994), 17–18.

2. Arthur Shlesinger, Sr., "The Tides of National Politics," in *Paths to the Present* (Boston: Houghton Mifflin Company, 1964), 93.

3. Arthur Schlesinger, Jr., *The Cycles of American History* (Boston: Houghton Mifflin Co., 1986), 23–48.

4. Ibid., 28.

5. Ibid., 29.

6. Ibid., 51.

7. Frank Klingberg, *Cyclical Trends in American Foreign Policy Moods: The Unfolding of America's World Role* (New York: University Press of America, 1983).

8. Ibid., 8.

9. William Strauss and Neil Howe, *The Fourth Turning: An American Prophecy: What the Cycles of History Tell Us about America's Next Rendezvous with Destiny* (New York: Broadway Books, 1997).

10. Ibid., 313.

11. Arthur Schlesinger, Sr., "The Tides of National Politics," in *Paths to the Present*, 92.

12. Samuel Eliot Morison, *The Oxford History of the American People* (New York: Oxford University Press, 1965), 52.

13. Ibid., 181.

14. Ibid., 185.

15. Ibid., 187.

16. For figures, see Morison, *The Oxford History of the American People*, 190–91.

17. Morison, *The Oxford History of the American People*, 191.

18. Ibid., 222.

19. Jerome Agel, *Words That Make America Great* (New York: Random House, 1997), 275.

20. Virgil, *Aeneid* [Book VI, 848–79], trans. W. F. Jackson Knight (London: Penguin, 1958), 173.

21. David Spangler, *Conversations with John* (Elgin, Ill.: Lorian Press, 1980), 7–8.

22. Marianne Williamson, *The Healing of America* (New York: Simon and Schuster, 1997), 49.

23. Morison, *The Oxford History of the American People*, 336.

24. Quoted in Morison, *The Oxford History of the American People*, 337.

25. Agel, "Washington's Farewell Address," *Words That Make America Great*, 276.

26. Edmund Burke, *Reflections on the Revolution in France: In a Letter Intended to Have Been Sent to a Gentleman in Paris*, 1790. http://www.ovrcivilisation.com/burke/index.html

27. Quoted in Morison, *The Oxford History of the American People*, 346.

28. Thomas Bailey, *A Diplomatic History of the American People*, 8th ed. (New York: Appleton-Century-Crofts, 1969), 87.

29. Bailey, *A Diplomatic History*, 73.

30. Ibid., 77.

31. Ibid., 94.

32. Quoted in Bailey, *A Diplomatic History*, 101.

33. Ibid., 119.

34. Ibid., 168.

35. John Gabriel Hunt, ed., *The Inaugural Addresses of the Presidents* (New York: Random House, 1997), 63.

36. Quoted in Bailey, *A Diplomatic History*, 172.

37. Agel, *Words That Make America Great*, 281.

38. Paul Johnson, *A History of the American People* (New York: Harper Collins, 1997), 288.

CHAPTER 4

AMERICA'S SECOND HERO'S JOURNEY (1823–1855)——RULE OF LAW AND MANIFEST DESTINY

The declaration of the Monroe Doctrine in 1823 was the start of a new hero's journey for America. The bold announcement of the doctrine by President Monroe was an assertion by America that it was now an international power that had to be respected by European states. America would play a more assertive role in promoting moral norms in the international system. America's example as a beacon of liberty and democracy would mean that more and more peoples in the New World would either want to join the American Federation or incorporate these principles into their own countries. This meant that territorial expansion would be inevitable as territories rushed to join America. This was widely seen by Americans as a positive development and meant that the principles of liberty, democracy, and rule of law would operate in more and more territory in the New World. America's second hero's journey was based on promoting rule of law at the international level, and its manifest destiny in expanding the area of the New World that operated under the principles of liberty, democracy, and rule of law.

CALL TO ADVENTURE (1823–1831)—PROMOTING INTERNATIONAL LAW

One of the pillars of the American Republic since its establishment has been "rule of law." Basing national domestic and foreign policy on the moral principles and constitutional procedures that make up rule of law was and continues to be a fundamental goal of American policymakers. It was this commitment to morality, or "virtue" as Washington called it, that distinguished the American experiment: "Can it be that Providence has not connected the permanent felicity of a nation with its virtue? The experiment, at least, is recommended by every sentiment which ennobles human nature."[1] "Virtue" for America would be measured by how closely America's behavior toward other peoples and nations was based on rule of law. At the international level, rule of law was synonymous with international law where treaties would be observed, states behaved in accord with moral principles, states obeyed decisions handed down by bodies of arbitration, and most importantly, states would not arbitrarily interfere in the domestic affairs of other states. International law was therefore a serious subject for all American policymakers. Emmerich de Vattel's *The Law of Nations* became standard reading for American policymakers. Indeed, Frank Klingberg observed that Vattel's "principles, with their high moral and democratic basis, seemed almost designed for the new American republic."[2]

Applying rule of law meant that America was taking a very different foreign policy path compared to European states. Whereas European states practiced power politics, America behaved in accord with the moral principles that made up international law. Treaties ratified with foreign states or with indigenous Indian tribes would therefore be respected. International arbitration of disputes between states would also be respected if done in a fair and impartial manner. Most importantly, independent states in the Western hemisphere would be supported against foreign interference. This was vitally important to America, because the republican form of government it embodied was being eliminated in Europe through interventions by the Holy Alliance. The Holy Alliance would interfere in what was clearly the internal affairs of other European states. America needed to ensure that this would not be repeated in Latin America. Applying rule of law was therefore a rejection of the policies of intervention then being practiced by Europe's Holy Alliance in support of anti-Republican governments. American withdrawal was the first step of a new hero's journey in world politics.

Hearing the Call

In 1822, soon after signing a treaty with Spain that allowed the annexation of Florida, President Monroe finally extended recognition to the former Spanish colonies in Latin America. By now the threat of intervention by the Holy Alliance had receded. The Alliance between 1821 and 1822 had sanctioned interventions that restored absolute monarchies in Spain and Naples. Britain had distanced itself from these Holy Alliance interventions. Britain was especially concerned that France's intervention in Spain would result in the former attempting to be repaid in terms of territory in Latin America. Britain would profit handsomely from trade opportunities in Latin America and could be counted on to oppose Alliance intervention on behalf of Spain that would only restrict trade with Britain. Indeed, so confident had the American administration become that the Alliance would not intervene that Secretary Adams declared in 1823: "I no more believe that the Holy Allies will restore the Spanish dominion upon the American continent than that the Chimborazo [Ecuadorian peak 20,702 feet high] will sink beneath the ocean."[3] Under these less threatening circumstances President Monroe announced his famous doctrine:

[T]he American continents, by the free and independent condition which they have assumed and maintain, are henceforth not to be considered as subjects for future colonization by any European powers. . . . We should consider any attempt on their [Europeans] part to extend their system to any portion of this hemisphere as dangerous to our peace and safety. . . . [W]ith the governments who have declared their independence and maintained it, and whose independence we have, on great consideration and on just principles, acknowledged, we could not view any interposition for the purpose of oppressing them, or controlling in any other manner their destiny, by any European power in any other light than as the manifestation of an unfriendly disposition toward the United States.[4]

America had declared that any attempt to restore colonies in any portion of Latin America that had been recognized as independent would be "dangerous" to America's "peace and safety." America had proclaimed itself as guarantor of the newly won independence of the Latin American republics and would in theory oppose any attempt by Spain, with either French or Russian assistance, to retake its former colonies. America was taking a strong stance in support of noninterference in the internal affairs of other states. This was a principle of international law that had been developed in the Treaty of Westphalia that had ended the Thirty Years War in Europe (1618–1648). The Monroe Doctrine was an assertion that this principle of international law also would apply to the newly independent republics of Latin America. Britain's control of the Atlantic and its interests in eliminating Spanish and French influence in Latin America gave the Monroe Doctrine the extra teeth it needed to deter unwelcome European interference in Latin America.

The Monroe Doctrine was based firmly on the principle of noninterference, which was a central pillar in the evolution of international law. The Monroe Doctrine was therefore the "call to adventure" for a new hero's journey. There remained strong opposition, however, to America playing any vigorous role in laying down the Monroe Doctrine and acting as a guarantor for the independence of Latin American republics.

Refusal of the Call

In 1826, the Panama Congress was convened in order to support the newly won independence of South American states. Simón Bolívar, the

George Washington of South America, issued a number of invitations to the Congress: "There he proposed that they should form an organization to serve as a protector of their liberties against possible attack from Europe, as an interpreter of treaties and an umpire in disputes, and as a council for consultation in emergencies."[5] Here surely was an opportunity to promote principles of international law in the Western hemisphere. Henry Clay, Secretary of State (1825–1829), enthusiastically embraced the significance of the Panama Congress and persuaded President Adams to send delegates. Unfortunately, the delegates never arrived due to the delay created by intense political opposition in the Senate and House of Representatives led by Andrew Jackson and his supporters. Adams was unjustly criticized for wanting "to be the President of the human race."[6] The Panama Congress subsequently ended in dismal failure. None of its recommendations was implemented, none of its projected meetings ever held, and no Pan-American organization was created that would promote international law in the Western hemisphere. Here was a "refusal of the call" by America to lend anything other than rhetorical support to principles of international law in Latin America.

Crossing the First Threshold

The Treaty of Ghent ending the 1812–1814 war had left unanswered a number of boundary questions between Britain and America. One of these concerned the precise dividing line between the territories of New Brunswick and Maine. In order to find an answer to a dispute that could easily have festered and led to attempts to find a military solution, the Andrew Jackson administration agreed to submit the issue to international arbitration. In 1831, the King of the Netherlands arbitrated the dispute and announced a compromise. Unfortunately for the Jackson administration, the King's decision was not to Maine's liking, and it refused to cede any territory. The Senate supported Maine's position and refused to accept the arbitration by the razor close vote of 21–20. The Jackson administration had recognized the importance of impartial arbitration for fostering international law, but was frustrated by the Senate's rejection. Nevertheless, the administration had crossed the first threshold. It would increasingly rely on principles and mechanisms based on international law for the settlement of international issues. It would be the Senate, then as today, that would finally decide whether such settlements would be ratified.

GREAT REMEMBERING (1831–1837)—THE ISSUES OF RELOCATION OF NATIVE AMERICANS, SLAVERY, AND TEXAS

The "great remembering" is an attempt to apply the moral vision of America's founding fathers and the principles of liberty, democracy, and rule of law to the outstanding political issues of the day. In the pre–Civil War era, these issues were how to deal with America's indigenous peoples, slavery, and the incorporation of Texas. In finding a response to these issues, America would establish a foundation for a more vigorous intervention in support of the moral vision and principles at the heart of its national identity.

Slaying the Dragon

Basing domestic and foreign policy on "rule of law" principles and morality led to heated debate on treatment of the Indian tribes with whom solemn treaties had been violated. Soon after Andrew Jackson's inauguration in 1829, the states of Georgia, Alabama, and Mississippi claimed jurisdiction over Indian reservations. These reservations had all been established by treaties with the federal government. Indian tribes were regarded as sovereign nations, and all relations with them were handled by the Department of State. It was only in 1890 that the Department of the Interior began exercising jurisdiction over the Indians. Allowing the three states to remove the Indians from their rightful territory was surely as flagrant a violation of rule of law and principles of international law as could be imagined. However, Jackson did not stop the states breaking these treaties. Indeed, the federal troops sent by President Adams to protect the Indian territories from whites that coveted their lands were removed by Jackson. In 1830 Jackson passed the Indian Removal Act that used federal funds in relocating the hapless Indian tribes. Jackson believed that a state's rights trumped federal rights, even if virtue rested with federal policy. The worst case involved the removal of the Cherokee nation, the most "civilized" of the tribes:

The Cherokee . . . invented a simple form of writing and printing the Cherokee language; Bibles, other books and even a weekly newspaper. . . . These Indians welcomed Christian missionaries, built roads, houses, and churches, adopted a constitution for the Cherokee nation, and elected a legislature. They became more civilized than the Georgia "crackers" and "hill-billies" who coveted their lands.[7]

The Supreme Court in *Cherokee Nation v. Georgia* handed down decisions in 1831 and 1832 that ruled in favor of the Cherokee against the Georgia government. President Jackson failed to enforce these rulings. In a moving speech before the Senate in 1835, Henry Clay denounced the treatment of the Cherokee. Georgia, he argued, had violated numerous federal treaties and the basics of rule of law. Clay "drew tears from the eyes of the senators, but they did nothing for the Cherokee except to expedite their removal."[8] The "dragon" of white greed at the expense of the Indian community could not be slain by moral argument. Only federal government protection could save the Indians, and this was something Jackson stead-fastly refused.

Instead, the Jackson administration supported the relocation of the tribes for their "own protection" with the Indian Removal Act. The thinking at the time was that progress was inevitable and that the Indian tribes would eventually be squeezed out by growing white communities eager to use Indian lands. The prospect of increasing tension between white and Indian communities led to many supporting the "humane" policy of removing the Indians over protecting them against white settlers. Indeed, Samuel Morison argued in 1965 that "it is now evident of the irresistible push of westward movement, Indian removal was the lesser evil."[9]

The question of honoring treaties with the Indian tribes became a litmus test for morality in American politics. Instead of meeting the problem of honoring the treaties, the Jackson administration used moral sophistry in justifying the removal of the Indians in order to "protect" them from the inevitable forces of westward expansion. Rule of law principles in honoring treaties would not be honored for the Indian tribes. "Slaying the dragon" of white settler greed for Indian territory was effectively ignored by the Jackson administration. Failure to slay the dragon was a poor foundation for American territorial expansion.

Sacred Marriage

Even though debate over the treatment of Indians was intense and emotional, it did not threaten the American Union. However, the controversy over slavery was reaching levels of intensity that presented a dire threat to the Union. Slavery was increasingly being abolished by civilized nations around the world. Most of the newly independent states from South America had emancipated the slaves. Britain was active on the high seas in eliminating the slave trade. Slavery was being seen by more and more civilized peoples as morally repugnant. This gradual change in attitudes on slavery was having a divisive effect in America. Petitions against slavery were growing in number and significance. A gag order was introduced in the House of Representatives between 1836 and 1844 to prevent antislavery petitions from being introduced. These had proved to be divisive and only increased tensions between pro- and antislavery forces rather than contributing to a solution. In the interest of national unity, slavery petitions were not discussed in the House of Representatives. America's "sacred marriage" meant that in the interest of national unity, all issues that related to slavery had to be dealt with very carefully. This was especially the case with the Mexican state of Texas, which had announced its independence in 1836 and was looking for admittance into the Union.

Atonement

In the early 1800s, Texas had its own legislature and independent governor under Mexico's federal constitution. When General Santa Anna came to power, he abolished the autonomy of the states and centralized the political system. Initially, Texas wanted to have the former constitution restored, but changed this to outright independence when it became clear that this would be the only way it would get support from America. In April 1836, General Sam Houston defeated a Mexican army led by General Santa Anna. Santa Anna was captured, and he was forced to sign documents recognizing Texan independence.

Texas met all the criteria of a state that deserved immediate support for its independence. Texas had a representative form of government that secured the liberty of its citizens and was based on rule of law. These were qualities that were absent in Mexico due to the centralizing efforts of the authoritarian President Santa Anna. Recognition of Texas independence, however, ran the risk of becoming involved in a war with Mexico intent on regaining Texas and restoring national honor. However, public opinion was strongly in favor of supporting Texan independence. Mexico was viewed to be authoritarian and unrepresentative, and rule of law was not something that was argued to come easily to the Mexican temperament. This was all too clear with the ease with which Santa Anna centralized power and revoked the autonomy of Mexican states. Independent Texas populated with white colonists from southern states in America had a greater chance of building a state based on "rule of law" principles.

Texas immediately sought either annexation by America or recognition as an independent state. A plebiscite was held on whether Texas should join America as a new state. There was almost unanimous support for immediate annexation. Texas permitted slavery, however, and this would have affected the balance that existed in Congress between pro- and anti-slavery forces. If America could not admit Texas to the American Union due to the growing slavery controversy, at least recognition of Texas's independence could be given. President Jackson formally recognized Texan independence on his last day of office in March 1837. This gave some assurance that Texas would be aided in the event of Mexico attempting to retake Texas. In recognizing Texas's independence, America was prepared to risk war with Mexico in support of a state that was more likely to be based on "rule of law" principles. America's decision to recognize Texan independence was an act of atonement consistent with the principles of liberty, democracy, and rule of law at the core of American national identity.

THE RETURN TO INTERNATIONAL SOCIETY
(1837–1845)—MANIFEST DESTINY

The debate over the inclusion of Texas into America proved to be the midwife to the idea of "manifest destiny." The historian Frederick Merk explained the concept as follows:

It meant expansion, prearranged by Heaven, over an area not clearly defined. In some minds it meant expansion over the region to the Pacific; in others, over the North American continent; in others, over the hemisphere. . . . It meant opportunity to gain admission to the American Union. Any neighboring peoples, established in self-government by compact or by successful revolution, would be permitted to apply.[10]

Supporters of the doctrine of Manifest Destiny believed that eventually all the peoples of the Western hemisphere would be united under the one flag. The greatest proponent of manifest destiny was John O'Sullivan, who wrote in 1845:

Away, away with all these cobweb tissues of rights of discovery, exploration, settlement, contiguity, etc . . . [The American claim] is by the right of manifest destiny to overspread and to possess the whole of the continent which Providence has given us for the development of the great experiment of liberty and federative self government entrusted to us. It is a right such as that of the tree to the space of air and earth suitable for the full expansion of its principle and destiny of growth—such as that of the stream to the channel required for the still accumulating volume of its flow.[11]

O'Sullivan believed that America had to take up with gusto the opportunities that Providence would arrange in order to spread the virtues of liberty and self-governance to oppressed peoples in the Americas. Such views had powerful supporters in Congress. John Wentworth, the congressional representative from Illinois, outlined his hopes for fulfilling America's manifest destiny in a powerful speech to Congress:

Many of this body would live to hear the sound from the Speaker's chair, "the gentleman from Texas." He wanted them also to hear "the gentleman from Oregon." He would even go further, and have "the gentleman from Nova Scotia, the gentleman from Canada, the gentleman from Cuba, the gentleman from Mexico, aye, even the gentleman from Patagonia." . . . He did not believe the God of heaven, when he crowned the American arms with success [in the Revolutionary War], designed that the original States should be the only abode of liberty on earth. On the contrary, he only designed them as the great center from which civilization, religion, and liberty should radiate and radiate until the whole continent shall bask in their blessing.[12]

If America's manifest destiny was to establish an expanded republic, freeing the oppressed peoples in the Americas, there were those who were not prepared to do this.

Refusal of the Return

Texas presented a special problem to the American public in 1836. Supporting Texan independence was popular due to the principles of liberty, self-government, and rule of law that Texas embodied and Mexico threatened. This then raised the dilemma over Texas's future because it would always feel insecure about Mexico and needed some form of alliance with a third power. The only two choices were admittance to the American Union or an alliance with Great Britain. The Texans had expressed their preference in a plebiscite in 1836 where they almost unanimously desired to join the Union. However, admitting Texas to the Union would only have strengthened the hand of pro-slavery forces. Indeed, a Northern abolitionist wrote a pamphlet arguing that "the Texas revolution was a conspiracy to gain new territory for slave-grown cotton."[13] Abolitionists believed that Texas would be divided into as many as six or eight states giving pro-slavery forces a dominant majority in Congress. Antislavery groups organized petitions against the annexation of Texas. It was claimed that up to 600,000 had signed the petitions. The state legislatures of eight northern states had passed resolutions against admitting Texas into the Union.

If America would not permit Texas to join the Union, then Britain could be Texas's major protector. The years 1836–1845 therefore saw Texas negotiating with both Great Britain and America for protection against any attempt from Mexico to retake Texas. As it became clear that Britain might in fact succeed in its efforts, Southern states began to feel alarmed. President Tyler negotiated a treaty with Texas President Sam Houston on admitting Texas to the American Union that looked sure to sail through the Senate ratification process. Due to intense partisan politics, however, the treaty failed to get the necessary two-thirds majority in June 1844. In fact, it failed to get a simple majority, and the final vote was 35 against to 16 for the treaty. America's refusal to admit Texas to the Union was a "refusal of the return"—it was a rejection of the idea of manifest destiny.

Crossing the Return Threshold

The Texas annexation issue became a key issue in the 1844 elections. The elections saw a narrow victory for James Polk who was committed to annexation of Texas and indeed to the idea of manifest destiny. President Tyler in the time remaining before change of administrations in March 1845, arranged for a joint resolution from Congress for the admittance of Texas into the Union. This was possible due to the constitutional clause that "new States may be admitted by the Congress into this Union." A joint resolution would be easier than gaining the two-thirds majority required for Senate ratification of a treaty. Such a majority would have been difficult to achieve due to strong opposition from antislavery Northern states. Indeed, the resolution admitting Texas passed in the Senate by only a 27–25 majority. The joint resolution was passed, and Texas was formally invited into the Union when President Tyler signed the Joint Resolution on March 1, 1845.

Master of the Two Worlds

Another opportunity to support America's manifest destiny presented itself in the case of the Oregon territory. In order to expand its form of government to all the territories in which American citizens lived, negotiations began between the Polk administration and British governments over the territory of Oregon in 1845. Americans had mainly populated areas south of the 49th parallel, while Britain had substantial financial interests in the form of the Hudson Bay Company that had initially encouraged American immigration into the area. In Polk's inaugural address, he outlined his policy on Oregon:

Nor will it become in a less degree my duty to assert and maintain by all constitutional means the right of the United States to that portion of our territory which lies beyond the Rocky Mountains. Our title to the country of the Oregon is "clear and unquestionable," and already are our people preparing to perfect that title by occupying it with their wives and children. . . . The world beholds the peaceful triumphs of the industry of our emigrants. . . . The jurisdiction of our laws and the benefits of our republican institutions should be extended over them in the distant regions which they have selected for their homes.[14]

Polk's claim to all of Oregon was not acceptable to Britain, so the 49th parallel was used as the boundary line between British and American negotiating positions on Oregon. This was a concession by America because it meant relenting on claims to all Oregon. The British concession was in letting go portions of Oregon around the Colombine river. Again, as in the case of Texas, the popular will of the territory's inhabitants was strongly in favor of annexation by America. America had committed herself to the idea of manifest destiny and had significantly increased her territory on principles of liberty, self-governance, and rule of law.

The annexation of Texas and the successful conclusion of a treaty with Britain dividing the Oregon territory had seen a considerable expansion of American territory. America had expanded the areas over which liberty, self-government, and "rule of law" principles had applied. America's power and prestige had increased significantly. It now was a powerful beacon of liberty, self-government, and "rule of law" principles throughout the Americas. America had achieved these without having gone to war, and with the significant support of the inhabitants of the annexed territories.

Supporters of manifest destiny were elated over the incorporation of Texas. They wanted to show how American expansion differed morally from that of European power politics. John O'Sullivan elaborated at some length at how American territorial expansion was distinguished by its fidelity to the moral principle of a people determining their own destiny:

There are some things this nation will never do. It will never be the forcible subjugator of other countries; it will never despoil surrounding territories; it will never march through the blood of their unoffending inhabitants; it will never admit within its own Union those who do not freely desire the boon. The parallel of its territorial extension will not be found in the history of the dismemberment of Poland or of the British conquests in India; and no patriots will ever rally upon their native hills to protect their own rights or their country's liberties from our rapacity.[15]

The contrast between territorial expansion done at the request of the inhabitants as opposed to European expansion that ignored the will of a territory's population was exemplified in the case of Texas:

Texas was the exemplification of the American method of expansion. She had applied repeatedly for admission, and only after her people and her Congress had shown a wish to enter by virtually unanimous votes, had she been taken in. Poland was the horrid example of the European process of expansion—a destruction by partition of a nationality and a people by three greedy neighboring monarchs.[16]

America was "master of the two worlds" insofar as it could expand its territories just as European powers were doing, but America did so in accord with the genuine wishes of the inhabitants of the territories. In short, power and morality were consistently applied in the acquisition of Texas and Oregon. America's second grand synthesis was based on combining the liberty of a territory's population to choose its government and America's territorial expansion.

DEEP FORGETTING (1846–1855)—AMERICAN IMPERIALISM

"Manifest destiny" had shown itself, so far, as being an idea that could lead to power and morality combining. In the territories of Texas and Oregon, largely populated by American immigrants who overwhelmingly desired incorporation into the Union, "manifest destiny" was a godsend. In other territories, where other peoples lived who did not desire incorporation into the Union, "manifest destiny" became shorn of its moral dimension and became little more than imperialism.

Fear

California was a sparsely populated area under Mexican sovereignty. In contrast to Texas, the population was mainly of Spanish descent, though the number of American born was on the rise. After the acquisition of Texas, President Polk was concerned that Britain might try to cut a deal with Mexico over California in order to curb further American expansion. If Polk waited until American immigration made possible a repeat of Texas's admission, it might be too late. As Julius Pratt writes, Polk's "anxiety for an early acquisition of that territory, therefore, was founded largely upon a genuine fear that if the United States failed to acquire it, Great Britain would do so."[17] Polk set out a three-pronged strategy to acquire California. The first was to persuade the Californians of Spanish descent to rebel for independence, and then seek admission into America. Polk forwarded to Thomas Larkin, the confidential American agent in California, instructions that if California rebelled, America would support the Californians. The instructions outlined Polk's strategy:

Whilst the President will make no effort and use no influence to induce California to become one of the free and independent States of this Union, yet if the people should desire to unite their destiny with ours, they would be received as brethren, whenever this can be done without affording Mexico just cause of complaint.[18]

Unfortunately, for Polk, Larkin failed to make much headway with the bona fide Californians who, while having genuine grievances with Mexico, were not ready to raise the flag of rebellion.

The second strategy used by Polk was to persuade Mexico to sell California. He sent John Slidell of Louisiana to bargain with Mexico's President Herrera in November 1845 with instructions not only to settle the question of the admittance of Texas and her boundaries, but also to buy the territories of California and New Mexico. Unfortunately, for Polk and the Slidel mission, Mexico was in the midst of revolutionary upheaval. Herrara refused to consider the offer because this would have only strengthened the hand of his revolutionary opponents. Nevertheless, revolution still broke out, and on January 2, 1846, General Paredes became Mexico's new president. Paredes also refused to receive Slidell. Polk's second strategy was also becoming a failure. This led to Polk's third and most desperate strategy, a contrived war with Mexico in which not only the question of Texas would be settled, but California and New Mexico would be forcibly acquired.

Imperialism

Despite Mexico's refusal to recognize Texas's annexation into America, withdrawal of its ambassador from Washington, and repeated notices that it would view annexation as a *casus belli*, Mexico was in no position to go to war for Texas. In November 1844, a revolution had led to the banishment of General Santa Anna, and another revolution was looming.[19] In the case of Texas, Mexican pride had been wounded. Time, good diplomacy, and perhaps some financial compensation may have been all that was required to get Mexican approval. President Polk, however, had ambitions to gain California and other Mexican territories. A war with Mexico would make possible further American expansion. As Samuel Morison explains: "If Polk had been content with Texas and had not reached for California, there is no reason to suppose that Mexico would have initiated hostilities, although she would long have delayed acknowledging the loss of Texas."[20]

In declaring its independence, Texas claimed that its territory extended to the Rio Grande rather than to the river Neuces. Texas under Spanish and Mexican rule had never extended beyond the river Neuces, so it is doubtful that independent Texas's claim would ever have held up under impartial arbitration.[21] The joint resolution on Texas had merely affirmed that the boundaries of Texas needed to be negotiated. Mexico was in no mood to discuss boundary issues while it was still smarting from the loss of Texas, and was in the midst of revolutionary turmoil.

Polk, despairing of any diplomatic settlement and lacking the patience for when Mexico might be stable enough to conduct negotiations, decided to move to his military option. He ordered American military forces led by Zachary Taylor to cross the river Neuces into what historically was the Mexican state of Tamaulipas. Taylor proceeded to the Rio Grande and set up a fortified base opposite the town of Matamoros. Denied permission by Mexico to use the Rio Grande as a supply line, Taylor blockaded the Rio Grande thereby denying its use to Matamoros.[22] President Paredes then proclaimed on April 23 a "defensive war," and two days later a Mexican force attacked Taylor's troops. On hearing of the attack on May 9, President Polk met with his Cabinet and issued a war message to Congress:

The cup of forbearance had been exhausted even before the recent information from the frontier of the Del Norte. But now . . . Mexico has passed the boundary of the United States, has invaded our territory and shed American blood upon American soil. She has proclaimed that hostilities have commenced, and that the two nations are now at war.[23]

Congress duly declared war on Mexico on May 13, 1846. American forces met no significant resistance and by January 1847 acquired all the territories sought by Polk: the Rio Grande boundary, New Mexico, and California. Mexico refused to sign a treaty ceding the conquered areas and continued to resist. An army of 10,000 under General Scott began fighting its way through to Mexico City. Mexico City fell on September 14. A treaty was finally signed on February 2, 1848, ceding all the territories sought by Polk with monetary compensation to the Mexican government.

The war was partly driven by fear of losing California and by the increased power that California and other Mexican territory would give to America. Never before had America embarked on such a naked course of imperialism. Polk's war aroused immediate opposition. Albert Gallatin, an antiwar advocate, was scathing in his remarks on what he saw as American imperialism:

[A]n appeal has been made to your worst passions; to cupidity; to the thirst of unjust aggrandizement by brutal force; to the love of military fame and false glory; and it has even been tried to pervert the noblest feelings of your nature. The attempt is made to make you abandon the lofty position which your fathers occupied, to substitute for it the political morality and heathen patriotism of the heroes and statesmen of antiquity.[24]

William Jennings Bryan used biblical language to warn against the perils of territorial expansion by military conquest:

Other nations may dream of wars of conquest and of distant dependencies governed by external force; not so with the United States. The fruits of imperialism, be they bitter or sweet, must be left to the subjects of monarchy. This is one tree of which the citizens of a republic may not partake. It is the voice of the serpent, not the voice of God, that bids us eat.[25]

The idea of "manifest destiny" was used to explain the remarkable American military conquests. However, morality and power were not both present in the war against Mexico. The justification for the war was a shameful example of how Polk had contrived a military confrontation when diplomacy was the appropriate way of dealing with the boundary problem. America had expanded her territory but had done so as an imperial power. Texas and Oregon were examples of admittance into the Union based on the support of the inhabitants of these territories. In contrast, California and New Mexico were achieved through military conquest rather than the free will of the inhabitants of these territories.

Materialism

America had acquired California and Oregon and now had a Pacific coast. With trade treaties signed with China and Japan in 1844 and 1854 respectively, an overland rail route would greatly help commerce between America's east and west coasts. The shortest and cheapest route would be one crossing from Texas, through Mexican territory, into California. In order to construct the railroad, the Mexican territory would have to be acquired. This was done through purchase with the weak and unstable

Table 4.1
America's Second Hero's Journey—Rule of Law and Manifest Destiny (1823–1855)

Phase of Hero's Journey	Step of Hero's Journey	Key Events	
CALL TO ADVENTURE Promoting International Law (1822-1831)	Hearing the Call	1.	Recognition of Latin American Republics (1822)
	Refusal of the Call	2.	America's division & delay in participating in Panama Congress of Western Hemisphere Republics (1826)
	Crossing the First threshold	3.	Submission of Maine-New Brunswick territorial dispute with Britain to international arbitration by King of Netherlands (1831)
GREAT REMEMBERING Relocation of Native Americans, Slavery & Texas (1831-1837)	Slaying the Dragon	• •	Indian Removal Act (1830) & subsequent forced removal Supreme Court rules against Georgia in Cherokee Nation vs Georgia - decision not enforced by President Jackson (1831-1832)
	Sacred Marriage	4.	Gag Order on anti-slavery petitions in House of Representatives (1836-1844)
	Atonement	5.	Recognition of Texas Independence
RETURN TO INTERNATIONAL SOCIETY Manifest Destiny (1837-1845)	Refusal of the Return	•	Refusal to admit Texas into Federal Union (1836-1845)
	Cross Return Threshold	•	Joint Congressional Resolution admitting Texas into Federal Union (1845)
	Master of the Two Worlds	• •	Oregon Territory admitted into Federal Union (1845) **Second Grand Synthesis: Self-Determination & Territorial Expansion**
DEEP FORGETTING American Imperialism (1846-1855)	Fear	•	British efforts to acquire California lead to failed American effort to purchase California (1845-1846)
	Imperialism	•	War against Mexico (1846-1848)
	Materialism	•	Purchase of Mexican populated territory from weak Mexican government (1854)

Mexican government led once again by General Santa Anna. In June 1854, the required territory was purchased. Here additional territory was purchased without any regard for the wishes of the inhabitants. America had once again profited due to the ineptness of the Mexican government. In gaining the territory, profit was more important than any political principle such as liberty or self-government.

In summary, the fear of losing the territory of California to Britain, the increased power that would come through acquiring Mexican territory, and the material benefits of Mexican territory for American settlers—all were part of Polk's imperialistic war against Mexico. America was again undergoing a deep forgetting of what distinguished the American republic from the European imperial powers! Thus ends the second hero's journey of the American Republic, which is summarized in Table 4.1

NOTES

1. Jerome Agel, *Words That Make America Great* (New York: Random House, 1997), 275.

2. Frank Klingberg, *Cyclical Trends in American Foreign Policy Moods: The Unfolding of America's World Role* (New York: University Press of America, 1983), 56.

3. Quoted in Thomas Bailey, *A Diplomatic History of the American People*, 8th ed. (New York: Appleton-Century-Crofts, 1969), 182.

4. Agel, *Words That Make America Great*, 281.

5. Julius Pratt, *A History of United States Foreign Policy* (Newark, N.J.: Prentice Hall, 1955), 181.

6. Ibid.

7. Samuel Eliot Morison, *The Oxford History of the American People* (New York: Oxford University Press, 1965), 447.

8. Ibid., 451.

9. Ibid.

10. Frederick Merk, *Manifest Destiny and Mission in American History* (New York: Knopf, 1963; Westport, Conn.: Greenwood Press, reprint 1983), 24

11. Ibid., 31–32.

12. Quoted in Merk, *Manifest Destiny and Mission in American History*, 28.

13. Morison, *The Oxford History of the American People*, 553.

14. John Gabriel Hunt, ed., *The Inaugural Addresses of the Presidents* (New York: Random House, 1997), 151.

15. Quoted in Merk, *Manifest Destiny and Mission in American History*, 107–8.

16. Ibid.

17. Pratt, *A History of United States Foreign Policy*, 242.

18. Quoted in Pratt, *A History of United States Foreign Policy*, 243.

19. In December 1845, General Paredes led another revolution. For details, see Pratt, *A History of United States Foreign Policy*, 238.

20. Morison, *The Oxford History of the American People*, 559.

21. See Pratt, *A History of United States Foreign Policy*, 238.

22. For details see Pratt, *A History of United States Foreign Policy*, 247.

23. Ibid., 248.

24. Quoted in Merk, *Manifest Destiny and Mission in American History*, 262–63.

25. William Jennings Bryan "Noboth's Vineyard," in *Great American Speeches 1898–1963*, ed. John Graham (New York: Appleton-Century-Crofts, 1970), 13.

CHAPTER 5

AMERICA'S THIRD HERO'S JOURNEY (1855–1891)—CIVIL WAR AND THE MONROE DOCTRINE

America's third hero's journey was dominated by the issue of ending slavery while preserving the federal union. The slavery issue that Thomas Jefferson had prophesied would bring devastation to the Union finally erupted into full-scale civil war. Confronting the issue of slavery while preserving the Union was a hero's journey that consumed America's energies and brought it as close as it ever has to the brink of national ruin.

CALL TO ADVENTURE (1855–1861)—ENDING SLAVERY AS A MORAL IMPERATIVE

During the years of America's rapid territorial expansion, the slavery issue was never far away in congressional debates. Indeed, Northern anti-slavery forces were strongly against acquiring any further territory from a weak Mexico that might lead to more slave territory. For example, regarding a treaty with the "liberal" Mexican government that gave America the right to intervene in protecting a proposed American railroad over Mexican territory, Northern Senators rejected it on the grounds that it was a fig leaf for gaining more slave territory. The movement away from schemes at further expansion of American territory reflected the growing opposition to slavery in the North. Slavery was becoming an issue that could no longer be ignored by political compromise.

Hearing the Call

In order to get Southern support for a railroad across the center of America, Senator Frederick Douglas of Illinois proposed that the Great Plains territories be opened to settlement, and the territory's future population would decide whether it would permit slavery. He called this "popular sovereignty." This was an implicit rejection of the Missouri Compromise of 1820 that had allowed slavery to be established in states south of 36° 30' parallel. Douglas's view had the advantage that both pro- and antislavery forces could benefit from opening the territories. The Kansas-Nebraska Act was passed on May 25, 1855. The Act violated various treaties with the Indians who had been solemnly told that the territory would remain theirs "as long as the grass shall grow and the water run."[1] This was hardly noticed, however, and the race was now on between pro- and antislavery forces to populate the new territory. Tensions between the two groups were high. A radical abolitionist, John Brown, and his supporters killed five pro-slavery sympathizers in the Pottawotami massacre in 1856. A vote was finally held on a pro-slavery constitution in 1858. It was overwhelmingly rejected. Antislavery forces were elated, pro-slavery groups alarmed. The "call to adventure" had been heard. Slavery was an anachronism that all the "Sons of Liberty" had to oppose.

Refusal of the Call

Extremists on both sides of the slavery debate were very active. None were more so than John Brown and his followers who led a daring raid on October 16, 1859. Taking the federal arsenal at Harper's Ferry, Brown wanted to start a slave insurrection in the American South. His small group was finally overwhelmed, and Brown was tried and sentenced to be hanged in December. Politicians condemned Brown and saw that nothing less than his execution would satisfy Southern opinion. Many abolitionists, however, admired his bravery and dedication and believed that execution was unjust. Ralph Waldo Emerson wrote of Brown: "That new saint, than whom nothing purer or more brave was ever led by love of men into conflict and death . . . will make the gallows glorious like the cross."[2] For many abolitionists, the execution of Brown was one more sign that the politicians were prepared to compromise with the evil of slavery.

Crossing the First Threshold

The Dred Scott decision of 1857 made it clear that slaves were not citizens and were the property of their owners, irrespective of where the owners chose to live. This meant that slavery was legal throughout the length and breadth of America. The Missouri Compromise was unconstitutional. The Scott decision made it appear that a final showdown between pro- and antislavery forces was imminent. The 1860 elections focused on the slavery issue. The Republican contender, Abraham Lincoln, was well known for his antislavery views, and believed it would die a natural death without interfering with the practice of slavery in the Southern states:

I hold it a paramount duty to us in the free States, due to the Union of the States, and perhaps to liberty itself (paradox though it may seem), to let the slavery of the other states alone; while on the other hand, I hold it to be equally clear that we should never knowingly lend ourselves, directly or indirectly, to prevent that slavery from dying a natural death—to find new places for it to live in, when it can no longer exist in the old.[3]

The victory of Abraham Lincoln was unacceptable to the South. Seven slave states promptly declared secession and formed the Confederate States of America on February 8, 1861. A number of compromises were attempted to bring the secessionist states back into the Union. The most far-reaching was a constitutional amendment that would have forever prevented interference with slavery in any state. The amendment was passed in the House of Representatives by a two-to-one majority and ratified by Ohio. The secessionist states were not satisfied. With this last attempt at political compromise unsuccessful, the North was ready to act to preserve the Union. President Lincoln ordered that the federal garrison at Fort Sumter, South Carolina, be resupplied. Southern forces surrounded Fort Sumter and began firing on April 12, 1861. The "first threshold" had been crossed. The North would fight to preserve the Union and in the process bring an end to one of the final bastions of slavery in the New World.

GREAT REMEMBERING (1861–1867)—FIGHTING TO PRESERVE THE UNION AND EMANCIPATION

The "great remembering" is a time when a nation reinterprets its historic mission and founding principles in the contemporary circumstances in which it finds itself. No time in American history had witnessed the principles of liberty, democracy and rule of law being as widely interpreted according to competing political interests as they had during the slavery debate. Liberty was interpreted in the North as the individual rights of slaves and the moral imperative of their emancipation. In contrast, the South saw liberty in the collective sense of state rights versus federal rights. Democracy was seen in the North as embodied in the will of state representatives in Congress. The Southern states interpreted democracy as the right to have the popular will implemented even if this meant secession. Rule of law, according to the federal government, meant its will and capacity to maintain national unity and enforce Congressional acts. For the South, rule of law was vested in the institutions of the seceding states and the Confederal system they established under Jefferson Davis. The Great Remembering for America was that the Northern perspective was to remain viable and coherent enough to maintain the costly and damaging struggle at a time when Northern dissent may have spelled doom for the federal Union.

Slaying the Dragon

The Civil War represented in archetypal terms the confrontation between the self and shadow of America. If America was to be a beacon of liberty for all the world to see, no political compromise with slavery could any longer be accepted. Rather than settle the issue of slavery, the long history of compromises beginning with the Missouri Compromise of 1820 had failed to put an end to the heated moral and political debates over slavery. Abolitionists believed that slavery was a moral evil that ought to play no part in American society. They therefore opposed all forms of political compromise. Henry David Thoreau believed that noncooperation with the state of Massachusetts was warranted as long as it permitted for escaped slaves to be rounded up and returned to the South as stipulated in the Missouri Compromise:

I do not hesitate to say, that those who call themselves abolitionists should at once effectually withdraw their support, both in person and property, from the govern- ment of Massachusetts, and not wait till they constitute a majority of one, before they suffer the right to prevail through them, I think that it is enough if they have God on their side, without waiting for that other one. Moreover, any man more right than his neighbors, constitutes a majority of one already.[4]

At the other end of the debate, opinion was just as strong, as revealed in a speech by Daniel DeJarnette in the House of Representatives:

The free suffrage and free labor of the North . . . has so shattered the framework of society, that society itself exists only in an inverted order. African slavery fur- nishes the only basis upon which republican liberty can be preserved. There is more humanity, there is more unalloyed contentment and happiness, among the slaves of the South, than any laboring population on the globe.[5]

Some Southern politicians believed that the Confederate States could carve out an empire from Mexico and establish "a civilization teeming with orators, poets, philosophers, statesmen and historians, equal to those of Greece and Rome."[6]

Each side, perhaps surprising to some today, was convinced of the moral justice of its cause. This accounts for the long and costly Civil War. Slavery, however, was an anachronism that had to be obliterated. The North's de- feat of the South was victory for the belief that domestic policy had to be based on moral principles that ran the length and breadth of American territory. America had finally put to rest the dragon of slavery that had for so long compromised its moral purity.

The Sacred Marriage

The attack on Fort Sumter was the initial military engagement of the Civil War, but it was not the end of attempts to find some political compromise. Lincoln at first tried to find some formula that would satisfy Southern aspirations while maintaining the Federal Union. This meant that there would be no repudiation of the slavery as long as compromise was possible. Such a compromise would have likely involved the South still maintaining slavery. Lincoln had stated: "If I could save the Union without freeing any slave . . . I would do it, and if I could save it by freeing all the slaves I would do it; and if I could save it by freeing some and leaving others alone I would also do that."[7] At the same time as he held on to hope of a political compromise, he pursued a determined military campaign to pressure the rebellious states back into the Union.

Lincoln was probably influenced by the view that if not war now with a rebellious South that was battling for international legitimacy and support, war would be inevitable at a later date with an expanding Southern Confederacy that would then enjoy all the advantages that international legitimacy brought to a state. This view gave added emphasis to Lincoln's belief that national unity was the key to the success of the American experiment. Strong support for the stand Lincoln had taken could be found in George Washington's farewell speech, where the latter claimed:

The unity of government which constitutes you one people is also now dear to you. It is justly so, for it is the main pillar in the edifice of your real independence, the support of your tranquillity at home, your peace abroad, of your safety, of your prosperity, of that very liberty which you so highly prize. . . . It is of infinite moment that you should properly estimate the immense value of your national union to your collective and individual happiness . . . discountenancing whatever may suggest even a suspicion that it can in any event be abandoned, and indignantly frowning upon the first dawning of every attempt to alienate any portion of our country from the rest or to enfeeble the sacred ties which now link together the various parts.[8]

Lincoln's initial dual track strategy of seeking political compromise while earnestly prosecuting the war was an attempt to maintain the "sacred ties which . . . link together the various parts" of America. The North's will to fight the Civil War enjoyed broad public support in terms of strong enlistment for the war effort and favorable newspaper coverage of the war. There was a shared understanding in the North that unity was the key to

America's future greatness. The Civil War was a renewal of the archetypal encounter of the sacred marriage.

At the end of the Civil War in 1865, the infrastructure of the South had been ruined and poverty was widespread. Southern resentment over military defeat was powerful, and there was widespread anxiety that emancipated slaves would be let loose on "civilized white society." It is worth remembering that, at the time, the Black population outnumbered the White in most Southern states. The reconstruction policy established by Lincoln and continued by his successor, Andrew Johnson, was mild toward the defeated South. Federally appointed provisional governors convened state constitutional conventions to formally renounce secessionist acts passed during the confederacy, to abolish slavery, and to amend state constitutions. No emancipated slaves were allowed to vote for delegates to the conventions or were allowed to attend. By January 1866, civil administrations were functioning in every former Confederate state except Texas. Former Confederate officials were allowed to hold public office as long as they swore allegiance to the Union. President Johnson declared by August that the insurrection was at an end, "and that peace, order, tranquility and civil authority now exist in and throughout the whole of the United States."[9] Lincoln's and Johnson's mild reconstruction policies were a continuation of the archetypal encounter of the sacred marriage that had all along guided the North's war goals. In a remarkably short time, Southern states were being integrated into the Union.

Atonement

The North's main goal in the Civil War was preservation of the Union. As the war raged on and the hope of an early end faded, it became clear that there was not going to be any political compromise. Either the North would maintain the Union by force of arms, or the South would be victorious and go her own way. Therefore on September 22, 1862, five days after the North's victory at Antietam, Lincoln issued his famous Emancipation Proclamation:

That on the 1st day of January, A.D. 1863, all persons held as slaves within any State or designated part of a State the people whereof shall then be in rebellion against the United States shall be then, thenceforward, and forever free; and the executive government of the United States, including the military and naval authority thereof, will recognize and maintain the freedom of such persons and will do no act or acts to repress such persons, or any of them, in any efforts they may make for the actual freedom.[10]

Freeing the slaves was all along the implicit goal of the Union, and now it became an explicit goal and official policy. The Proclamation meant that there would now be no possibility of a political compromise with the secessionist South. The Emancipation Proclamation turned the war into a moral crusade and boosted Northern morale. Importantly, it helped cement worldwide liberal opinion in favor of the North and helped prevent the Confederacy from gaining international recognition. The Civil War after the Emancipation Proclamation became for the North an act of atonement. America was putting into effect Jefferson's revolutionary belief in the Declaration of Independence "that all men are created equal." At the end of the war in 1865, the 13th amendment to the Constitution was passed, which forever abolished slavery. America had finally become the land of the free for all its inhabitants.

After the Civil War, President Johnson's reconstruction policy came under increasing attack due to Southern acts of defiance by former Confederate officials. The governor of Mississippi, for example, refused to fly the national flag on the state capitol and made insulting speeches about "Yankee vandals." Most provocative were "black codes" passed by Southern legislatures in 1865–1866. These codes did not give Blacks the right to vote, possess firearms, perform jury service, and other rights taken for granted by American citizens. For many Southern Whites, the codes were liberal and generous and were passed by people who "understood the colored."[11] For Northern radicals, the "black codes" were an attempt to evade the Emancipation Proclamation and an attempt to make emancipated slaves second-class citizens. Increasing numbers of Blacks were being murdered by White mobs without the perpetrators being brought to justice. Johnson narrowly escaped removal from office, and Congress began passing legislation that ushered in the era of "radical reconstruction." As Samuel Morison wrote:

Lincoln had grasped a great truth . . . that reconstruction of a shattered empire must be approached with wisdom rather than strict justice; the defeated foe must be helped to his feet and treated more like the prodigal son than a convicted felon. Lincoln and Johnson had tried this Christian policy on the South; the South (so it seemed) had contemptuously declined the friendly hand and defied the victors. Woe, then, to the South![12]

In March 1867, by Act of Congress, military rule had replaced the civil administrations that Johnson had created in the South. Five military governors reported directly to General Grant rather than to President Johnson. Thousands of local officials and the governors of six states were removed. Military courts replaced civil courts in hearing cases of violence against Blacks that had gone unpunished. Congress passed the 14th Amendment to the Constitution (1868) barring former Confederate officials from holding public office and the 15th Amendment (1870) guaranteeing the right to vote to the Black population. Emancipated slaves were allowed to vote and indeed many became members of Southern state legislatures. For the defeated Southerners, it was humiliating to see former slaves play leading roles in the appointed governments ruling over them during the era of Radical Reconstruction (1867–1875). For Northerners, allowing emancipated slaves to fill important government posts served two important functions. First, it would give effect to the moral goal of the North and ensure that emancipated slaves had the same rights as all American citizens. Second, the policy would serve as a reminder that no defiance would be permitted and that the North was very much in charge.

General Grant continued radical reconstruction when he won the presidency in 1868. Any Southern resistance to efforts to fully integrate the states into the Union or to oppose the rights of emancipated slaves would not be tolerated. Despite the excesses of the radical reconstruction era, it did exemplify how America took seriously the task of emancipating slaves and ensuring that their rights were respected. Radical reconstruction was a continuation of the national act of atonement begun by the Emancipation Proclamation—liberty would be enjoyed by all of America's inhabitants.

The long and costly Civil War finally ended in a decisive victory for the North. Lincoln had succeeded in forever slaying the dragon of slavery that had for decades divided America. In the process, America's sacred marriage was renewed and the foundation established for a stronger Federal Union. Lincoln's and Johnson's reconstruction policies were a reflection of the sacred marriage. At the same time, the emancipation of slaves became an act of atonement. This was reflected in the radical reconstruction policies of Congress and the Grant administration when the South did not do enough to effect Black rights. In the four years of the Civil War and up to and including the beginning of the radical reconstruction, America had undergone the "great remembering." The moral and political visions of the Founding Fathers were realized and played a decisive role in making possible the North's great victory.

THE RETURN TO INTERNATIONAL SOCIETY (1867–1875)—REASSERTING THE MONROE DOCTRINE

In the midst of the Civil War, a dire challenge to the Monroe Doctrine had been posed by military intervention by France in Mexico. Here was as clear a challenge to the principle of noninterference by European powers in Latin America as could be imagined. A European autocrat, Napoleon III of France, was attempting to establish by force of arms a puppet state ruled by another monarch, Prince Maximilian of Austria. In the process, the Mexican republican government was forcibly removed, and it began a desperate guerrilla struggle against the French-supported regime. Despite the urgencies of the Civil War and its immediate aftermath, America began slowly to give effect to the Monroe Doctrine and forever establish in the mind of European states that it was serious about excluding them from Latin America.

Refusal of the Return

As a result of yet another series of political crises, the Mexican republic was forced to default on a number of loans to European states in July 1861. The largest creditors—Britain, Spain, and France—agreed in October to launch a joint military expedition to force the Mexican government to pay its debts. The joint military expedition took over the port city of Santa Cruz with the objective of raising the debt from the customs duties. In disgust over the behavior of the French occupation forces, Britain and Spain decided to pull out of the joint military venture. France under the Emperor Napoleon III, however, had ambitions of reviving its colonial empire in Latin America. He planned to take over Mexico and install a puppet government. French forces began to fight to depose the Mexican government led by President Juarez that put up a stubborn resistance. In June 1863, French forces occupied Mexico City, and the republican government now began a desperate guerrilla campaign. With support from the Mexican aristocracy, France contrived a plebiscite in which the Mexican population supposedly desired a monarchical form of government under the Austrian prince, Maximilian. The unfortunate Maximilian was duped into believing that the population genuinely desired a European monarchy. In April 1864 he took up with zeal the responsibility he believed Providence had thrust upon him.

Napoleon's unfolding plans for Mexico were not unnoticed by members of Congress. Senator Summer from Massachusetts in early 1864 denounced Napoleon: "Trampler upon the Republic in France, trampler upon the Republic in Mexico, it remains to be seen if the French Emperor can prevail as trampler upon this Republic."[13] Public opinion continued to harden against France, and a week before the coronation of Emperor Maximilian, the House of Representatives adopted by a vote of 109–0 a resolution containing a veiled threat to France:

The Congress of the United States are unwilling by silence to leave the nations of the world under the impression that they are indifferent spectators of the deplorable events now transpiring in the republic of Mexico, and that they therefore think fit to declare that it does not accord with the policy of the United States to acknowledge any monarchical Government erected on the ruins of any republican Government in America under the auspices of any European Power.[14]

All these events were watched cautiously by President Lincoln and his Foreign Secretary William Henry Seward. The desperate nature of the Civil War meant that little more than a diplomatic protest could be launched to deter France from so brazenly violating the Monroe Doctrine. In a letter in May 1864 to the American Consul General in Paris, Seward wrote that "with our land and naval forces in Louisiana retreating before the rebels instead of marching toward Mexico, this is not the most suitable time we could choose for offering idle menaces to the Emperor of France."[15] For the moment, America would have to undertake a "refusal of the call" insofar as it was in no position to pose a legitimate military threat to France. The Monroe Doctrine would not be enforced in case it would trigger French intervention on behalf of the desperate South.

Crossing the Return Threshold

The successful conclusion of the Civil War meant that American policymakers could now turn their full attention to Napoleon's activities in Mexico. Of all the major European powers, France had given most support to the Confederacy. To make matters worse, in the final months of the South's resistance Maximilian had ill-advisedly given aid to the South. This had further alienated Northern public opinion and the American government against Maximilian and his French supporters. General Grant ordered an army of 50,000 under General Sheridan to march to the border. Secretary Seward ordered General Schofield to France with instructions that could be summarized in the words: "I want you to get your legs under Napoleon's mahogoney and tell him he must get out of Mexico."[16] America was giving a serious warning that unless France left Mexico, it might have to face a costly war with America. The threat was real, and despite the devastating Civil War, America had the resources to forcibly eject France from Mexico. America crossed the "return threshold" and displayed its willingness to enforce the Monroe Doctrine.

Master of the Two Worlds

A combination of the costs of fighting the ongoing guerrilla war waged by the ejected Mexican government, possible intervention by America, and signs that war with Prussia was not far off led to Napoleon's decision to withdraw from Mexico. In April 1866, a period of nineteen months was specified as the time withdrawal was to take. With the departure of his French protectors in Spring 1867, the unfortunate Maximilian was captured by Mexican republican forces and executed in June 1867. In convincing Napoleon to withdraw from Mexico, America demonstrated that it had the will and capacity to uphold the Monroe Doctrine. Never again would a European power so brazenly intervene in Latin America. The historian Thomas Bailey summed up the significance of these events for the Monroe Doctrine:

With the Civil War, the Monroe Doctrine came of age. In the 1830's it had been ignored, if not forgotten; in the 1840's it had been reasserted without commanding much respect; and in the 1850's it had come to be rather generally accepted by the Democratic Party. But in the 1860's, embraced by the Republican administration of Lincoln, it attained the dignity of a national heritage. Respected at home and acknowledged abroad, it was never again to be challenged so boldly and frontally. If Monroe enunciated the Doctrine and Polk, a Democrat, resurrected it, Seward, a Republican, vindicated it.[17]

With its success in asserting the Monroe Doctrine against France, America was now master of the two worlds. It had achieved its third grand synthesis through its efforts to ensure the political independence of Latin American states. It could use its now proven military capabilities in deterring European intervention in Latin America on the basis of the principle of nonintervention. At the same time, Congress took the lead in rejecting any further attempts at territorial aggrandizement. When President Grant took office in March 1869, he briefly considered ways for increasing American territory. He explored the option of annexing the island of Santo Domingo that had declared independence from Spain. A treaty was signed with the political leaders of the island and a plebiscite was held with the result that there was almost unanimous support for annexation. Grant, however, was frustrated by the Senate's refusal to ratify the treaty. Senator Bayard of Delaware declared that "such a scheme of empire, if indulged in, will destroy our republican system of government."[18] This and other attempts at expanding American territory were frustrated. Summing up the public mood, Secretary of State Seward, declared,

Public attention continues to be fastened upon the domestic questions which have grown out of the late civil war. The public mind refuses to dismiss these questions even so far as to entertain the higher but more remote questions of national extension and aggrandizement. . . . The leaders of each party therefore seem to shrink from every suggestion which may involve any new national enterprise, and especially any foreign one.[19]

In 1872, President Grant declared that there would be no further attempts to purchase territory. America had shown that both politically and morally it was opposed to intervention in the sovereign affairs of Latin American states.

DEEP FORGETTING (1875–1889)—IGNORING THE PLIGHT OF INDIANS AND EMANCIPATED SLAVES

The years after the Civil War saw America concentrate her energies on industrialization and westward expansion. The historian Foster Rhea Dulles observed that the 1870s and 1880s "found interest in foreign affairs at the lowest ebb in all American history, with the public almost totally absorbed in the overriding domestic problems arising from industrial expansion and the final settlement of the West."[20] Westward expansion was having a devastating effect on the remaining lands left to the Native American population. Initial concern over the fair treatment of emancipated slaves in the Southern states that was present in the era of radical reconstruction (1866–1875) gave way to increasing apathy and disinterest.

Fear

If fear was a characteristic of American foreign policy during this era of inactivity, it was because America became self-conscious of its inability to influence global events outside of the Western hemisphere. Indeed, noninterference and isolationism was the order of the day as President Rutherford B. Hayes made clear in his 1877 inaugural address: "[W]e are reminded by international complications abroad, threatening the peace of Europe, that our traditional rule of noninterference in the affairs of foreign nations has proved of great value in past times and ought to be strictly observed."[21] Despite the moral issues involved in European conflicts over principles of self-determination, reunification, and colonial expansion, America became isolationist. America's fear was that being sucked into the moral vortex of issues that involved European states would spell doom for the well-being of the American republic.

Imperialism

Though America undertook no scheme of territorial expansion and conquest against other states, there was conquest against the Native American population. As mentioned earlier, Indian tribes were treated as sovereign nations by Congress with whom treaties had to be made and respected. Federal governments had ratified treaties with the Indians assuring them that the remaining lands they occupied would be untouched. These treaties were ignored as the building of transcontinental railroads brought larger and larger numbers of Whites to settle adjacent lands and to mine the mineral-rich hills. These wars against Indians were therefore imperialism insofar as America ignored the responsibility of living up to treaties with the sovereign Indian nations. The Commissioner of Indian Affairs, General Francis Walker, stated the following in his annual report to Congress:

Every year's advance of our frontier takes in a territory as large as some of the kingdoms of Europe. We are richer by hundreds of millions, the Indian is poorer by a large part of the little that he has. This growth is bringing imperial greatness to the nation; to the Indian it brings wretchedness, destitution, beggary.[22]

The Indian tribes fought back, sometimes with devastating results. Colonel George Custer and his entire command of 265 were killed at Little Big Horn in 1876 by 2,500 braves led by Crazy Horse. Victory, however, was to be short-lived. Crazy Horse and his followers were soon defeated. With successive defeats of the Native American population, America was indeed becoming an imperial power at the expense of weaker Indian nations.

Materialism

The election of a Democrat-controlled Congress in 1874 brought an end to the era of radical reconstruction. Northern public opinion was losing interest in ensuring that the Southern Black population was protected. Federal garrisons were reduced, and Black militias were disbanded. This led to the White Southern population increasingly resorting to intimidation and violence against the Black population in election campaigns. Samuel Morison described the situation in Mississippi, for example:

Any meeting of Negro voters was apt to be set upon by armed white men; and in these clashes Negroes, still timid and unresourceful, were invariably worsted. Governor Ames appealed to President Grant for federal troops, but was told by the attorney general, "The whole public are tired of these annual autumnal outbreaks in the South."[23]

In Southern states, lynchings continued to be widespread and went unpunished. Blacks were quickly learning that the Emancipation Proclamation was a dead letter as long as not energetically supported by the federal government. The cost of maintaining a federal presence in the South would no longer be borne by the American taxpayer.

Similarly, solemn treaties ratified with Indian tribes were ignored by the federal government that was unwilling to hold back the tide of White encroachment on Indian lands. What motivated White settlers, miners, and railway companies in encroaching upon Indian lands was purely the material benefits to be gained. Greed rather than the need to civilize or protect the Indians was what motivated the Indian wars.

Grant's second term in office (1873–1877) became known as the most corrupt of all presidential administrations. Mark Twain called this the "Guilded Age" "for when the gilt wore off one found only base brass; everyone was trying to make a 'fast buck.' "[24] America underwent a period of rapid expansion with the building of transcontinental railroads that enabled commerce and people to move the length and breadth of America. Enormous opportunities were at hand, and the majority of Whites in America became more concerned about making a "fast buck" than about the rights of their Black brethren or the Native American population.

With an absence of interest in moral issues that arose in European con-

Table 5.1
America's Third Hero's Journey—Civil War and the Monroe Doctrine (1855–1891)

Phase of Hero's Journey	Step of Hero's Journey	Key Events	
CALL TO ADVENTURE Ending Slavery as a Moral Imperative (1855-1861)	Hearing the Call	1.	Vote to abolish pro-slavery constitution in Kansas (1858)
	Refusal of the Call	2.	Execution of John Brown after Harper's Ferry Raid (1859)
	Crossing the First threshold	3.	Federal troops refuse to evacuate Fort Sumter, South Carolina and return fire after Confederate attack (1861)
GREAT REMEMBERING Fighting to Preserve the Union and Emancipation (1861-1865)	Slaying the Dragon	4.	Civil War (1861-1865)
	Sacred Marriage	5. 6.	Fighting to preserve the Federal Union (1861-1865) Mild reconstruction policies under Presidents Lincoln and Johnson (1865-1867)
	Atonement	7. 8.	Emancipation Proclamation (1863) Radical Reconstruction (1867-1877)
RETURN TO INTERNATIONAL SOCIETY Reasserting the Monroe Doctrine (1867-1875)	Refusal of the Return	9.	America does not pressure France to stop intervening in Mexico through support of the puppet Emperor Maximilian (1864-1865)
	Cross Return Threshold	10. 11.	General Grant reaches the Mexican border with 50,000 troops (1865) General Schofield sent to Paris to negotiate with Napoleon III (1865)
	Master of the Two Worlds	• •	American military threats lead to France withdrawing troops and support of Maximilian (1866-1867) **Third Grand Synthesis, America's willingness to enforce the Monroe Doctrine through military means ensures independence of Western hemisphere states.**
DEEP FORGETTING Ignoring the Plight of Native Americans & Emancipated Slaves (1875-1889)	Fear	12.	Isolationism (1875-1889)
	Imperialism	13.	Violation of Indian Treaties and military campaigns waged against Plains Indians. Colonel Custer and 265 troops killed at Little Big Horn (1876)
	Materialism	14.	Mark Twain refers to this as the 'Guilded Age' of corruption and fast bucks (1873-1877)

flicts, territorial expansion at the expense of the Indian tribes, and unwillingness to pay the cost of protecting the rights of emancipated slaves in the South, America had once more undergone a deep forgetting. America's third hero's journey, summarized in Table 5.1, had come to a mindnumbing end.

NOTES

1. Samuel Eliot Morison, *The Oxford History of the American People* (New York: Oxford University Press, 1965), 589.

2. Quoted in Morison, *The Oxford History of the American People*, 602.

3. Lincoln quoted in Dan Nimmo and James Combs, *Subliminal Politics: Myths and Mythmakers in America* (Englewood Cliffs, NJ: Prentice Hall), 1980. 54.

4. Henry David Thoreau, "On Civil Disobedience," in *The Pacifist Conscience*, ed. Peter Mayer (London: Penguin Books, 1966), 148.

5. Quoted in Morison, *The Oxford History of the American People*, 606.

6. Ibid.

7. John Graham, ed. Quoted in *Great American Speeches 1898–1963* (New York: Appleton-Century-Crofts, 1970), 214.

8. Jerome Agel, *Words That Make America Great* (New York: Random House, 1997), 274.

9. John Graham, ed. Quoted in Morison, *The Oxford History of the American People*, 712.

10. "The Emancipation Proclamation," in *Great American Speeches 1898–1963*, 214.

11. Morison, *The Oxford History of the American People*, 713.

12. Ibid., 716.

13. Quoted in Thomas Bailey, *A Diplomatic History of the American People*, 8th ed. (New York: Appleton-Century-Crofts, 1969), 352.

14. Ibid., 352–53.

15. Ibid., 352.

16. Ibid., 354.

17. Bailey, *A Diplomatic History of the American People*, 358.

18. Julius Pratt, *A History of United States Foreign Policy* (Newark, N.J.: Prentice Hall, 1955), 324.

19. Ibid., 321.

20. Foster Rhea Dulles, *Prelude to World Power: American Diplomatic History, 1860–1900* (New York: Macmillan, 1965), vii.

21. John Gabriel Hunt, ed. *Inaugural Addresses of the Presidents* (New York: Random House, 1997), 224.

22. Quoted in Morison, *The Oxford History of the American People*, 751.

23. Morison, *The Oxford History of the American People*, 724.

24. Ibid., 732.

CHAPTER 6

AMERICA'S FOURTH HERO'S JOURNEY (1889–1912)—AMERICA'S RISE TO GREAT POWER STATUS

The years up to 1889 saw no attempt by American administrations to acquire foreign territory. This gradually changed, and by the end of the nineteenth century, America went through a very active and rigorous period in foreign affairs when it carved out for itself a foreign empire. It achieved a foreign empire while attempting at the same time to remain true to its principles of liberty and self-governance. This hero's journey eventually saw America fully step into the international arena as a new Great Power. The seeds for America's journey to great power status lay in a renewed effort to promote the Monroe Doctrine.

CALL TO ADVENTURE (1889–1895)—REASSERTING THE MONROE DOCTRINE

Hearing the Call

William Harrison was elected in 1888 and was determined to prevent possible European interference in the Western hemisphere. The key to maintaining isolation from Europe was the Monroe Doctrine. In his inaugural address in 1889, Harrison affirmed that this would be the central pillar of his foreign policy:

We have not sought to dominate or to absorb any of our weaker neighbors, but rather to aid and encourage them to establish free and stable governments resting upon the consent of their people. We have a clear right to expect, therefore, that no European government will seek to establish colonial dependencies upon the territory of these independent American states. That which a sense of justice restrains us from seeking they may be reasonably expected willingly to forego.[1]

President Harrison wanted to legitimate the Monroe Doctrine, and hosted a Pan-American meeting in Washington in October 1889. The Secretary of State, Jim Blaine, worked energetically to get the meeting to support the two main goals of the creation of a customs union, and the establishment of an arbitration mechanism for settling international disputes. Both goals were voted down in the meeting. Though the results were disappointing, the meeting signaled America's willingness to support the independence of Western hemisphere states through Pan-American cooperation. President Harrison's willingness to assert the Monroe Doctrine was America's "call to adventure" for a new hero's journey.

Refusal of the Call

Acquisitions of strategically placed islands were seen as critical for maintaining the Monroe Doctrine. In the case of Hawaii, possession of this island chain would give America a huge strategic advantage in the Pacific Ocean. The opportunity to acquire the Hawaiian islands came in the final months of the Harrison administration. A pro-American revolutionary committee had deposed the Hawaiian Queen in January 1893. American marines soon landed, and a treaty of annexation was negotiated with Hawaiian representatives. This was submitted to the Senate for ratification on February 15. On coming into power on March 4, President Grover Cleveland promptly withdrew the treaty and recognized Hawaiian independence. Cleveland's action was a refusal of the call insofar as he dismissed the thinking that acquisition of Hawaii was necessary for giving further teeth to the Monroe Doctrine.

Crossing the First Threshold

In 1895 a boundary dispute between the colony of British Guiana and Venezuela came to a head. Venezuela, being the weaker state, had long wanted arbitration to settle the matter. Britain was content to continue to settle territory claimed by Venezuela and have arbitration with limits on the territory to be discussed. In a pamphlet titled *British Aggressions in Venezuela, or the Monroe Doctrine on Trial*, William Scruggs outlined the Venezuelan case. As the title suggested, the Monroe Doctrine was on trial and all Western hemisphere states were interested in seeing whether America would back the doctrine with force if necessary against Britain. American public opinion was solidly in support of forcing Britain to the negotiating table. In a diplomatic note, President Cleveland asked Congress for authorization to convene a commission to arbitrate the contested boundary. In considering the consequences of enforcing the decision of the commission, he delivered an ultimatum to Britain:

[W]hile it is a grievous thing to contemplate the two great English-speaking peoples of the world as being otherwise than friendly competitors in the onward march of civilization . . . there is no calamity which a great nation can invite which equals that which follows a supine submission to wrong and injustice and the consequent loss of national self respect and honor beneath which are shielded and defended a people's safety and greatness.[2]

Fully aware of the risk of war with Britain, Congress gave the necessary authorization for the commission to be created. Britain backed down and agreed to arbitration of the boundary. America had crossed the first threshold. It signaled its willingness to use force to maintain the Monroe Doctrine. As the *Chicago Tribune* triumphantly announced: "Never again will a European nation put forth claims to American territory without consulting the government of the United States."[3]

GREAT REMEMBERING (1895–1898)—SUPPORTING CUBAN INDEPENDENCE

The principle of self-determination was at the center of America's great remembering in its fourth hero's journey. Self-determination could be directly linked to the principle of liberty, the first of the three principles at the core of American national identity. Liberty was linked to the right of self-determination insofar as it meant that all peoples, including the Cuban people, had a right to be free of unjust or tyrannical government, and choose their own form of government. Under the administration of William McKinley, America moved decisively towards intervening in the Cuban independence struggle against Spanish rule.

Slaying the Dragon

In 1895, there had been a revolt against Spanish rule in Cuba. American public opinion shifted strongly toward support of the rebels, and the revolt became an election issue in 1896. The successful Republican candidate, William McKinley, adopted a "peace" policy because war with Spain was a costly and dangerous prospect with America still recovering from an economic depression. In his first inaugural speech, he said:

Our diplomacy should seek nothing more and accept nothing less than is due us. We want no wars of conquest; we must avoid the temptation of territorial aggression. War should never by entered upon until every agency of peace has failed;

peace is preferable to war in almost every contingency. Arbitration is the true method of settlement of international as well as local or individual differences.[4]

The sinking of the American warship *Maine* in Havana harbor with the loss of 260 men in February 1898 raised tension with Spain. Public opinion grew strongly in favor of American military intervention as Spanish forces continued to commit atrocities. Most disturbing of Spanish policies was herding rural Cubans into urban concentration camps from which they could be watched and stopped from aiding the rebels. It was estimated that up to 200,000 Cubans died in these camps out of a total population of 1,600,000. A report delivered in the Senate on March 17, 1898, by Senator Proctor of Vermont on these developments electrified Congress. On March 27, bowing to overwhelming public pressure and prospect of Republican losses in the forthcoming congressional elections, McKinley delivered an ultimatum to the Spanish government to negotiate with the insurgents. Spain's reply was unsatisfactory, and on April 11, 1898, McKinley reluctantly submitted to Congress a request for military intervention in Cuba.

There was intense debate over the motives for the intervention in Cuba. Was intervention purely humanitarian to help Cuban independence or was it an attempt to increase American economic interests in Cuba and perhaps even keep the island as a colony? So strong was sentiment that America should not establish Cuba as a colony, that a resolution was passed by Senator Henry M. Teller expressing America's intentions towards Cuba:

That the United States hereby disclaims any disposition of intention to exercise sovereignty, jurisdiction, or control over said Island except for the pacification thereof, and asserts its determination, when that is accomplished, to leave the government and control of the Island to its people.[5]

The "dragon" America was attempting to slay through the Teller Amendment was any vestige of European colonialism in its Cuba policy. America would assist Cuban insurgents driving out the Spanish government without any ulterior motive.

Sacred Marriage

An economic depression in America from 1893 to 1897 saw America concentrate her energies on finance and trade. The second Cleveland administration (1893–1897) was heavily preoccupied with the national economy and did not give great priority to international affairs. In his inaugural address of 1893, Cleveland pointed out the priority of his administration as follows:

Manifestly nothing is more vital to our supremacy as a nation and to the beneficent purposes of our government than a sound and stable currency. Its exposure to degradation should at once arouse to activity the most enlightened statesmanship, and the danger of depreciation in the purchasing power of the wages paid to toil should furnish the strongest incentive to prompt and conservative precaution. . . . We will be wise if we temper our confidence and faith in our national strength and resources with the frank concession that even these will not permit us to defy with impunity the inexorable laws of finance and trade.[6]

During the growing public furor over unfolding events in Cuba, President McKinley desperately attempted quiet diplomacy to settle the problem. Like his predecessor, McKinley wanted to concentrate on the domestic economy in order to bring America out of its economic depression. Indeed, at one point in the conflict, he declared that he would "not mobilize the army" if Congress declared war.[7] By 1897 a recovery had begun and American business interests in Cuba were warning that a war with Spain would end "the trade prosperity we are all enjoying."[8] In sum, the Cleveland administration and early part of the McKinley administration represented the "sacred marriage" insofar as achieving national unity through ending the economic depression and a diplomatic solution to the Cuban conflict were paramount.

Atonement

America's decision to militarily intervene in Cuba was done largely on humanitarian grounds. Julius Pratt explains that with a few exceptions, "trade journals and resolutions of boards of trade and chambers of commerce . . . advocated a hands-off policy."[9] Trade had suffered as a result of the rebellion, with exports to Cuba falling from $60,000,000 in 1895 to $15,000,000 in 1896.[10] The business community was eager to bring a quick end to the war even if this meant a restoration of Spanish rule. The long history of brutal suppression by Spain of Cuban independence movements, however, had created great public sympathy in America for the Cuban population. The current Cuban independence movement resonated deep within the American psyche of an oppressed people fighting for their liberty and self-government. Wasn't this, after all, what the American independence movement a century earlier had been all about? The support for liberty and self-government was at the heart of America's national identity. Helping Cuba achieve her independence would be a wonderful way of demonstrating America's global mission of supporting liberty and self-government. After diplomatic initiatives with the Spanish government had failed to achieve the goal of independence, President McKinley received Congressional resolutions supporting his request for military intervention. America declared war on Spain on April 25, 1898. America's decision to militarily intervene in support of Cuban independence movement was an act of "atonement."

THE RETURN TO INTERNATIONAL SOCIETY (1898–1903)—COMMITMENT TO SELF-DETERMINATION

The successful conclusion of the Spanish-American War confirmed America as a Great Power with an overseas Empire from which it could secure its national interests elsewhere. In contrast to the other Great Powers, however, America was perceived to be benevolent because it aimed to promote self-government in territories that had yet to reach political maturity. Cuba was soon given its freedom, and other captured territories would, so the thinking went, eventually be given theirs.

Refusal of the Return

At the end of the nineteenth century, the idea of Manifest Destiny had again become popular due to the widespread belief in Social Darwinism. Just as different animal species were in a biological contest of the survival of the fittest, so too were different "human races." This led to popular views that the Anglo-Saxon, with his political institutions and culture, was destined to dominate international affairs. Josiah Strong, a popular clergyman, wrote in 1885 that the Anglo-Saxon race

will spread itself over the earth. If I read not amiss, this powerful race will move down upon Mexico, down upon Central and South America, out upon the islands of the sea, over upon Africa and beyond. And can anyone doubt that the result of this competition of races will be the "survival of the fittest"?[11]

The idea that America's manifest destiny was to expand and establish overseas colonies raised intense public and congressional debate. Territorial expansion on the principles of liberty and self-governance in areas such as Texas, California, and Oregon where there were substantial numbers of American settlers could be justified. This clearly differed to European territorial expansion by which the wishes of the territory's population were not consulted. It was where America gained control of territories without significant numbers of American settlers that differences with European colonialism became less clear-cut. Nowhere did the debate over American expansion become so intense as in the question of what to do with the former Spanish colonies of the Philippines, Puerto Rico, and Guam at the end of the Spanish-American War. The Philippines case was especially intense given its great distance from America and its non-European population. Supporters of expansion such as Albert Beveridge argued:

The world is interested in the Philippines, and it has a right to be. . . . You can not take the Philippines out of the operation of those forces which are binding all mankind into one vast and united intelligence. When Circumstance has raised our flag above them, we dare not turn these misguided children over the destruction by themselves or spoliation by others, and then make answer when the God of nations requires them at our hands, "Am I my brother's Keeper?"[12]

Supporters of holding on to the Philippines and the other captured Spanish colonies had the belief that political control over subject populations that had not yet reached sufficient political maturity for self-governance was justified. Whereas Europe established colonies for economic and security benefits and intended to maintain political control, America's colonies would be prepared for self-governance and eventual independence. This was an important distinction indeed and was intended to show that America did not practice European colonialism.[13] Opponents of holding on to the Philippines such as Missouri's Senator Vest argued that "under the Constitution of the United States no power is given to the Federal Government to acquire territory to be held and governed permanently as colonies."[14] America's "refusal of the return" was a rejection of the belief that colonial peoples had the right to self-determination. They first had to be sufficiently "civilized" before gaining their freedom.

The consequences of America's "refusal of the return" were seen immediately in the Philippines. Once Filipinos learned that America intended to hold on to the Philippines, a bloody revolt began. American troops fought Philippine insurgents ironically using many of the same policies of the former Spanish colonial government. The brutality of the methods used by American troops is vividly displayed in a letter from a young soldier from Kingston, New York:

Last night one of our boys was found shot and his stomach cut open. Immediately orders were received from General Wheaton to burn the town and kill every native in sight; which was done to a finish. About 1,000 men, women and children were reportedly killed. I am probably growing hard-hearted, for I am in my glory when I can sight my gun on some dark skin and pull the trigger.[15]

It took three years (1899–1902) for American forces to crush the revolt with significant loss of life and property. This was exactly what was warned against by Democratic opponents of America's acquisition of overseas colonies. Rather than preparing the peoples for liberty and self-government, America would be oppressing the population and maintaining unpopular political rule. In refusing to consider self-determination for the Philippines, America was behaving as would any imperial power in keeping control over a territory despite the wishes of the population.

Crossing the Return Threshold

The success of the Spanish-American war led to America now beginning a process that would fulfill its pledge to give Cuba its independence. American military forces controlled Cuba but did not recognize the insurgent government. Instead, America appointed a military governor who would prepare Cuba for independence through a constitutional convention beginning in November 1900. In the meantime, America sponsored a range of programs in health, public works, education, and court reform that improved the quality of life for average Cubans. The Constitutional Convention signed a new constitution on February 21, 1901. The Platt Amendment was later added as an annex by the Convention. This gave America the right to militarily intervene: "for the preservation of Cuban independence, the maintenance of a government adequate for the protection of life, property, and individual liberty."[16] The new Cuban government was inaugurated on May 20, 1902, and American troops were withdrawn. A permanent treaty was ratified in 1903 between Cuba and America. America had "crossed the return threshold" insofar as it signaled that it would take seriously a people's right to self-determination in any acquisition of further American territory.

Master of the Two Worlds

In fulfilling its pledge to grant independence to Cuba, America had shown that it was "master of the two worlds." In the political sphere, America had the military means to successfully oppose a European power and force diplomatic changes. In the moral sphere, by carrying out its commitment to give Cuba its independence, America was true to its founding principles of liberty and self-governance. America had successfully achieved a new grand synthesis of power and morality in support of the principle of self-determination.

Despite the violence in repressing the Philippines revolt (1899–1901) and no commitment to granting independence to the Philippines and the other captured Spanish colonies, America provided for a generous degree of self-government for its colonies. A legislature was created for the Philippines in 1902 that was elected by popular vote. A similar policy was adopted for Puerto Rico. America was far more benevolent than European colonial powers in permitting a genuine degree of self-government to its colonial territories.

Another arena in which America could support its grand synthesis was in China. In 1900 groups of Chinese inspired by the Dowager Empress began attacking all foreigners in an effort to free China from external influence. The Boxer Rebellion resulted in an 18,000-man international rescue expedition that succeeded in ending the rebellion and saving the foreign legations. There was now every chance that China would be taken over by foreign powers as had earlier happened with the British takeover of India after the Sepoy Mutiny (1857–1859). Strongly opposed for commercial reasons to any carve-up of China in which America would gain a share, President McKinley and his Secretary of State, John Hay, instead preferred maintaining an "open door policy" in China. This preserved the status quo where China was locked into a series of treaties giving foreign powers open access and extensive commercial rights. Though this guaranteed foreign influence over the government, it at least preserved the territorial integrity of China. The principle of self-determination for the Chinese people was upheld by America's fifth grand synthesis.

With the assassination of the conscientious McKinley, the expansionist Theodore Roosevelt became president. Roosevelt was openly committed to the idea of America becoming a great power through the acquisition of external territories. He embraced the notion of manifest destiny with a passion and took America into a new 'deep forgetting'.

DEEP FORGETTING (1903–1912)—IMPERIAL AMERICA

In 1890, Captain (later Rear Admiral) Alfred Mahan argued in his famous book, *The Influence of Sea Power upon History, 1660–1783*, that sea power was the key to national greatness. To be able to increase its sea power, America needed overseas colonies. Otherwise, America's ships of war would "be like land birds, unable to fly far from their own shores. To provide resting-places for them, where they can coal and repair, would be one of the first duties of a government proposing to itself the development of the power of the nation at sea."[17] Influenced strongly by Mahan's theory, many in the Republican Party believed that America had to join the great march for acquiring colonial possessions, otherwise she would miss out with dire peril for the future. The "great nations," Henry Cabot Lodge wrote in 1895 (later Chair of the Senate Foreign Relations Committee), "are rapidly absorbing for their future expansion and their present defense all the waste places of the earth. It is a movement which makes for civilization and the advancement of the race. As one of the great nations of the world, the United States must not fall out of the line of march."[18] Securing American colonies or protectorates therefore became an important goal that could not be ignored. As "master of the two worlds," America under President McKinley had achieved its fourth grand synthesis of power and morality in the cases of Cuba and China. This grand synthesis began to unravel as it became clear that America would join in the race for overseas territories and influence. America would not change its policy of refusing self-determination for the captured Spanish territories of the Philippines and Puerto Rico.

Fear

The Spanish-American War had resulted in several of Spain's overseas colonies falling into American hands. Cuba became independent, but other Spanish territories—Guam, Puerto Rico, and the Philippines—were ceded by Spain to America. The capture of the Philippines presented a huge dilemma for President McKinley. They presented a great strategic asset because from the Philippines a power could extend its influence and power all across the Far East. Indeed, American participation in suppressing the Boxer Rebellion was possible due to the presence of military personnel in the Philippines. Granting self-determination to the Philippines would have led to its political independence. That would mean that America would have lost a significant strategic advantage in the great march for commercial and territorial influence in Asia. The fear that America would be overtaken by the other great colonial powers drove McKinley to accepting the inevitability of American control. America had taken the first fateful step towards becoming an imperial power.

Imperialism

The 1900 election saw imperialism as an important issue. The Democratic Party was opposed, and its foreign policy platform stated:

[W]e favor an immediate declaration of the Nation's purpose to give to the Filipinos, first, a stable form of government; second, independence; and third, protection from outside interference such as has been given for nearly a century to the republics of Central and South America.[19]

McKinley, however, won a second term with a policy permitting imperialism. The American public had embraced the idea that some races had inferior political traditions and institutions, and needed time to be educated for independence as a modern state. This was a view embraced by McKinley as revealed in his account of how he eventually decided to keep the Philippines:

The truth is I didn't want the Philippines and when they came to us as a gift from the gods, I did not know what to do about them. . . . I walked the White House night after night until midnight; and I am not ashamed to tell you, gentlemen, that I went down on my knees and prayed Almighty God for light and guidance more than one night. . . . And one night late it came to me in this way . . . (1) that we could not give them back to Spain—that would be cowardly and dishonorable; (2) that we could not turn them over to France or German—our commercial rivals in the Orient—that would be bad business and discreditable; (3) that we could not leave them to themselves—they were unfit for self-government—and they would soon have anarchy and misrule over there worse than Spain's was; and (4) that there was nothing left for us but to take them all, and to educate the Filipinos, and uplift and civilize and Christianize them. . . . And then I went to bed, and went to sleep and slept soundly.[20]

McKinley's fateful acceptance of imperialism was enthusiastically continued by his successor Theodore Roosevelt. On March 19, 1903, America signed and ratified a treaty with Colombia on building and controlling the Panama Canal. The Colombian Congress, however, refused to ratify the treaty on August 12, which they saw as a case of "Yankee Imperialism." In fact, Colombian politicians suspected getting a better deal than that negotiated in the treaty if they held out. President Roosevelt was infuriated. He regarded Colombian politicians as "foolish and homicidal corruptionists."[21] Roosevelt could have renegotiated the treaty or could have chosen the alternative Nicaragua route that was proposed. Instead, he tacitly gave support in private interviews for the territory of Panama to secede from Colombia by indicating that American forces would not allow Colombia to retake Panama.[22] On November 3, the predicted revolution occurred, and American naval forces were nearby in case Colombia tried to retake the territory. On November 18, a treaty was signed with an envoy of Panama, and approved by the Senate on February 23, 1904. With bewildering speed, President Roosevelt had tacitly sponsored, approved, and then recognized the secession of territory from a sovereign international state. This was a complete reversal of the position taken in the American Civil War as many Southern commentators were quick to point out. America's action was condemned as Yankee imperialism by Colombia, and continues to be a deep source of tension.

Events in Venezuela from 1902 to 1903, when Britain, France, and Germany blockaded the country due to it issuing defunct bonds, culminated in President Roosevelt's famous Corollary of the Monroe Doctrine. Announced on December 6, 1904, the Corollary stated that America would be an international police force for Western hemisphere states that misbehaved or did not fulfil their treaty obligations:

Any country whose people conduct themselves well can count upon our hearty friendship. If a nation shows that it knows how to act with reasonable efficiency and decency in social and political matters, if it keeps order and pays its obligations, it need fear no interference from the United States. Chronic wrongdoing, or an impotence which results in a general loosening of the ties of civilized society, may in America, as elsewhere, ultimately require intervention by some civilized nation, and in the Western Hemisphere, the adherence of the United States to the Monroe Doctrine may force the United States, however reluctantly, in flagrant cases of such wrongdoing or impotence, to the exercise of an international police power.[23]

The Roosevelt Corollary of the Monroe Doctrine was a clear statement of America as an imperial power in the Western hemisphere. America subsequently intervened militarily to ensure financial stability in the Dominican Republic (1905), Cuba (1906), and Nicaragua (1912).

As a great power fully engaged in imperialism, President Roosevelt also demonstrated that America could play a decisive role in the balance of power politics of the international system. He adopted a policy of "benevolent neutrality" toward Japan in the Russo-Japanese War of 1904–1905. He was mainly motivated by balance-of-power considerations. Russia was expanding her influence in Manchuria, Korea, and China. This was seen as a threat to American economic interests in the Far East. Russia was a threat, so a Japanese victory would serve American interests. As Japan's military victories swung the power pendulum towards it, Roosevelt was alarmed that Japan might become a major threat to American interests in the Far East. Roosevelt therefore welcomed the chance to mediate between the two countries and settle the conflict. A treaty was signed in September 1905, and Roosevelt subsequently won the Nobel Peace Prize. On hearing the terms of the treaty, many Japanese were furious because it did not have much in the way of territorial and financial compensation that Japan's victories seemed to merit. Roosevelt had successfully practiced balance of power in the Far East.

Roosevelt also showed that he was capable of intervening in European affairs to maintain a balance of power. The growth of Germany's power was threatening to disrupt Europe. If Germany had gotten her way in Morocco, the European balance of power could be threatened, so America intervened to maintain the balance. He permitted American participation in an international conference on the future of Morocco from January to April 1906. He was intervening in the European balance of power in order to maintain it, and reduce the chance of war. Under Roosevelt, America was becoming an accomplished imperial power in the international system. This was applauded by some European commentators such as the French writer, Andre Tardieu:

The United States is . . . a world power. . . . Its power creates for it . . . a duty—to pronounce upon all those questions that hitherto have been arranged by agreement only among European powers. These powers themselves, at critical times, turn toward the United States, anxious to know its opinion. . . . The United States intervenes thus in the affairs of the universe. . . . It is seated at the table where the great game is played, and it cannot leave it.[24]

Materialism

Under Presidents Roosevelt (1901–1909) and Taft (1909–1913), America's foreign policy was characterized by "dollar diplomacy," which the historian Julius Pratt describes as follows:

Dollar diplomacy had a dual character. On one side, it was the use of diplomacy to advance and protect American business abroad; on the other side, it was the use of dollars abroad to promote the ends of American diplomacy. In the first sense it was practiced by many an administration before Taft and since. The employment of American dollars to advance the political and strategic aims of diplomacy was a less familiar technique. . . . It was plainly seen in the refunding of the debt and the instituting of the receivership in the Dominican Republic under Theodore Roosevelt.[25]

Dollar diplomacy was a consequence of the Roosevelt Corollary for the Monroe Doctrine. Revolutions were common in Western hemisphere states, so that meant that the chances of defaulting on international loans or the loss of a foreign national's capital was quite high. To prevent European intervention in such situations, America would ensure that states would meet all of their financial obligations. America would act as an "international police force" to ensure good and financially responsible government in the Western hemisphere.

President Roosevelt had practiced dollar diplomacy in the Dominican Republic after costly revolutions saw it unable to service its national debt to a number of European and American companies and governments. In 1903 to 1904, America intervened in Nicaragua and took control of its customs houses. In 1907, a treaty was ratified by the Senate that allowed America to maintain control of Nicaragua's customs houses until its financial obligations were payed out. President Taft practiced dollar diplomacy in Nicaragua when a revolutionary government came to power in 1909. Again, America took control of a sovereign state's customs houses until it had payed out its debts.

America under dollar diplomacy placed or threatened to place Western hemisphere states under an American receivership. Though the logic of intervention was clear given the threat that Europeans would intervene, the great bulk of loans were often to American companies and interests. Essentially, America would intervene to ensure the payment of debts, many of which belonged to its own citizens. America's dollar diplomacy can therefore be described as a form of materialism where profits were more important than principles of international law.

In sum, McKinley's Philippines policy launched America toward becoming a full-fledged imperial power. Roosevelt continued this policy with greater success and in the process saw America enter as an important force in the international balance of power. Combined with the dollar diplomacy he and the Taft administrations presided over, it would be fair to say that morality was not a critical factor in American foreign policy. Indeed, aside from completing the task of making good the pledge to grant Cuba her independence, America underwent a deep forgetting of the moral principles that lie at the heart of its national identity. Its fourth grand synthesis of

Table 6.1
America's Fourth Hero's Journey—America's Rise to Great Power Status (1889–1913)

Phase of Hero's Journey	Step of Hero's Journey	Key Events	
CALL TO ADVENTURE Reasserting the Monroe Doctrine (1889-1895)	Hearing the Call	1. •	President Harrison Asserting the Monroe Doctrine (1889) Pan American meeting held in Washington (1889)
	Refusal of the Call	2.	President Cleveland's Rejection of Treaty annexing Hawaii and dismissing need to give teeth to the Monroe Doctrine (1893)
	Crossing the First threshold	3.	Britain backs down to American demand for impartial arbitration of the Britain-Venezuela dispute (1895)
GREAT REMEMBERING Supporting Cuban Independence (1895-1898)	Slaying the Dragon	4.	Spanish repression of Cuban insurgents becomes election issue (1896)
	Sacred Marriage	5.	Ending economic depression is a priority for second Cleveland administration (1893-1897)
	Atonement	6.	War declared against Spain (1898)
RETURN TO INTERNATIONAL SOCIETY Commitment to Self-Determination (1898-1903)	Refusal of the Return	7.	Refusal to consider self-determination for Philippines & Puerto Rico (1898)
	Cross Return Threshold	**8.**	America begins political process that culminates in Cuban independence (1900-1902)
	Master of the Two Worlds	**9.** 10.	American troops withdrawn and treaty signed with the Cuban government (1903) **Fourth Grand Synthesis: Using America's Diplomatic & Military Resources to Promote Self-determination**
DEEP FORGETTING Imperial America (1903-1912)	Fear	**11.**	Rivalry with Imperial Germany leads to America's refusal to grant independence to the Philippines (1901-1914)
	Imperialism	12. **13.**	President Roosevelt's encourages Panamanian revolt against Colombia to control Panama Canal (1903-1904) Roosevelt Corollary & Dominican Republic (1904-1905)
	Materialism	14.	Dollar Diplomacy (1904-1913)

morality and power quickly unraveled. The political and commercial advantages of overseas colonies were simply too great to follow a moral foreign policy based on liberty and self-determination. America's fourth hero's journey, summarized in Table 6.1, was at an end. A new hero's journey was needed to bring morality back to the center stage of American foreign policy.

NOTES

1. John Gabriel Hunt, ed., *The Inaugural Addresses of the Presidents* (New York: Random House, 1997), 258.

2. Quoted in Julius Pratt, *A History of United States Foreign Policy* (Newark, N.J.: Prentice Hall, 1955), 350.

3. Quoted in Thomas Bailey, *A Diplomatic History of the American People*, 8th ed. (New York: Appleton-Century-Crofts, 1969), 447.

4. Hunt, *The Inaugural Addresses of the Presidents*, 285.

5. Quoted in Pratt, *A History of United States Foreign Policy*, 380.

6. Hunt, *The Inaugural Addresses of the Presidents*, 268.

7. Quoted in David Burner, Virginia Bernhard, and Stanley Kutler, *Firsthand America: A History of the United States*, 4th ed. (St. James, N.Y.: Brandywine Press, 1996), 671.

8. Ibid., 670.

9. Pratt, *A History of United States Foreign Policy*, 376.

10. For figures see Pratt, *A History of United States Foreign Policy*, 375.

11. Quoted in Pratt, *A History of United States Foreign Policy*, 369.

12. Albert Beveridge, "The Star of Empire," in *Selected American Speeches on Basic Issues 1850–1950*, ed. Carl G. Brandt and Edward M. Shafter, Jr. (Boston: Houghton Mifflin, 1960), 229

13. For comparison of British and American imperialist discourses, see Jeff D. Bass and Richard Cherwitz, "Imperial Mission and Manifest Destiny: A Case Study of Political Myth in Rhetorical Discourse," *The Southern Speech Communication Journal* 43 (Spring 1978): 213–22.

14. Quoted in Pratt, *A History of United States Foreign Policy*, 389.

15. Quoted in Burner, Bernhard, and Kutlor, *Firsthand America: A History of the United States*, 678.

16. Quoted in Pratt, *A History of United States Foreign Policy*, 415.

17. Ibid., 370–71.

18. Ibid., 372.

19. Ibid., 393.

20. Quoted in Bailey, *A Diplomatic History of the American People*, 473–74.

21. Quoted in Pratt, *A History of United States Foreign Policy*, 405.

22. See Pratt, *A History of United States Foreign Policy*, 407.

23. Quoted in Pratt, *A History of United States Foreign Policy*, 417.

24. Quoted in Burner, Bernhard, and Kutler, *Firsthand America: A History of the United States*, 684.

25. Pratt, *A History of United States Foreign Policy*, 420.

CHAPTER 7

AMERICA'S FIFTH HERO'S JOURNEY (1913–1933)—MAKING THE WORLD SAFE FOR DEMOCRACY

Woodrow Wilson was opposed to the imperialistic policy of the Roosevelt and Taft administrations. He therefore did not approve of intervention purely for the sake of American political or economic interests. Instead, Wilson supported the creation of stable democracies in Western Hemisphere states. Wilson, in contrast to Roosevelt, detested power politics. For Wilson, morality was a critical feature in the development of American foreign policy, as he made clear in a speech in October 1913:

We dare not turn from the principle that morality and not expediency is the thing that must guide us and that we will never condone iniquity because it is most convenient to do so. . . . It is a very perilous thing to determine the foreign policy of a nation in terms of material interest. It not only is unfair to those with whom you are dealing, but it is degrading as regards your own actions.[1]

CALL TO ADVENTURE (1913–1914)—SUPPORTING DEMOCRACY IN THE WESTERN HEMISPHERE

The foreign policy practice of all presidential administrations since Thomas Jefferson was to recognize governments in the Southern Hemisphere no matter how they had come to power. This policy was abandoned by Wilson who did not approve of revolutions by authoritarian groups or the military against democratically elected governments.

Hearing the Call

The election of Woodrow Wilson in 1912 brought the Democratic Party to power. Opposed to the imperialism and dollar diplomacy of the Republicans, Wilson and the Democrats stood for supporting stable and democratic governments abroad. Principle rather than economic interests would be the determining factor in America's relations with its Western Hemisphere neighbors. In a speech given October 27, 1914, Wilson declared that "the United States will never again seek one additional foot of territory by conquest."[2] In America's colonies of Puerto Rico and the Philippines, Wilson did not believe in granting immediate independence. Orderly ballots had been conducted in these territories since America had taken control. Wilson believed that more time was needed to consolidate the virtues of democracy. This was more important than a hasty independence process that could lead to unstable revolutionary governments coming to power as they did elsewhere in the Western Hemisphere. Wilson's first obligation was "to teach the South American republics to elect 'good men'!"[3]

Wilson rightly believed that revolutions, which had become the norm for replacing unpopular rulers, was an unstable way of replacing governments. He believed that it was sensible to discourage revolutionary governments from coming to power, especially if they replaced popular and representative rulers with tyrants backed by a small part of the population. The key to this new direction was to teach the populations of Western Hemisphere states, that the ballot rather than the bullet was the correct way of replacing leaders and maintaining office. Wilson declared that America would only deal with "republican governments based upon law, not irregular force."[4] Wilson's new policy was put into immediate effect in responding to a revolution in Mexico.

In the last days of the Taft administration, a new Mexican government led by General Victoriano Huerta had come to power through a military coup in February 1913. The General arranged for the assassination of his predecessor, President Madero. Madero had earlier begun ambitious democratic and economic reforms that threatened American and European business interests. European governments and America under President Taft therefore had no qualms in tacitly supporting Huerta's coup. Britain, Japan, and major European powers quickly recognized the Huerta government. Taft had made no move to extend recognition, but this was to gain certain concessions from Huerta rather than opposition to his new government. On assuming office, Woodrow Wilson was aghast at the coup and the assassination of Madera. He viewed the new government as "a government of butchers." In a press release he said that cooperation with America's sister republics in the Western Hemisphere was possible "only when supported at every turn by the orderly processes of just government based upon law, not upon arbitrary or ir- regular force. . . . We can have no sympathy with those who seek to seize the power of government to advance their own personal interests or am- bition."[5] Wilson had made a dramatic break with the practices of earlier presidents who had recognized the governments of Western Hemisphere states regardless of its origins. For Wilson, "hearing the call" was for America to teach her neighbors the virtue of democracy and refusal to accept revolutions against democratically elected governments.

Refusal of the Call

Ever since the establishment of the American Republic there had been those who believed that there was nothing morally superior in America's democratic system because history showed that republics could also be in- volved in wars of conquest. As Alexander Hamilton wrote:

Sparta, Athens, Rome, and Carthage were all republics; two of them, Athens and Carthage, of the commercial kind. Yet were they as often engaged in wars, offensive and defensive, as the neighboring monarchies of the same times. . . . In the govern- ment of Britain the representatives of the people compose one branch of the national legislature. Commerce has been for ages the predominant pursuit of that country. Few nations, nevertheless, have been more frequently engaged in war.[6]

Opponents of Wilson's new policy included former President Theodore Roosevelt. They believed that American national interests would be harmed if it began a policy of crusading for democracy. Despite the sympathy of the American public for democratic government, policymakers believed that a crusade for democracy was dangerous. This paralleled the thinking later in the 1970s when policymakers were opposed to incorporating human rights into foreign policy making.

Crossing the First Threshold

Wilson demanded that Mexico's new leader, Huerta, immediately organ- ize free and fair elections, and not himself stand as a candidate. When Huerta refused, Wilson provided arms to Huerta's opponents and ordered American forces to take the port city of Vera Cruz. Huerta finally capitu- lated and resigned on July 14, 1914. Wilson insisted that the military in- tervention was not a war against Mexico but against the Huerta regime. Wilson had "crossed the first threshold" by his military intervention in support of establishing a democratic government in Mexico. A new regime led by Venustiano Carranza came to power and was eventually recognized by America in 1917.

GREAT REMEMBERING (1914–1917)—SUPPORTING EUROPEAN DEMOCRACIES

American interventionism in the Western Hemisphere was overshadowed by the beginning of World War I in Europe in 1914. Support for establishing democratic governments in the Western Hemisphere was replaced by concern for supporting European democracies in the war against German imperialism.

Slaying the Dragon

Wilson had repudiated dollar diplomacy but intervened in Nicaragua and several Caribbean states. He believed that these military interventions were warranted because "he had the best interests of these nations more at heart than the leaders of these nations themselves."[7] Who was to judge, however, what the best interests of these nations were? Even if foreign policy under Wilson was benevolent and aimed at promoting good stable government, wasn't this just a more refined version of Yankee imperialism? Wasn't Wilson merely maintaining under the guise of democracy the Roosevelt Corollary of the Monroe Doctrine by which an international police force would enforce good government practice?

Debate continues to this day over the inconsistencies of Wilson's policies. As Julius Pratt wrote, "Woodrow Wilson's policy toward Latin America presented curious contradictions, which are confusing to the historian and must have been still more confusing to Wilson's Latin American contemporaries."[8] In all, the dragon of Yankee imperialism was not an easy one for Wilson to slay.

The Sacred Marriage

During the first years of the European War, President Wilson was concerned to maintain neutrality. Opinion on entering the war was strongly divided between supporting one or the other side. The overwhelming majority, however, thought the war was a European affair and America should not become involved. Wilson issued a formal neutrality statement on August 4, 1914, warning of the danger of taking sides in the war. Otherwise, Americans might "be divided in camps of hostile opinion, hot against each other, involved in the war itself in impulse and opinion if not in action."[9] Memories of the Civil War were still fresh. In the absence of some events that might unify the nation in entering the war, neutrality was the preferred option. In his second inaugural address, Wilson outlined how avoiding entanglement would help unify America:

We are being forged into a new unity amidst the fires that now blaze throughout the world. In their ardent heat we shall, in God's Providence, let us hope, be purged of faction and division, purified of the errant humors of party and of private interests, and shall stand forth in the days to come with a new dignity of national pride and spirit.[10]

America experienced the archetypal encounter of the sacred marriage during the lead up to World War I by maintaining its national unity at a time when the divisive effects of the European war were being felt.

Another aspect to the sacred marriage was the booming American economy due to the war in Europe. Munition sales to allied powers, increasingly financed by American loans, led to an influx of capital and economic growth. For example, exports of explosives jumped in value from $6,000,000 in 1914 to $470,000,000 in 1916. America rapidly went from being a debtor nation to a creditor nation. The growth of the American economy prospered, and maintenance of national unity corresponded to the archetypal encounter of the sacred marriage.

Atonement

In his neutrality message of August 1914, President Wilson proclaimed: "The United States must be neutral in fact as well as in name. . . . We must be impartial in thought as well as in action, must put a curb upon our sentiments as well as upon every transaction that might be construed as a preference of one party to the struggle before another."[11] Despite this commitment to neutrality, Wilson's sympathy with the allied powers grew with time. After all, Britain and France were well-established democratic governments fighting for their very survival against German domination. If Imperial Germany was to succeed, then the war would be a major setback for democracy in Europe. The Western Hemisphere could not remain insulated for long from the political culture of a Europe dominated by victorious Germany.

Though the causes and factors driving the war were complex, Wilson increasingly came to see it in terms of democracies fighting against a German version of autocracy. Indeed in May 1915, he confided that "England is fighting our fight."[12] Even though America was too divided to enter the war outright, it could support the democracies by exporting munitions and other war materials. Once the Allies ran out of funds, they could raise American loans to finance these exports. These policies violated Wilson's commitment to put "a curb upon . . . every transaction that might be construed as a preference of one party to the struggle." These unneutral policies under Wilson were clear signals that America was moving toward supporting the democracies of Europe.

THE RETURN TO INTERNATIONAL SOCIETY (1917–1919)—FIGHTING FOR SELF-DETERMINATION, DEMOCRACY, AND A NEW WORLD ORDER

America finally did enter World War I. Wilson justified it as a crusade to support the principles of self-determination and democracy. He believed that only creating a new world order based on these principles could justify the massive American commitment to the Allied effort. These principles took form in terms of Wilson's support for creating a League of Nations and supporting the freedom of new states from the empires of the defeated powers.

Refusal of the Return

As earlier mentioned, America took a policy of neutrality toward World War I. This was consistent with Washington's policy of avoiding entanglement in European affairs. Despite Wilson's sympathy for the European democracies, the British adopted a policy in July 1916 of blacklisting companies that traded with Germany. This began to alienate American public opinion. The pro-British *New York Times* described it as "quite the most tactless, foolish, and unnecessary act of the British government during the war."[13] What alienated Wilson and many Americans even more was the Allies' stubborn determination to maintain their colonial empires. When Britain ruthlessly repressed the Irish rebellion in 1916, for example, support for the democracies reached its lowest ebb. Wilson campaigned in the 1916 election with the slogan "He kept us out of the war." Despite the threat posed to democracy in Europe if Germany won the war, and Wilson's commitment to democracy, America refused to intervene. In terms of the hero's journey, Wilson's refusal to intervene in the war amounted to a "refusal of the return."

Crossing the Return Threshold

On February 4, 1915, Germany declared the waters around the British Isles a war zone and that merchant vessels in the zone would be sunk on sight. This immediately led to tension with America, which declared that it would take the necessary measures "to safeguard American lives and property and to secure to American citizens the full enjoyment of their acknowledged rights on the high seas."[14] Freedom for neutral countries to trade on the high seas was a principle that America had supported over a century earlier during the Napoleonic Wars. An undeclared naval war with France (1798–1800) and the 1812–1814 war with Britain were both based on America's support for neutral shipping and liberty of its merchant seamen on the high seas. Military conflict with Germany would be inevitable if it attacked neutral shipping with subsequent loss of life and property. After crises sparked by sinking the passenger ships *Lusitania* (1915) and *Sussex* (1916), Germany relaxed its policy and pledged to respect the rules of international law in its submarine policy.

When Germany resumed a policy of unrestricted submarine warfare on February 1, 1917, in an effort to bring a quick and final blow to Britain, military conflict with America became inevitable. The sinking of three American merchant ships on March 18 was the catalyst for President Wilson asking Congress for a declaration of war. On April 6, Congress resolved: "That the state of war between the United States and the Imperial German Government which has been thrust upon the United States is hereby formally declared."[15] For the first time in its history, America would commit its men and resources to fighting a war in Europe. For Wilson, America had "crossed the return threshold." It was now committed to actively fighting in support of the European democracies.

Master of the Two Worlds

The principle of defending neutral shipping to belligerent nations was what motivated America in an undeclared war with France and a declared war with Britain during the Napoleonic era. Although this same principle was what essentially led to America's entry into World War I, more lofty principles were sought by Wilson to justify American intervention. Wilson believed that moral principles had to be consistently applied in world politics rather than purely economic or political interests such as freedom on the high seas. In an address to both houses of Congress on January 8, 1918, he outlined his principles in his famous "Fourteen Points" speech. Wilson was outlining a "New World Order" that was a more modern rendition of the "New Order of the Ages" (Novus Ordo Seclorum) that had profound symbolic value for America's Founding Fathers in designing the Great Seal.

The two pillars of the New World Order would be self-determination and democracy. "Self-determination" was outlined in point five of Wilson's Fourteen Points:

A free, open-minded and absolutely impartial adjustment of all colonial claims based upon a strict observance of the principle that in determining all such questions of sovereignty, the interests of the populations concerned must have equal weight with the equitable claims of the government whose title is to be determined.[16]

Self-determination would be a moral imperative for deciding the future of the numerous ethnic communities in the former Hapsburg, German, and Ottoman empires. Wilson declared: "We set this Nation up to make men free, and we did not confine our conception and purpose to America, and now we will make men free. If we did not do that, all the fame of America would be gone, and all her power would be dissipated."[17] Wilson was especially opposed to the bartering of peoples among imperial powers as though they were mere chattels or pawns:

No peace can last, or ought to last, which does not recognize and accept the principle that governments derive all their just powers from the consent of the governed and that no right anywhere exists, to hand peoples about from sovereignty to sovereignty as if they were property. . . . Peoples and property are not to be bartered about from sovereignty to sovereignty as if they were mere chattels and pawns in the game. . . . Peoples may now be dominated and governed only by their own consent. Self determination is not a mere phrase. It is an imperative principle of action, which statesmen will henceforth ignore at their own peril. . . . The settlement of every question . . . (must be) upon the basis of the free acceptance of that settlement by the people immediately concerned.[18]

Wilson's vision of order in the New Order of the Ages was to be expressed through the creation of a "universal association of nations" as described in his fourteenth point: "A general association of nations must be formed under specific covenants for the purpose of affording mutual guarantees of political independence and territorial integrity to great and small [states] alike."[19]

So committed was Wilson in his vision that subsequent biographies have commented on the religious zeal he showed in bringing into life his bold new vision convinced as he was that he was directly guided by the hand of God.[20] Wilson was doing no more than displaying the same religious faith as America's Founding Fathers in designing the Great Seal that America had a special role to play in ushering in a "New Order of the Ages" (*Novus Ordo Seclorum*) and that "God Favors our Undertaking" (*Annuit Coeptis*). Wilson's Fourteen Points and the worldwide popularity he personally enjoyed led to America being "Master of the Two Worlds." Under Wilson, America's successful entry into World War I and his partial success in incorporating his vision in the Treaty of Versailles was fusion of power and morality. The Wilsonian vision of foreign policy based on self-determination and democracy was America's fifth grand synthesis. The synthesis would begin what Wilson believed would be a new age:

[T]his age is an age . . . which rejects the standards of national selfishness that once governed the counsels of nations and demands that they shall give way to a new order of things in which the only questions will be: "Is it right?" "Is it just?" "Is it in the interest of mankind?"[21]

Wilson's vision of a global cooperation through a League of Nations might offer the kind of peace hoped for by many shocked at the horror of World War I.

DEEP FORGETTING (1919–1933)—ISOLATIONISM TRIUMPHANT

Wilson was able to successfully tap into the idealism of the American public that supported a New World Order based on principles of self-determination, democracy, and rule of law. However, he badly miscalculated the political process necessary for gaining America's ratification of the Treaty of Versailles. He alienated powerful political opponents by his high-handed way of dealing with them in the discussions over the terms of the peace settlement in Paris. The single most important element that his opponents used was the latent fear of the American public in committing America to peace in Europe.

Fear

For the League of Nations to work, it had to have the capacity to respond to international aggression. This was encapsulated in Article X of the League's Covenant:

The Members of the League undertake to respect and preserve as against external aggression the territorial integrity and existing political independence of all Members of the League. In case of any such aggression or in case of any threat or danger of such aggression the Council shall advise upon the means by which this obligation shall be fulfilled.[22]

The Senate Foreign Relations Committee was dominated by isolationists and others opposed to America joining the League of Nations. American sovereignty and independence was held to be too precious to be risked in any way by membership in an international organization such as the League of Nations. Some argued that the League would become a super-state that would dominate America. Held by Republicans after the 1918 Congressional elections and chaired by Senator Henry Cabot Lodge, the Committee proposed an extensive list of reservations to the League's Covenant. The most serious reservation was that concerning Article 10:

The United States assumes no obligation to preserve the territorial integrity or political independence of any other country or to interfere in controversies between nations—whether members of the league or not—under the provisions of article 10, or to employ the military or naval forces of the United States under any article of the treaty for any purpose, unless in any particular case the Congress, which, under the Constitution, has the sole power to declare war or authorize the employment of the military or naval forces of the United States, shall act or joint resolution so provide.[23]

The objection makes clear the view that only Congress could authorize American military intervention in the affairs of sovereign states. This was consistent with America's past policies of military intervention in the Western Hemisphere and the Far East under the McKinley, Roosevelt, Taft, and Wilson administrations. These presidents had asked for and received congressional approval for a variety of military interventions. Would such a practice, however, be feasible in an international body that would be acting as an international police force? Wouldn't executive approval, with some form of consultation with Congress, be enough? Could the proposed Council of the League really be effective in responding to an international crisis if America or any other country had to first get explicit approval of its national legislature? France, the most security conscious of the League's Council members, would have objected that such a reservation did not address its security needs over a resurgent Germany. President Wilson, realizing that the proposed revision to Article 10 and other major revisions to the Covenant would not be accepted by other Allied states, tried to have the Covenant passed essentially as it stood. Two attempts to have the Treaty of Versailles, which contained the League Covenant, ratified by a two-thirds Senate majority failed. America would not become a member of the League of Nations. Senate Republicans were able to successfully exploit fears that American participation in the League would lead to unwanted military interventions in support of imperial European states.

While oppressed peoples embraced his vision, the important Allied statesmen of his time failed to support him. The Treaty of Versailles, which only selectively applied his principles and was fraught with moral inconsistencies, was based on a retributive vision and perpetuated an alliance system that was bound to break down. The U.S. Senate refused to ratify the treaty and to join the League of Nations. Capturing the sentiment of many in the U.S. Senate, William Borah claimed in a speech before that body on November 19, 1919:

But your treaty does not mean peace—far, very far, from it. If we are to judge the future by the past it means war. Is there any guarantee of peace other than the guarantee which comes of the control of the war-making power by the peoples? Yet what great rule of democracy does the treaty leave unassailed? The people in whose keeping alone you can safely lodge the power of peace or war nowhere, at no time and in no place, have any voice in this scheme for world peace. Autocracy which has bathed the world in blood for centuries reigns supreme. Democracy is everywhere excluded. This, you say, means peace.[24]

An editorial in *New Republic* outlined why refusal to ratify the League Covenant and subsequent withdrawal from the international system were warranted:

Americans would be fools if they permitted themselves now to be embroiled in a system of European alliances. . . . The peace cannot last. America should withdraw from all commitments which would impair her freedom of action. Article Ten [of the League's Covenant] obliged the United States to defend an unjust territorial settlement. America could not play that game. It would be the height of folly to commit a great people as the guarantor of a condition which is morbidly sick with conflict and trouble.[25]

America's absence doomed the League to ineffectiveness in issues involving major powers. The Senate's fears of what League membership entailed led to the collapse of Wilson's vision. The 1920 elections resulted in a landslide for the Republican candidate, Warren Harding, who had been part of the Republican faction most strongly opposed to the League. A deep forgetting of America's global mission had once more begun.

Imperialism

In terms of Latin America, America found itself in the embarrassing position of trying to justify interventions that appeared increasingly out of step with the changing times. The charge "Yankee imperialism" was regularly leveled against America. Following his triumph at the 1928 elections, President-elect Hoover embarked on a goodwill tour of Latin America and got the following advice from one Cuban journal:

If Mr Hoover wants to conquer the immediate sympathy of Latin America, he should at once announce a change in the policy of his country, declaring that the Monroe Doctrine does not mean that the American continent is only for the United States, that Haiti will be evacuated, that Nicaragua shall be freed from foreign yoke, that Cuba will see the quick abrogation of the Platt Amendment, that our commercial treaties will cease being one-sided affairs, that our countries will be free to manage their own affairs as they deem fit, and that the Unites States is a real friend in fact, and not a conqueror.[26]

Political upheaval and violence broke out in Nicaragua in 1927, which led to America adopting the kind of Yankee imperialism that so threatened Western Hemisphere nations. President Coolidge sent several thousand Marines to restore law and order, and protect American business interests. Armed resistance by the Nicaraguans was led by the popular Augusto Sandino, but his forces were comprehensively defeated and he was killed. America set up a protectorate that was led by the ruthless Anastasio Somoza soon after American forces departed in 1933.

Japan, America, and Britain conducted an extensive naval buildup in the Pacific soon after the end of World War I. America was concerned to balance Japan's growing power and capacity to damage American economic interests in China and elsewhere in the Far East. Britain was concerned over America's growing naval power. To address these concerns over naval power in the Pacific, a conference on building capital ships was held in Washington from November 1921 to February 1922. Ratios were decided upon for major naval powers with interests in the Pacific. America was deeply involved in maintaining a balance of power in the Pacific where British, Japanese, and American interests were paramount. This meant that none of these countries would interfere in how one another operated in their territories and respective spheres of interest in the Pacific. Balancing competing naval power was more important than ensuring good governance and the right of self-determination for populations under colonial control. For example, Japan's political influence in territories such as Manchuria, nominally part of China; American control of the Philippines; and British colonial practice did not come under sustained criticism. Indeed, Mahatma Gandhi's independence struggle in India did little to affect British-American relations. As an imperial power, America had deeply forgotten the principles of self-determination and democracy that had been championed by President Wilson.

Materialism

America prior to World War I was a net debtor. It often had to raise loans from Europe to build its national infrastructure and payed for these through its exports. At the end of the war, America for the first time was a net creditor. This produced a boom economy for much of the 1920s. American firms invested heavily abroad and made profits out of building heavy industries in countries such as Japan, Germany, and Italy. As one writer put it, "Our financial mechanism was busily creating future targets for our bombers."[27] Formally outside of the League of Nations, America returned to Washington's policy of avoiding entanglement in European affairs. For the American public, these were boom times when large profits could be made by thrifty individuals. The boom times came to a thundering end with the 1929 Wall Street Crash. America entered the Great Depression and became preoccupied with providing basic services for its vast unemployed. There was little public concern for problems in the international arena.

Wilson's vision of a new world order based on a world association of nations and self-determination was truly forgotten by the American public. America was once again in a "deep forgetting." Fear of the consequences of entanglement in European affairs was the main factor behind America's triumphant mood of isolationism that ended its fifth hero's journey, summarized in Table 7.1. Another international crisis would be needed before America would awaken from its deep forgetting and start a new hero's journey.

Table 7.1
America's Fifth Hero's Journey—Making the World Safe for Democracy (1913–1933)

Phase of Hero's Journey	Step of Hero's Journey	Key Events	
CALL TO ADVENTURE Supporting Democracy in the Western Hemisphere (1913-1914)	Hearing the Call	1.	President Wilson refuses to recognize coup leaders overthrowing democratically elected Mexican government (1913-1914)
	Refusal of the Call	**2.**	Criticism of Wilson's refusal to recognize new Mexican government (1913-1914)
	Crossing the First threshold	3.	Wilson orders military intervention in support of democratic opposition & occupies Vera Cruz (1914)
GREAT REMEMBERING Supporting European Democracies (1914-1917)	Slaying the Dragon	**4.**	Wilson & American Imperialism in the Western Hemisphere (1914-1917)
	Sacred Marriage	**5.**	Wilson announces America's Neutrality to maintain National Unity during First World War (1914)
	Atonement	6.	Moral Support for Britain & France, Wilson announces in speech "England is Fighting Our War!" (1915)
RETURN TO INTERNATIONAL SOCIETY - Fighting for Self-Determination, Democracy & New World Order (1917-1919)	Refusal of the Return	**7.**	National election campaign features major candidates pledging to keep America out of the War, Wilson campaigns on slogan "he kept us out of the war"(1916)
	Cross Return Threshold	8.	Germany's unrestricted submarine warfare leads to sinking of American merchant ships with heavy loss of lives. Congress declares War (1917)
	Master of the Two Worlds	9. 10.	Wilson announces his 14 points as the basis for ending the War. **Fifth Grand Synthesis: Self-Determination, Democracy & a New World Order**
DEEP FORGETTING Isolationism Triumphant (1919-1933)	Fear	11.	Fear of entanglement in future European wars leads to Senate refusal to ratify Treaty of Versailles (1919)
	Imperialism	**12.**	Military Intervention in Nicaraqua (1926-1933)
	Materialism	13.	Roaring Twenties and the Great Depression (1929-1941)

NOTES

1. Quoted in Thomas Bailey, *A Diplomatic History of the American People*, 8th ed. (New York: Appleton-Century-Crofts, 1969), 556.

2. Quoted in Julius Pratt, *A History of United States Foreign Policy* (Newark, N.J.: Prentice Hall, 1955), 432.

3. Ibid., 422.

4. Quoted in David Burner, Virginia Bernhard, and Stanley Kutler *Firsthand America: A History of the United States*, 4th ed. (St. James, N.Y.: Brandywine Press, 1996), 752.

5. Quoted in Pratt, *A History of United States Foreign Policy*, 428.

6. Quoted in Henry Kissinger, *Diplomacy* (New York: Simon and Schuster, 1994), 33.

7. Alexander George and Juliette George, *Woodrow Wilson and Colonel House: A Personality Study* (New York: Dover Publications, 1964), 173.

8. Pratt, *A History of United States Foreign Policy*, 431.

9. Quoted in Pratt, *A History of United States Foreign Policy*, 467–68.

10. John Gabriel Hunt, ed., *The Inaugural Addresses of the Presidents* (New York: Random House, 1997), 332.

11. Quoted in Pratt, *A History of United States Foreign Policy*, 468.

12. Ibid.

13. Ibid., 477.

14. Ibid., 474.

15. Ibid., 482.

16. Jerome Agel, *Words That Make America Great* (New York: Random House, 1997), 286.

17. Quoted in Kissinger, *Diplomacy*, 50.

18. Quoted in Lawrence T. Farley, *Plebiscites and Sovereignty: The Crisis of Political Illegitimacy* (Boulder, Colo.: Westview Press, 1986), 5

19. Agel, *Words That Make America Great*, 287.

20. George and George, *Woodrow Wilson and Colonel House*, 120.

21. Quoted in Kissinger, *Diplomacy*, 51.

22. Quoted in Pratt, *A History of United States Foreign Policy*, 510.

23. Ibid., 517.

24. William Borah, "Against the League of Nations," in *Selected American Speeches on Basic Issues, 1850–1950*, ed. Carl G. Brandt and Edward M. Shafter, Jr. (Boston: Houghton Mifflin, 1960), 401.

25. Quoted in Ronald Steel, *Walter Lippman and the American Century* (New York: Vintage Books, 1980), 159.

26. Quoted in Bailey, *A Diplomatic History of the American People*, 681.

27. Quoted in Pratt, *A History of United States Foreign Policy*, 564–65.

CHAPTER 8

AMERICA'S SIXTH HERO'S JOURNEY (1933–1974)—THE DEMOCRATIC STRUGGLE AGAINST FASCISM AND COMMUNISM

America's fifth hero's journey had seen it attempt to develop a foreign policy based on support of democratic government, self-determination, and a world association of states. Woodrow Wilson largely was responsible for this foreign policy approach that differed greatly from anything attempted by his predecessors. Despite the grandeur and depth of Wilson's vision, he badly managed the political process needed to give birth to his vision. By alienating key Republicans in the Senate, his vision was doomed. The painful failure to ratify the Treaty of Versailles and the League Covenant led to a period of "deep forgetting" under successive Republican administrations. It would be another Democratic president who would rise to the occasion and finally fulfill Wilson's vision: Franklin Delano Roosevelt.

CALL TO ADVENTURE (1933–1939)—OPPOSING INTERNATIONAL AGGRESSION AND SUPPORTING SELF-DETERMINATION

America had not joined the League of Nations and therefore was not part of its formal efforts to deter international aggression. Even though America had withdrawn from formal efforts at deterrence, it was still deeply committed to the principles of non aggression and respect for self-determination. As the 1930s unfolded and witnessed more examples of these principles being violated, America began to move slowly toward a stronger stance against their violation.

Hearing the Call

After World War I, Manchuria fell under Japan's sphere of interest even though the territory was nominally part of China. Japan dominated Manchuria with ownership and control of a strategic railway line and had troops in a special zone around the railway to protect it. A Chinese nationalist government under Chiang Kai-shek swept into power over 1926–1928. The nationalist government was determined to strengthen and reunify China, and attempted to strengthen its authority in Manchuria. This alarmed the Japanese government, which saw Manchuria as its economic lifeline. An incident was staged on September 18, 1931, in which Japan claimed that Chinese soldiers had attempted to blow up a Japanese owned and controlled railway line. Japanese troops attacked and took over Chinese garrisons in the territory. Japan then began a campaign of expelling the Chinese government and army, and taking over the whole territory. China appealed to the League of Nations for support.

Even though it was not a member to the League, America sent an observer to the Council session to debate what course of action the League should take. A League resolution calling for Japan's withdrawal to the railway zone was ignored by Japan. Japan continued to consolidate its hold on Manchuria and, by September 1932, had created the puppet state of Manchuko. The League Assembly passed a resolution in February 1933 for all its members not to recognize Manchuko. Japan promptly gave its two-year notice of withdrawal from the League.

The Manchurian crisis led to America being confronted with two courses of action in protecting long-established trading privileges in Manchuria. In the words of Secretary of State Cordell Hull:

One was to withdraw gradually, perhaps with dignity, from the Far East. . . . The other course was to continue to insist on the maintenance of law, on our legitimate rights and interests in the Far East, and on observance of the treaties and declarations that guaranteed an independent China and pledged equality to all nations, nonintervention, non-aggression, and peaceful settlement of disputes in the Orient. This meant a firm, though not an aggressive, policy toward Japan. . . . It meant adequate military preparedness. . . . It meant close contact and parallel action with the other powers interested in the Orient, particularly Great Britain. It meant friendship and cooperation with China. . . . The President and I choose the second course.[1]

The policy to take a "firm, though not an aggressive, policy toward Japan" was a "call to adventure." The principles of nonaggression and self-determination would be supported; though, for the time being, not through armed force or economic sanctions. To demonstrate its commitment to self-determination in its own colonial possessions, Congress passed legislation in 1934 that provided for Philippines independence.

Refusal of the Call

If a firm rather than aggressive policy was what characterized America's response to Japanese militarism, America chose a neutral rather than firm response to Italian and German militarism. The main reason for such a response was that American public opinion was disappointed by the behavior of its European allies after World War I. As Julius Pratt wrote:

All in all, as the average American saw it, the United States had participated in World War I for altruistic reasons and at great costs. Then its former associates had used the war and the peace settlement for their own selfish advantage, had repudiated the ideas for which America had fought, and had shown neither gratitude for American aid nor a disposition to pay their just debts. This was a partial and distorted view of history. . . . It pointed unmistakably to the conclusion: Our entry into World War I was a grave mistake; we must never repeat it.[2]

Consequently, Congress passed three Neutrality Acts from 1935 to 1937. These made illegal the shipping of arms, munitions, or other war material to either side in a conflict. This policy overlooked the moral issues posed by not actively opposing aggressor states, or at least arming the state or government defending itself.

Italy, under Benito Mussolini, invaded Ethiopia in October 1935. In response, America declared that a state of war existed between Italy and Ethiopia, and promptly applied the August 1935 Neutrality Act. All shipment of arms, ammunition, and other war material would be prohibited to either side. This decision of course overlooked the entire question of military aggression. It implied American neutrality and disinterest in who initiated the war and what the proper response should be. America took no action to stop oil exports to Italy but declared a "moral embargo," which was largely ineffective. In May 1936, Ethiopian resistance had collapsed and Italy annexed Ethiopia. In July, the League formally withdrew economic sanctions it had placed on Italy, and members began recognizing Italian sovereignty in Ethiopia.

Adolph Hitler came to power in January 1933, and by October had announced Germany's withdrawal from the Disarmament Conference and the League of Nations. Hitler then began disregarding clauses in the Treaty of Versailles preventing German rearmament. Taking advantage of the Italian invasion of Ethiopia, Hitler repudiated the whole treaty in March 1936. He also announced the militarization of the Rhineland.

In July 1936, an insurrection led by General Francisco Franco began to topple the Spanish Republican government. Franco and the nationalist movement he led were Fascist in orientation and were supported by Italy and Germany. The Spanish Republic was democratic in orientation and had the sympathy of France, Russia and, to a lesser extent, Britain. Over the three years of the war, the Fascist powers increasingly sent men and material to support Franco, while the democracies maintained a strict policy of nonintervention. America accepted this noninterventionist policy despite the attempt by the Fascist forces to destroy democracy in Spain.

America's Neutrality Acts were viewed by President Roosevelt as encouraging aggression because, in his words, they "may actually give aid to an aggressor and deny it to the victim."[3] After Germany's absorption of Czechoslovakia in 1938 and Italy's invasion of Albania in April 1939, Roosevelt sided with France and Britain in wanting to protect other small European states from aggression. In order to deter Hitler and Mussolini, Roosevelt wanted to repeal the arms embargo in the Neutrality Acts. This would send a message to Hitler that America would give military aid to France and Britain in any European war. The Senate, led by the isolationist Senator Borah, refused to consider repeal of the arms embargo. Despite the clear challenge posed by Fascist countries to democracies and self-determination, America refused to heed the call to adventure.

Crossing the First Threshold

World War II began with Germany's invasion of Poland on September 1, 1939. On September 5, America declared its neutrality, which meant, in theory, that it would not supply either belligerent in accord with Congress's Neutrality Acts. President Roosevelt was convinced that victory by Nazi Germany would mean economic strangulation of America, and that Germany and America would eventually go to war. He therefore believed it better to support the Allies with all material means possible in the struggle against Hitler's legions. America under Roosevelt began a gradual transition from a policy of neutrality to nonbelligerency. The latter meant the status of not being at war but giving military aid to one side. Roosevelt did this by modifying the three previous neutrality acts with a fourth neutrality act that allowed the sale of war material to any belligerent that could pay for the material and carry it away. Because only Britain and France had this "cash and carry" ability, this effectively was to support Britain and France in the same manner as had been done in World War I. Mussolini's attack on France on June 10 led to Roosevelt dismissing any vestiges of neutrality in an address on the same day:

In our American unity, we will pursue two obvious and simultaneous courses: we will extend to the opponents of force the material resources of this nation, and at the same time we will harness and speed up the use of those resources in order that we ourselves in the Americas may have equipment and training equal to the task of any emergency and every defense.[4]

The fall of France on June 22 meant that only Britain stood between Hitler and complete victory. Roosevelt decided in September, without consulting Congress, to lend fifty aging destroyers to Britain for America's right to lease a number of British possessions for building American military bases. According to Winston Churchill, this was "a decidedly unneutral act by the United States" and should, "according to all the standards of history, have justified the German Government in declaring war."[5] Hitler, however, remembered well the lesson from World War I when America's entry saved Britain and France. He did not even bother to make an official protest over the lend-lease deal.

GREAT REMEMBERING (1939–1941)—FROM NEUTRALITY TO NONBELLIGERENCY

The main problems confronted by Roosevelt were similar to those faced by Wilson in World War I. Could American unity be maintained in the face of divided public opinion over the merits of staying out of or entering the war? How should European democracy be supported in a struggle against countries wanting to extinguish the candle of democracy and impose some form of authoritarianism on unwilling populations? America's "great remembering" involved a gradual process of coming to terms with each of these questions.

Slaying the Dragon

As mentioned earlier, isolationism was a powerful force in America that dated back to President Washington's own view that America should avoid becoming entangled in European wars. Isolationists in the World War II era had the view that America had been duped into entering World War I and this "evil" should not be repeated. Isolationist forces were led by a group called the America First Committee and were supported by the *Chicago Tribune*, the Hearst newspapers, and other journals. The widely popular Charles Lindbergh, the first person to fly across the Atlantic, outlined four principles the Committee stood for in a powerful speech in Iowa before 8,000 people:

1. The United States must build an impregnable defense for America.
2. No foreign power, nor group of powers, can successfully attack a *prepared* America.
3. American democracy can be preserved only by keeping out of the European war.

4. "Aid short of war" weakens national defense at home and threatens to involve America in war abroad.[6]

Isolationism was strong right up until the bombing of Pearl Harbor in December 1941. President Roosevelt, personally convinced of the importance of actively combating Hitler, was constantly frustrated in getting more active Congressional support for the Allied war effort. The decision to lease fifty destroyers to Britain, for example, was completed as a deal between the British and American governments. Roosevelt did not dare risk having the deal approved first by Congress, which could well have voted against it. Isolationism was a powerful force for the Roosevelt administration to contend with openly. It was the bombing of Pearl Harbor that led to the Roosevelt administration finally "slaying the dragon" of isolationism.

The Sacred Marriage

The 1940 election campaign was in many ways a rerun of the 1916 campaign in the midst of divided public opinion over World War I. National unity was emphasized in an environment where serious division existed between isolationists and those supporting joining the war on the side of the democracies. Given these differences, both parties campaigned to stay out of "any foreign war" in the 1940 campaign. Roosevelt, under attack from Republicans as pro-war, kept on repeating the pledge: "Your boys are not going to be sent into any foreign wars."[7] America experienced the archetypal encounter of the sacred marriage during the lead-up to World War II by maintaining its national unity despite the divisive effects of the war.

Atonement

After the 1940 election campaign, Roosevelt came out more forcefully than ever in support of American aid for Britain. His famous fireside chat on December 28 that America must become an "Arsenal of Democracy" outlined why he believed the move toward a policy of "dynamic nonbelligerence" was justified:

Never before since Jamestown and Plymouth Rock has our American civilization been in such danger as now. The Nazi masters of Germany have made it clear that they intend . . . to enslave the whole of Europe, and then to use the resources of Europe to dominate the rest of the world. . . . There is far less chance of the United States getting into war if we do all we can now to support the nations defending themselves against attack by the Axis than if we acquiesce in their defeat, submit tamely to an Axis victory, and wait our turn to be the object of attack in another war later on.[8]

The majority of the American public slowly began to move to agreement with Roosevelt's view over the question of military aid. By the end of 1940, a poll revealed that over 60 percent of Americans supported aid to Britain, even at the risk of war. With this shift in public opinion, Roosevelt was more confident of congressional approval for his policy of nonbelligerence. He initiated legislation that would make possible vast military assistance to Britain. This would be done through the innovative idea of leasing war equipment to Britain rather than providing loans that Britain could not afford to pay back after the war. He justified this novel policy by using the metaphor of a garden hose and a fire:

Suppose my neighbor's home catches fire. . . . If he can take my garden hose and connect it up with his hydrant, I may help him to put out his fire. Now, what do I do? I don't say to him before that operation, Neighbor, my garden hose cost me $15; you have got to pay me $15 for it . . . I don't want $15—I want my garden hose back after the fire is over. . . . In other words, if you lend certain munitions and get the munitions back at the end of the war . . . you are all right.[9]

The Lend-Lease Act was approved by Congress and became law on March 11, 1941. America had dispensed with all pretense of neutrality in the war between Britain and Nazi Germany. In the absence of some act of German aggression that would unite Americans behind a war declaration, America would do all it could to help Britain materially and morally. Democracy was threatened, and America was conscious of its national mission as Roosevelt made clear in his third inaugural address on January 20, 1941:

There are men who believe that democracy, as a form of government and a frame of life, is limited or measured by a kind of mystical and artificial fate—that, for some unexplained reason, tyranny and slavery have become the surging wave of the future—and that freedom is an ebbing tide. But we Americans know that this is not true. . . . In the face of great perils never before encountered, our strong purpose is to protect and to perpetuate the integrity of democracy. For this we muster the spirit of America, and the faith of America.[10]

Roosevelt's dynamic policy of nonbelligerence in support of Britain against Nazi Germany was an act of atonement.

THE RETURN TO INTERNATIONAL SOCIETY (1941–1956)—WORLD WAR II AND THE COLD WAR

In his third inaugural address, Roosevelt had clearly made up his mind about the Nazi menace to democracy in Europe and ultimately to America. He was unable to get America to enter the war until Japan's attack on Pearl Harbor, and Hitler's and Mussolini's declarations of war against America. America was now a full participant in the war. America would play a powerful role in protecting democracy and promoting self-determination. For America's hero journey, this was a return to active military support of the principles inherent in its national identity.

Refusal of the Return

Despite the clear danger to democracy in Europe and ultimately America posed by Nazi Germany's success in Europe, America did not enter the war in aid of struggling Britain. On June 22, 1941, Stalin's attempt to sit out the war while the capitalist powers exhausted themselves was rudely shocked by Nazi Germany's attack. The Soviet Union was now fighting along with Britain and began receiving American support. Roosevelt's policy of nonbelligerence was as far as he could go in getting Congressional support for active opposition to Nazi Germany. Isolationism was still a powerful force, and public opinion was overwhelmingly against America entering the war. A poll conducted by the American Institute of Public Opinion on November 5, 1941, showed that 63 percent were opposed to Congress passing a resolution declaring a state of war between America and Germany.[11] Congress was still unsure of the wisdom of Roosevelt's policy of nonbelligerence. It passed in both houses a resolution supporting the arming of American merchant ships only by the slim majority of 262 in favor to 231 against the measure. If Roosevelt had introduced a resolution for a declaration of war, either defeat or a slim majority would have been disastrous for the war effort. Roosevelt declined to take the risk. In terms of the hero's journey, America had "refused the return."

Crossing the Return Threshold

In July 1941, Japan intervened in Indochina and established air and naval bases. In response, Roosevelt froze all Japanese assets in America. Negotiations aimed at ending the deadlock between America and Japan failed on December 7, 1941. Japan attacked Pearl Harbor on the same day. Congress responded with a declaration of war on December 8. On December 11, Germany and Italy declared war on America.

America gave priority to the war against Nazi Germany. It was feared that the German scientists were building secret weapons that could result in Nazi victory. In Albert Einstein's 1939 letter to President Roosevelt supporting research on building atomic weapons, he warned that German scientists had begun research on uranium and could be building an atomic bomb. American forces helped turn the tide against Nazi Germany. Hitler had gambled disastrously in both attacking the Soviet Union and declaring war against America. By April 1945, both countries had large armies racing into Germany in the final days of Hitler's Third Reich. Japan too had erred as American forces closed in on the Japanese mainland. By August the Axis threat had been completely defeated. The democracies had triumphed in the struggle against Fascism and Japanese militarism.

Master of the Two Worlds

America emerged from World War II with its economy intact, large armies in Europe and Asia, and a decisive edge in military technology with the atomic bomb. Thus began a remarkable period in American history when America was able to successfully fuse power and morality in defending democracy, promoting the principle of self-determination, and supporting the creation of a world body with the power to prevent international aggression. Woodrow Wilson's vision finally had been realized. America had achieved its sixth grand synthesis.

In implementing Wilson's vision, Roosevelt had learned well from his predecessor's mistakes. Bipartisan delegations of senators and congressmen participated at all stages in planning for a world association of states to be called the United Nations. At the San Francisco conference, from April 25 to June 26, 1945, the American delegation was bipartisan with the result that ratification was approved by July 28 by an overwhelming majority.

It gradually became clear after the end of the war that the Soviet Union repudiated the principles of democracy and self-determination in the Nazi occupied territories it controlled. The Soviet Union had no intention of keeping its pledges to allow the populations of countries "liberated" by its armies to choose their own form of government. It was determined to hold on to territories in Central and Eastern Europe by turning them into satellite states with highly centralized political systems that had communist parties in power. Winston Churchill was the first Western leader to see the ominous intent of the Soviet Union in his famous "Iron Curtain" speech in 1946:

From Stettin in the Baltic to Trieste in the Adriatic, an iron curtain has descended across the Continent. Behind that line lie all the capitals of the ancient states of central and eastern Europe. Warsaw, Berlin, Prague, Vienna, Budapest, Belgrade, Bucharest, and Sofia, all these famous cities and the populations around them lie in the Soviet sphere and all are subject in one form or another, not only to Soviet influence but to a very high and increasing measure of control from Moscow. . . . The Communist parties, which were very small in all these Eastern states of Europe, have been raised to preeminence and power far beyond their numbers and are seeking everywhere to obtain totalitarian control.[12]

The Cold War had begun.

Presidents Roosevelt and Truman initially believed that the West had to continue to cooperate despite the Soviets breaking their pledges. When Soviet intentions became clear, Truman took belated action to prevent further

Soviet moves in Greece, Turkey, Iran, and in Berlin during the Soviet block-ade. He declared what has become controversially known as the Truman Doctrine in February 1947: "I believe that it must be the policy of the United States to support free peoples who are resisting attempted subju-gation by armed minorities or by outside pressures."[13] It was only the fu-sion of power and morality in America's sixth grand synthesis that would be successful in responding to Soviet attempts to further increase its influ-ence and control in Europe. Under the Truman Doctrine, America would throw its military resources and forces, if needed, in support of democracies resisting Soviet influence.

If military assistance was one tool to constrain Soviet expansion, another was massive economic assistance. President Truman asked Congress for permission to begin such a program in December 1947:

I am proposing that this Nation contribute to world peace and to its own security by assisting in the recovery of sixteen countries which, like the United States, are devoted to the preservation of free institutions and enduring peace among nations.[14]

The Marshall Plan was criticized by the Soviet Union as a form of "American imperialism." In fact, it was an enlightened attempt by America to use its economic power to help democratic states rebuild their war-shattered economies. This extended even to the defeated Axis powers. Never before in history had a country helped former foes rebuild their economies. America had demonstrated the depth and vision found in its sixth grand synthesis of power and morality.

The United Nations was empowered through its Charter to prevent in-ternational aggression and to support the principle of self-determination. The U.N. Security Council, however, soon became ineffective due to Cold War tensions. The Soviet Union increasingly used its veto against resolu-tions it did not approve. The boycott of the Security Council by the Soviet Union from January to August 1950 enabled the Security Council to re-spond promptly to the surprise North Korean invasion of South Korea. America played a lead role in getting U.N. support for a military force to help the South Koreans. Without such intervention, the South would have been absorbed by the North under a communist government. This was despite the wishes of the South Koreans, and probably most northerners as well, who desired a democratic form of government free of Soviet control. American and U.N. intervention therefore was consistent with the principle of self-determination in the Korean War.

America also supported self-determination in its own colonial territory of the Philippines and for territories of the other colonial powers, Britain, France, and the Netherlands. The Philippines was granted its independence in 1946, and first Britain and then the other colonial powers began granting independence. America went as far as possible in encouraging the formation of democratic governments and supporting the principle of self-determination.

The impressive period of America being "master of the two worlds" from its entry into World War II in 1941 until 1956 can be explained by a number of factors. European states either under or threatened by Soviet influence genuinely desired their independence. In these cases, American military and economic support was consistent with the principle of self-determination. Importantly, America maintained national unity while it pursued foreign policy goals that were consistent with its vision of freedom and democracy. America was able to prevent itself from slipping into the "deep forgetting" due to it sustaining the archetypal encounters essential in the "great remembering." In short, the lesson is that a grand synthesis of power and morality can be maintained as long as America renews the archetypal encounters that make up its "great remembering."

DEEP FORGETTING (1956–1974)—IGNORING SELF-DETERMINATION IN THE CRUSADE AGAINST COMMUNISM

The Truman doctrine laid the seeds of what would become America's "deep forgetting." The doctrine pledged support for governments against armed minorities influenced or controlled by foreign states. If these armed minorities only had the support of small segments of the population, then American intervention would be consistent with the principle of self-determination. If the armed minorities in fact had the support of a majority of the population, then America was not acting in support of self-determination. In the case of Europe, communism was genuinely unpopular given the democratic heritage of European states, and the undemocratic way in which Central and Eastern European states had been turned into Soviet satellites. Self-determination had clearly been violated in these cases. The same, however, could not be said for communism in Asia. Communist ideology was widely adopted by nationalists as a tool for liberating peoples from colonial control and exploitation from colonial elites. Communism promised revolutionary changes that would redistribute wealth and land controlled by colonial elites. Attempts at encouraging democracy were dismissed as a means of former colonial powers maintaining a more indirect means of control through local elites—neocolonialism. To maintain or impose democratic governments on populations suspicious of neocolonialism ultimately was to deny the principle of self-determination.

America's misguided attempt to roll back popular nationalist movements that used elements of communist ideology in their programs forced these movements to rely more heavily on the Soviet Union and China for support. America's opposition to such movements, beginning with the case of North Vietnam, led to it supporting corrupt and unpopular "democratic" regimes.

The "crusade against communism" irrespective of the wishes of populations for the revolutionary changes proposed by nationalists was a dangerous combination of fear and imperialism. Another deep forgetting had begun.

Fear

America's fear of communism was rooted in the belief that communism posed a direct threat to liberty and other key principles found in the Declaration of Independence and the Constitution. In Truman's Inaugural Address on January 20, 1949, he spelled out the threat of communism to liberty:

[T]he United States and other like-minded nations find themselves directly opposed by a regime with contrary aims and a totally different concept of life. That regime adheres to a false philosophy which purports to offer freedom, security, and greater opportunity to mankind. Misled by this philosophy, many peoples have sacrificed their liberties only to learn to their sorrow that deceit and mockery, poverty and tyranny, are their reward. That false philosophy is communism.[15]

The Truman Administration then adopted in 1950 National Security Council Document 68 as an authoritative rationale for American foreign policy. The document described the Soviet Union as "animated by a new fanatic faith, antithetical to our own, and seeks to impose its absolute authority over the rest of the world."[16] The former ambassador to Moscow, George Kennan, further argued that "there can be no middle ground or compromise between the two."[17] These views led to the policy of containment implemented by the Truman administration that guided American foreign policy right up to the Reagan-Gorbachev era. In both of the inaugural addresses of Dwight D. Eisenhower, for example, he showed his complete agreement with Truman over the antithetical nature of communism to the American ideals: "The designs of that power [international communism], dark in purpose, are clear in practice. It strives to seal forever the fate of those it has enslaved. It strives to break the ties that unite the free."[18]

America's fear of communism peaked during the Eisenhower administrations (1953–1961). The public's fear of communism initially was fueled by Senator Joseph McCarthy who in the 1952 national elections claimed to be holding a list of communist sympathizers in the State Department. Senior State Department figures were purged on spurious charges of not being earnest enough in the fight against communism. In 1957, the Soviet Union launched Sputnik and took an early lead in the space race and in missile technology. Fear of Soviet nuclear superiority led to an expensive U.S. effort to close the "missile gap." All global conflict was seen through the lens of communist expansion, which had to be contained wherever possible. This fear of communist expansion was best illustrated in terms of the domino theory for Southeast Asia.

The watershed event in the transformation of America from being "master of the two worlds" where it supported the principles of democracy and self-determination, to giving lip service to these principles in an anticommunist crusade was the collapse of French Indochina. From the end of World War II, France began fighting a losing war against the popular nationalist forces of Ho Chi Minh. America under Presidents Truman and Eisenhower had given military assistance to France in the hope it could install an independent and democratic government. Faced with imminent defeat at the strategic crossroad of Dienbienphu, France appealed for direct American military intervention. President Eisenhower refused due to a lack of support from Britain and because of his own anticolonial scruples, as he wrote in his memoirs:

[T]he standing of the United States as the most powerful of the anti-colonial powers is an asset of incalculable value to the Free World. . . . Thus it is the moral position of the United States was more to be guarded than the Tonkin Delta, indeed than all of Indo-China.[19]

A conference in Geneva in July 1954 decided the future of Vietnam and the rest of French Indochina. For the moment, Vietnam would be divided into two, with the North held by Ho Chi Minh and the South held by the French-installed Vietnamese government. Elections were scheduled for 1956, which, if held, would most likely have resulted in the victory of Ho Chi Minh.

Lying at a strategic crossroads on the Asian continent, a united Vietnam under Ho Chi Minh sparked American fears that communism would soon sweep down throughout Southeast Asia. In 1950, National Security Council Document 64 stated that Indochina was "a key area of South East Asia and is under immediate threat."[20] This was the beginning of the domino theory and the idea that if Vietnam and Indochina fell, Burma, Thailand, and Indonesia would soon follow. All Southeast Asia would then be in danger of falling under communist control. This would have been catastrophic for the interests of America and its allies as President Eisenhower outlined in a letter to Winston Churchill in 1954:

If . . . Indochina passes into the hands of the Communists . . . it is difficult to see how Thailand, Burma and Indonesia could be kept out of Communist hands. This we cannot afford. The threat to Malaya, Australia and New Zealand would be direct. The off-shore island chain would be broken. The economic pressure on Japan which would be deprived of non-Communist markets and sources of food and raw material would be such, over a period of time, that it is difficult to see how Japan could be prevented from reaching an accommodation with the Communist world which would combine the manpower and natural resources of Asia with the industrial potential of Japan.[21]

Due to the fears of the domino theory, America began a foreign policy that would deny Ho Chi Minh control of the South. The elections scheduled for 1956 that would reunify the country were never held. American fears of communist expansion drove it into an anticommunist crusade in which it behaved as an imperial power.

Imperialism

The belief in the moral, political, social, and economic superiority of democracy over its ideological rival communism may be something to which a majority of citizens in democratic countries could easily agree. After all, the most technologically and materially advanced countries in the world after World War II were and continue to be democratic. All major indicators of quality of life in terms of health, education, housing, per capita income, and life expectancy continue to be highest in democratic countries. On the other hand, the relatively low level of quality of life indicators in Asia, Africa, and Latin America, combined with the legacy of colonialism, made communism an attractive ideology. For many attracted to communist thought, democracy was synonymous with capitalism, which was oppressive and would eventually be surpassed by communism. America's attempts to impose democracy through governments controlled by local elites that used a mixture of repression and corruption was doomed to failure. In the developing world after World War II, America was losing the battle for hearts and minds in the crusade against communism.

In the case of Vietnam after the withdrawal of France, America gave vital military and economic assistance to the "democratic" government of South Vietnam. Led by Ngo Dinh Diem after 1955, the government had no intention of allowing the internationally supervised elections called for in the 1954 Geneva conference that would unify the country. Diem's government was corrupt, practiced nepotism, and became increasingly unpopular. According to one commentator: "The cities became generators of inflation and vice while the countryside became an open field for the settlement of private grudges and for extortionate demands which drove the peasants into the arms of the communist opposition."[22] In committing itself to an unpopular and corrupt regime that was undemocratic in all but name, America made anticommunism rather than democracy or self-determination the top priority of its Vietnam policy. By 1960, nearly 700 military advisors were in Vietnam. The slippery road to full-scale military intervention in Vietnam had begun. In 1961, President Kennedy authorized large numbers of military personnel to assist directly South Vietnamese forces. A year later American bombing missions had begun. America kept escalating its commitment to maintaining South Vietnam as an independent anticommunist state. Eventually, America was forced to seek an escape route from the quagmire in which it found itself. In 1973, the Paris Peace Accord was signed which enabled America to "withdraw with honor." Fighting began again not long after the American withdrawal. The South Vietnam government finally fell in 1975. Over two million people had been killed in the war.

America's anticommunist crusade was a form of imperialism insofar as it denied any possibility that nationalists operating under communist principles and Soviet or Chinese support could bring about needed socioeconomic changes in many developing countries. The slogan "better dead than red" epitomized the belief that individual liberty should never be surrendered. For those struggling in conditions of dire poverty and poor education, political rights were secondary to the necessities of employment, education, and health. America's hubris over the superiority of its tradition of liberty and democracy in all conditions made possible a debilitating anticommunist crusade in developing parts of the war. Francis Fukuyama has been shown to be correct in his analysis that historical forces have demonstrated the superiority of liberal democracy over communism as an effective way of organizing societies.[23] Rather than support unpopular "democratic" regimes in the developing world, America would have been better placed to allow nationalists to come to power irrespective of the communist beliefs they held. Historical forces would have driven these regimes away from the Soviet camp and toward the liberal democratic camp. The nonaligned movement was a vivid demonstration that nationalists, when they came to power, would not automatically fall into the Soviet camp. America's imperialism did not allow it to see how communism offered short-term benefits that would inevitably translate into deep support for liberal democratic reforms.

Under President Richard Nixon, America began shifting toward a foreign policy based on power politics rather than anticommunism. In an interview in January 1972, Nixon stated:

We must remember the only time in the history of the world that we have had any extended periods of peace is when there has been balance of power. It is when one nation becomes infinitely more powerful in relation to its potential competitor that the danger of war arises. So I believe in a world in which the United States is powerful. I think it will be a safer world and a better world if we have a strong, healthy United States, Europe, Soviet Union, China, Japan, each balancing the other, not playing one against the other, an even balance.[24]

In a vivid demonstration that power politics rather than anticommunism would be the guiding motive of his administration, Nixon implicitly supported China in its border conflict with the Soviet Union in 1969. Along the Ussuri river, more than forty Soviet divisions assembled for what U.S. intelligence forces believed could be an invasion of China. Such intervention would have been based on the Brezhnev Doctrine of the Soviet Union's right to protect communist states. Kissinger explained the significance of the conflict as follows:

Soviet military intervention in China would signal the most serious threat to the global balance of power since the Cuban missile crisis. The application of the Brezhnev Doctrine to China would mean that Moscow would try to make the government in Beijing as submissive as Czechoslovakia's had been obliged to become the previous year. The world's most populous nation would then be subordinate to a nuclear superpower—an ominous combination which would restore the dreaded Sino-Soviet block, the monolithic nature of which had inspired such fear in the 1950's. Whether the Soviet Union was capable of realizing so vast a project remained far from clear. What was obvious, however—especially to an administration basing its foreign policy on a geopolitical conception—was that the risk could not be run. If the balance of power is taken seriously, then the very prospect of geopolitical upheaval must be resisted; by the time the change has occurred, it may well be too late to oppose it.[25]

That America could support Communist China in its conflict with the Soviet Union was a vivid sign that anticommunism was now replaced as the pivot of foreign policy. Even communist states could conflict with one another, thereby raising the possibility of strategic alliances for America. President Nixon began a process of normalizing relations with China. This culminated in a visit to China by President Nixon in 1972 and America's formal recognition of mainland China, rather than Taiwan, as a permanent member of the U.N. Security Council.

In 1975, in another demonstration of power politics, President Ford and Kissinger colluded in the Indonesian invasion of the Portuguese colony of East Timor. The island of Timor had been divided by the Dutch and the Portugese into their respective colonial empires. When Indonesia became independent, West Timor became part of Indonesia. Pledges to rapidly abandon its sprawling colonial empire by the new Portuguese government in 1974 meant that East Timor was likely to gain independence. A 1975 civil war led to the victory of the dominant East Timor political party, Fretilin. Fretilin in fact was a rainbow of political parties ranging from extreme left to moderates who would be described today as social democrats. The possibility of East Timor going communist rang alarm bells in the Indonesian and American governments. Coming so soon after the traumatic fall of Saigon, and the seeming reality of the domino principle, these governments were determined to prevent East Timor from becoming Southeast Asia's Cuba. A visit to Jakarta by President Ford and Secretary of State

Henry Kissinger in 1975 was followed two days later by a massive air, sea, and land invasion of East Timor by the Indonesian military. Balance of power dictated that East Timor could not slip into the communist camp! East Timor was a vivid demonstration that, under the influence of Henry Kissinger, America's foreign policy was based firmly on principles of power politics rather than morality. Under Kissinger, America's sixth hero's journey had truly ended in a deep forgetting.

Materialism

As Europe and elsewhere slowly recovered from World War II thanks to the Marshall Plan (1947), there was a need for American goods and services. American banks, the manufacturing sector, and agriculture all benefited from the revival of Europe and the increased global trade. This began an era of unprecedented economic growth for America that made possible the ever-increasing defense budget in the anticommunist struggle. Opening overseas markets and protecting global trade therefore was vital to America's national interest and the anticommunist struggle. This bred a form of American consumerism that was seen as the embodiment of Western capitalism. A consumer culture based on the relentless acquisition of more and more consumer goods was deeply alienating to the Third World, which was more concerned with issues of social justice, equitable development, and preserving traditional cultures than in embracing the capitalist world in the battle against communism.

If the communist world was seen as oppressive of the most talented of a society, the capitalist world was viewed as breeding a form of heartless materialism that crushed the aspirations of the less fortunate. America and other major trading nations, for example, consistently resisted calls for restructuring the global economy to assist the Third World in developing their economies in a just and sustainable manner. Attempts at global economic reform were led by seventy-seven developing countries at the first U.N. Conference on Trade and Development (UNCTAD) in 1964. Rather than agree to reform the global economy, America and its major trading partners instead encouraged short-term measures such as loans, aid, and development assistance that were wholly unsuited for addressing the deep inequities of global trade.

In sum, fear of communism and the imperialism resulting from an anticommunist crusade launched America into its sixth deep forgetting. Materialism, in the form of a consumer culture that sustained the expansion of the American economy, bred the belief that democracy and capitalism went hand in hand. If countries were to join the free democracies in the struggle against communism, then they were encouraged to open their markets to global capitalism. America was deeply enmeshed in a deep forgetting

Table 8.1

America's Sixth Hero's Journey—The Democratic Struggle against Fascism and Communism (1933–1974)

Phase of Hero's Journey	Step of Hero's Journey		Key Events
CALL TO ADVENTURE — Opposing International Aggression & Promoting Self-Determination (1933-1939)	Hearing the Call	1.	America condemns Japanese aggression in Manchuria (1933)
		2.	America declares timetable for Phillipines Independence (1934)
	Refusal of the Call	3.	Congress passes three Neutrality Acts (1935-1937)
		4.	Congress refuses to repeal arms embargo to democratic nations under threat from Fascism (1939)
	Crossing the First threshold	5.	President Roosevelt initiates Fourth Neutrality Act which effectively gives military aid to Britain & France (1940)
		6.	Roosevelt 'lends' fifty destroyers to Britain (1940)
GREAT REMEMBERING — From Neutrality to Non-Belligerency (1939-1941)	Slaying the Dragon	7.	Roosevelt contends with America First Committee & Isolationism (1939-1941)
	Sacred Marriage	8.	1940 elections have both parties pledging to stay out of the war and maintain national unity
	Atonement	9.	Roosevelt's 'Arsenal of Democracy' speech (1940)
		10.	Lend-Lease Act permits vast quantities of arms and military supplies for Britain (1941)
RETURN TO INTERNATIONAL SOCIETY — The Second World War & the Cold War (1941-1956)	Refusal of the Return	11.	America First Committee lobbies against entering the War. Polls show majority of Americans do not support declaration of War on Germany(1939-1941)
	Cross Return Threshold	12.	After attack on Pearl Harbor, America declares War against Japan and Axis powers (1941)
	Master of the Two Worlds	13.	Truman Doctrine (1947) & Marshall Plan (1948)
		14.	America leads response to North Korean invasion (1950)
		15.	**Sixth Grand Synthesis: Self-determination, democracy & global cooperation through United Nations**
DEEP FORGETTING — Ignoring Self-Determination in the anti-Communist Struggle (1956-1974)	Fear	16.	Domino Theory in Southeast Asia (1956-1974)
		17.	Soviet Union launches Sputnik (1957)
	Imperialism	18.	Military intervention in Vietnam (1961-1973)
		19.	Power politics under Nixon/Kissinger (1969-1977)
	Materialism	20.	Industrialized nations ignore Group of 77 demands to reform international trading system (1964-)

during its anticommunist crusade that ended its sixth hero's journey, summarized in Table 8.1.

NOTES

1. Quoted in Julius Pratt, *A History of United States Foreign Policy* (Newark, N.J.: Prentice Hall, 1955), 589.

2. Pratt, *A History of United States Foreign Policy*, 597.

3. Quoted in Pratt, *A History of United States Foreign Policy*, 631.

4. Ibid., 637.

5. Ibid., 638.

6. Jerome Agel, *Words That Make America Great* (New York: Random House, 1997), 512.

7. Quoted in Pratt, *A History of United States Foreign Policy*, 638.

8. Agel, *Words That Make America Great*, 296.

9. Ibid., 295.

10. John Gabriel Hunt, ed., *The Inaugural Addresses of the Presidents* (New York: Random House, 1997), 390, 393.

11. Pratt, *A History of United States Foreign Policy*, 643.

12. Agel, *Words That Make America Great*, 454.

13. Quoted in Pratt, *A History of United States Foreign Policy*, 720.

14. Ibid., 721.

15. Hunt, *Inaugural Addresses of the Presidents*, 403.

16. Quoted in David Campbell, *Writing Security: United States Foreign Policy and the Politics of Identity* (Minneapolis: University of Minnesota Press, 1992), 25.

17. Ibid., 27

18. Hunt, *Inaugural Addresses of the Presidents*, 420–21.

19. Quoted in Henry Kissinger, *Diplomacy* (New York: Simon and Schuster, 1994), 632.

20. Ibid., 623–24.

21. Ibid., 632.

22. Peter Calvocoressi, *World Politics since 1945*, 4th ed. (London: Longman, 1982), 307.

23. Francis Fukuyama, "The End of History?: The New Shape of World Politics: Contending Paradigms in International Relations," *Foreign Affairs* (1997): 2, 4; originally published in *The National Interest* (Summer 1989).

24. Quoted in Kissinger, *Diplomacy*, 705.

25. Kissinger, *Diplomacy*, 722.

CHAPTER 9

AMERICA'S SEVENTH HERO'S JOURNEY (1974–)—HUMAN RIGHTS, HUMANITARIAN INTERVENTION, AND A NEW WORLD ORDER

America's sixth hero's journey began as an express commitment for principles of nonaggression, self-determination, and support of democracy. Fear over the power and influence of the Soviet Union eventually led to an anticommunist crusade where America supported corrupt repressive regimes that were by no means democratic. More importantly, America interpreted the principle of self-determination selectively. It would be applied for removing colonial powers, or for bringing about democratic governments. Self-determination would not be recognized, however, if it meant that communist governments would come into power as a result. The Vietnam war led to a deep re-evaluation of American policy in supporting "democratic" allies in the anticommunist crusade. American support would increasingly be based on how well human rights were respected. Consequently, the transition from the sixth to the seventh hero's journey saw attempts by America to support human rights and democracy.

CALL TO ADVENTURE (1974–1981)—HUMAN RIGHTS DIPLOMACY

The Vietnam war saw the American public deeply divided. Many Americans deplored the human rights violations brought about by America's policy of supporting a corrupt and repressive Vietnamese government. Congress began passing legislation supporting greater respect for human rights. The Nixon and Ford administrations had effectively ignored these Congressional resolutions. Annual State Department reports on how well allied governments had implemented human rights norms contained nothing that would offend loyal allies. The decisive shift toward a more moral American foreign policy that emphasized human rights culminated in the election of Jimmy Carter. Carter elevated human rights to the center stage of American foreign policy. Although the struggle against communism still continued, to get American support, a regime would have to do more than rest on its anticommunist credentials. More respect had to be shown for human rights and for establishing democratic reforms based on free and fair elections in a multiparty system. Carter's human rights policy was a "call to adventure." America had begun its seventh hero's journey.

Hearing the Call

The American public had been shocked by the human rights violations committed during the Vietnam war by both the South Vietnamese government and American military forces. In response to this shift in public opinion, Congress passed in 1974 a resolution that tied military assistance to respect of human rights. The resolution became law in 1978 and stated that "no security assistance may be provided to any country the government of which engages in a consistent pattern of gross violations of internationally recognized human rights."[1] The resolution went on to state that exemptions could only be made when "the President certifies in writing . . . that **extraordinary circumstances exist** warranting provision of such assistance [emphasis added]." Legislation was also passed in 1974 that made economic assistance conditional on a government's respect for human rights. The legislation stated that no assistance shall be provided "to the government of any country which engages in a consistent pattern of gross violations of internationally recognized human rights . . . unless such assistance will directly benefit the needy people in such country."[2] In addition, Congress authorized creation of the Bureau of Human Rights (renamed Bureau of Democracy, Human Rights and Labor in 1994) in the State Department with special focus on promoting human rights around the globe.

These congressional initiatives in 1974 reflected widespread public opinion on the importance of human rights in American foreign policy. No longer could anticommunist policies shield governments from criticism over the former's human rights excesses. Both American military and economic assistance would depend on its anticommunist allies having greater respect for human rights. Respect for human rights was a "hearing of the call" that Congress had initiated as a result of a decisive shift in the mood of the American public. A new hero's journey was about to begin.

Refusal of the Call

If the American public had shifted toward a greater focus on human rights, this was not reflected in the Ford administration. The top branches of executive government involved in foreign policy making shared a view of human rights that is starkly pointed out by the international lawyer, Louis Henkin:

[L]eading members of the traditional foreign policy establishment, notably the career foreign service, tended to find the new international human rights movement "unsophisticated," and at best a nuisance. They were inclined to consider human rights conditions in any other country that country's business, and active concern with those conditions by the United States, or by international institutions, to be meddlesome, officious, unprofessional, disturbing of "friendly relations" and disruptive of sound diplomacy.[3]

As Secretary of State, Henry Kissinger exemplified the lack of attention for human rights among policymakers. For Kissinger's balance-of-power worldview, what counted was the distribution of global resources and power. Moral concerns such as human rights would be considered as long as they did not negatively impact on the global balance of power. For instance, in discussions with Soviet bloc countries in negotiating the Helsinki Accords in 1975, human rights were part of the third basket of issues in crafting an end to a range of territorial, economic, and moral issues between the two Cold War blocs. Human rights, for Kissinger, were not a moral imperative. Human rights were simply one set of competing interests that needed to be balanced with other interests. Effectively, this meant that countries would not be criticized for human rights violations if they formed significant alliances with America in the global balance of power.

State Department reports on human rights performance of states that received American military and/or economic assistance began in 1977. The first report coming at the end of the Ford administration was muted in its criticism and indeed contained hardly anything that offended important allies. For example, nothing was done to highlight the human rights abuses being done by the government of Indonesia in its repression of East Timor since the 1975 invasion. In fact, American military assistance was crucial in helping Indonesia overcome the surprisingly strong resistance shown by East Timorese military forces. Though Congress reflected a broad public embrace of human rights, the executive branch of government did little to give effect to this. Under the influence of Henry Kissinger, the Ford administration reflected a "refusal of the call to adventure."

Crossing the First Threshold

It was the election of Jimmy Carter that gave effect to Congressional initiatives in a way that has made human rights a key element of American foreign policy. In Carter's inaugural address, he stated what he believed would be a bold departure from the foreign policy of his predecessors:

The world itself is now dominated by a new spirit. Peoples more numerous and more politically aware are craving and now demanding their place in the sun—not just for the benefit of their own physical condition, but for basic human rights. The passion for freedom is on the rise. Tapping this new spirit, there can be no nobler nor more ambitious task for America to undertake on this day of a new beginning than to help shape a just and peaceful world that is truly humane.[4]

In embracing human rights in American foreign policy, Carter took a number of steps. The most important was quiet diplomacy. For the first time, American diplomatic staff began to vigorously press for improved human rights in discussions with foreign governments. Carter succeeded in making human rights part of regular diplomatic business. The second step was to raise human rights publicly. This was to make America's position clear and to put America's allies on notice. The third step was to instruct the Bureau of Human Rights to release more candid assessments of the human rights performance of its allies. The annual State Department reports on human rights became an important instrument in signaling to foreign governments that they were under constant scrutiny. And finally, Carter cut off economic assistance to a number of countries notorious for human rights violations. He also pressured the World Bank, the International Monetary Fund, and the Inter-American Development Bank to cut off economic assistance.

The most prominent of the regimes that collapsed due to America's new human rights policy was the Somoza family in Nicaragua. The Somozas had run Nicaragua since 1934. The Somoza family had alienated all segments of the population due to the brutality of the National Guard. Jimmy Carter ended all assistance to Nicaragua and joined other states in calling for the replacement of the Somoza regime. Other states that felt the effects of Carter's human rights policy were the Philippines, South Korea, Chile, Brazil, and Argentina.

Carter institutionalized human rights in the executive branch of government. No longer would human rights be simply viewed as a concern of foreign policy "amateurs" in Congress responding to an unsophisticated public. Human rights were now the business of foreign policy professionals in the State Department. America had crossed the first threshold on a new hero's journey. Human rights was an essential part of what would eventually become a new attempt by America to fuse power and morality in creating a New World Order.

GREAT REMEMBERING (1981–1993)—HUMAN RIGHTS AND NEW WORLD ORDER

The American Congress and President Carter had demonstrated a firm rejection of Kissinger's amoral balance-of-power politics. American foreign policy had to be based on a set of clear moral principles that coincided with its strategic national interests. America's seventh "great remembering" involved making clear the moral principles that would be promoted by American power.

Slaying the Dragon

Criticism of President Carter's human rights policy came from those that believed deserting loyal allies would allow communist regimes to come to power. Despite the human rights abuses of America's allies, it was argued that such abuses would only be worse under communist regimes. The historian Paul Johnson caustically wrote:

Carter actually added to American weakness by well-meaning but ill-thought-through ventures. One of them was his human rights policy. . . . [I]t played a major role in the overthrow of the Somoza regime in Nicaragua. . . . [A] Marxist and pro-Soviet regime [emerged], whose attitude to human rights was even more contemptuous.[5]

The election of Ronald Reagan saw a resurrection of the anticommunist rhetoric from the Truman and Eisenhower administrations. He saw Soviet communism as the "focus of evil in the modern world" and said Soviet leaders would "lie, steal, cheat, and do anything else to advance their goals."[6] In a surprisingly accurate twist to conventional political thinking, Reagan announced that freedom and democracy were the waves of the future, and would leave "Marxism-Leninism on the ashheap of history."[7] Francis Fukuyama was to make the same argument later in his famous "End of History" paper in 1989.

Rather than ignore human rights in the struggle against Soviet communism as Truman and Eisenhower had done, Reagan made it a centerpiece of the anticommunist crusade. Human rights and democracy, according to Reagan, were most threatened by communism. Reagan took every opportunity to criticize the human rights performance of Soviet Bloc countries. This increased pressure on the Soviet Union, which now found itself responding to human rights abuses in its satellite countries where America had little influence. Though less vigorous than the Carter administration in criticizing human rights among allies, key figures in the Reagan administration did succeed in pressuring allies in promoting human rights and introducing democratic reforms. For example, whereas nearly all Latin America countries were under military governments when Reagan took office in 1981, nearly none were when he left office in 1989. Reagan had exerted pressure on General Pinochet to step down from power in Chile and for President Marcos to hand over power to the victorious opposition parties in the Philippines.

President Reagan's foreign policy was based on the idea of the Soviet Union as the "evil empire." Soviet communism was the dragon America had to slay. Promoting human rights and democratic reforms was the means of achieving this. In slaying the communist dragon, Reagan's basic strategy was to support a host of anticommunist groups that were supposedly fighters for human rights and democracy. This led to the birth of the Reagan Doctrine: "The United States would help anticommunist counterinsurgencies wrest their respective countries out of the Soviet sphere of influence."[8] The idea behind the Reagan Doctrine was that the Soviet Empire had overextended and was straining under the forces of freedom and democracy. Secretary of State George Shultz explained in 1985:

For many years we saw our adversaries act without restraint to back insurgencies around the world to spread communist dictatorships. . . . Any victory of communism was held to be irreversible. . . . Today, however, the Soviet empire is weakening under the strain of its own internal problems and external entanglements. . . . The forces of democracy around the world merit our standing with them. To abandon them would be a shameful betrayal—a betrayal not only of brave men and women but of our highest ideals.[9]

The Reagan Doctrine was exemplified with all its alarming consequences in the Contra insurgency against the Sandinista government in Nicaragua. The Nicaraguan Contra rebels contained significant elements of Somoza's disgraced National Guard who had a brutal reputation under the former regime. A policy began of arming and funding these unsavory groups who did little more than target innocent civilians and the social services created by the Nicaraguan government. Similarly, in Ethiopia, Angola, and Afghanistan, Reagan supported counterinsurgency groups that were anticommunist rather than democratic. In 1983, in his boldest move yet, he ordered an invasion of Grenada to reverse a left-wing coup. Reagan had elevated human rights and democracy to the center stage against the dragon of Soviet communism. In slaying this dragon, inconsistencies appeared in the Reagan Doctrine that led to increasing friction between Congress and the Reagan administration.

Sacred Marriage

When Ronald Reagan used the ailing American economy as the strategic focus of his 1980 presidential campaign, he saw this as the means of defeating President Carter whose popularity had suffered as a result of the ailing American economy. As a result of the Iranian revolution and a cutback in Iranian oil production, oil prices had soared from a low of $16 in 1979 to $36 in 1981. The impact was immediately felt in the world economy with trade declining with devastating effects on the American economy. Reagan's focus on the economy had unconsciously tapped into an underlying sentiment that America needed to experience again the "sacred marriage" to restore confidence in its own virtue and proficiency in order to resume its national mission. His first inaugural address stressed the theme of economic recovery by cutting taxes and cutting back on "big government" spending programs.

Under Reagan's supply side economics, the American economy underwent a full recovery by 1983. Rather than cuts in income taxes and social service programs being the sole factors that drove the recovery, lower energy costs contributed enormously. As a result of the Iran-Iraq war and both countries' need for revenue, oil production increased dramatically. Oil prices dropped from a high of $36 a barrel in 1981 to $21 in 1984; and by 1985 the price had plummeted to $8. Americans found themselves with much more disposable income and when asked in the 1984 elections whether they were better off than they were four years earlier, the electorate voted overwhelming for re-electing Reagan. Reagan's supply side economics symbolized the archetypal encounter of the sacred marriage.

Atonement

The collapse of Eastern bloc countries occurred in 1989. The Soviet Union under Gorbachev had abandoned the Brezhnev Doctrine and had committed itself to a policy of political openness and economic restructuring. A period of unprecedented cooperation began between the Soviet Union and Western countries. This level of cooperation between major world powers led to President Bush arguing before the U.N. General Assembly in October 1990 that a New World Order had finally begun.

We have a vision of a new partnership of nations that transcends the Cold War. A partnership based on consultation, cooperation, and collective action, especially through international and regional organizations. A partnership united by principle and the rule of law and supported by an equitable sharing of both cost and commitment. A partnership whose goals are to increase democracy, increase prosperity, increase the peace, and reduce arms.[10]

In short, America was committed to cooperating with other countries through the United Nations in creating a New World Order based on democracy, human rights, and free trade.

When Iraq invaded Kuwait in August 1990, Bush's idea of a New World Order was put to a severe test. Iraq had been a close ally of the Soviet Union during much of the Cold War. The question now was whether the Soviet Union would cooperate in Security Council resolutions against Iraq. Despite Soviet attempts to seek a diplomatic solution, it agreed in the Security Council that only the credible threat of force would persuade Hussein to pull his forces out of Kuwait. When force was finally used to oust Iraq from January 16 to February 27, 1991, Bush had achieved a stunning success. He had dispelled the ghost of Vietnam and his popularity temporarily soared to as high as 89% in a March Gallup poll.

Unfortunately for Bush, his foreign policy successes did not protect him from electoral defeat in the 1992 Presidential elections. Under Reagan and Bush, America's national deficit had steadily increased as a result of cutting taxes while increasing defense spending and maintaining social services that the Congress, controlled by Democrats, were unwilling to eliminate. The government was able to manage the national deficit through issuing bonds. Reagan's arms buildup and anticommunist policies strained the American economy but were a major factor in Soviet leaders bringing about major reforms and ultimately in the collapse of the Soviet Union. The Soviet Union's collapse was seen by the political scientist Paul Kennedy and others as a pyrrhic victory for America. By 1991 America was again in recession and challenged by the economic vitality of Japan and then the European Community (now European Union). Kennedy believed: "The task facing American statesmen over the next decades . . . [will be] to 'manage' affairs so that the relative erosion of the United States' position takes place slowly and smoothly."[11] The state of the American economy became Bill Clinton's focus in the 1992 elections just as it had been twelve years earlier for Ronald Reagan.

After his inauguration in 1993 Clinton wanted to show that he would continue Bush's vision of a New World Order. In a major foreign policy speech to the U.N. General Assembly in September 1993, Clinton stated:

In a new era of peril and opportunity, our overriding purpose must be to expand and strengthen the world's community of market-based democracies. During the Cold War, we sought to contain a threat to survival of free institutions. Now we seek to enlarge the circle of nations that live under those free institutions, for our dream is of a day when the opinions and energies of every person in the world will be given full expression in a world of thriving democracies that cooperate with each other and live in peace.[12]

The idea of a New World Order enthusiastically promoted both by Bush and Clinton was America's act of atonement insofar as it signaled America's renewed commitment to human rights, democracy, and rule of law.

THE RETURN TO INTERNATIONAL SOCIETY (1993–   )—HUMANITARIAN INTERVENTION AND NEW WORLD ORDER

Bill Clinton won the 1992 presidential campaign by concentrating on the domestic economy and the need for national renewal. Clinton nevertheless wanted to continue an interventionist foreign policy program that would focus on democracy and human rights. Disaster in Somalia brought a halt to the early optimism that American power would achieve desirable foreign policy. When American inaction made international humanitarian crises only worse, Clinton finally came around to taking decisive foreign policy actions in the Balkans. Ironically, Clinton ended his second term with foreign policy rather than domestic policy successes.

Refusal of the Return

When the state of Somalia disintegrated in early 1992, famine and civil war threatened a humanitarian catastrophe. The American public demanded military intervention to restore peace and feed the starving population. In one of his last foreign policy actions, President Bush succeeded in gaining U.N. Security Council support for military intervention for famine relief. A U.N.-authorized military force intervened in Somalia in December 1992 and was embarrassingly greeted at designated landing points on Somali beaches by the international media. The intervention, Operation Restore Hope, proceeded well to begin with and achieved its mandate of ensuring the delivery of humanitarian supplies to the Somali population. In fact, the mission had succeeded so well that Security Council members decided to change the U.N. mandate in midstream. In the words of Ambassador Albright, America urged the United Nations to restore "an entire country as a proud, functioning, and viable member of the community of nations."[13] The U.N. peacekeeping mission that replaced the U.S.-led intervention force in March 1993 was now asked to disarm Somali militias and begin building the political and economic infrastructure of a new state. This immediately led to conflict with one of the major warlords—General Mohammed Farah Aidid—who controlled the capital. Aidid's forces ambushed and killed twenty-four Pakistani peacekeepers. American military forces joined in the manhunt for Aidid, and in a firefight in October, seventeen Army rangers were killed. The picture of one of the dead U.S. Rangers being stripped naked and dragged through the streets of Mogadishu to cheering crowds and television cameras was too much for the American public. Clinton and his foreign policy staff decided that Somalia was fast becoming a quagmire. The manhunt for Aidid was called off, the campaign of disarming the militias was abandoned, and America decided to pull out all its troops from Somalia by March 1994. The U.N. mission ended a year later in dismal failure, raising acrimony between U.N. members.

Somalia had turned into a foreign policy disaster for the Clinton administration, which observed how quickly public support could evaporate for a peacekeeping mission. As Warren Strobel wrote:

If policy is not well anchored, the temptation to respond to the calculation of the moment can be overwhelming. CNN, in particular, gives opponents of policy—

whether in the U.S. Congress or in the streets of Mogadishu—a platform to make their views known instantly, thus complicating the life of today's policy maker.[14]

The Somalia fiasco led to strict criteria for any further participation in peacekeeping missions. In May 1994, not long after the last American troops left Somalia, the Clinton administration's policy on future U.N. peacekeeping efforts was released. Presidential Decision Directive 25 made future American participation dependent on a range of criteria. The most important were the following: clear objectives, realistic criteria for ending the operation, and American leadership of American forces.

The Somalia experience eliminated Clinton's enthusiasm for committing American forces to creating a New World Order. The unfolding crisis in Rwanda led to the Clinton administration doing little to stop what was fast turning into a genocidal campaign by the Hutu ethnic majority against the Tutsi minority. Using primitive weapons, Hutus were encouraged by the government to hunt down and kill their Tutsi neighbors. From April to June 1994, up to 750,000 people were killed in the genocidal campaign. America and other U.N. Security Council members were very slow to commit forces that could easily have stopped the genocide. French forces began arriving in July, too late to stop the genocide and unable to prevent invading Tutsi rebel forces from taking over the country.

In Bosnia too, the Clinton administration dragged its feet in a crisis that European states were clearly unable to manage. Fighting had begun in 1991, and the better-armed Serbs began unleashing devastation upon the hapless Muslims and Croats who together made up two thirds of the population. Television cameras captured the irony of European peacekeepers providing humanitarian relief in the midst of a civil war where the Muslim and Croat population were being slowly killed off. This prompted sarcasm from Bosnian Muslim leaders that the Europeans were merely fattening them up to be killed by the Serbs. Despite success in restoring democratic government in Haiti without loss of American military personnel, the Clinton administration up to mid-1995 was reeling from criticism over its foreign policy failures in Somalia, Rwanda, and Bosnia.

Crossing the Return Threshold

Soon after Clinton took office in 1993, the American economy had begun to recover. Rather than "relative decline" as Paul Kennedy and others had predicted for the American economy, America instead began to surge ahead of Europe and Japan. The European Union and Japan experienced their own recessions in the mid-1990s, and Japan again went into recession in 1998. As Mortimer Zuckerman explained:

America was all but written off in the 1980s because of its apparently uncontrollable fiscal deficit and its products' steady loss of competitiveness in the global economy. Downsizing and restructuring depressed everyone, but that valley is now largely traversed. . . . [T]he United States lost some 44 million jobs in the process of adjusting its economy but simultaneously created 73 million private-sector jobs— a net gain of over 29 million jobs since 1980. A stunning 55 percent of the total work force today is in a new job, some two-thirds of them in industries that pay more than the average wage. Contrast all of continental Europe, with its larger economy and work force. It has created an estimated 4 million jobs in the same time period, virtually all of which are in the public sector. Since 1991, the European Union has lost about 5 million jobs while the U.S. economy has created more than 14 million new ones.[15]

The surprising recovery of the American economy enabled Americans to direct more of their attention to what was happening in the world. Under President Clinton, America was ready to cross the return threshold and support human rights and democracy.

American and international public opinion was appalled by the murderous Bosnian conflict. Serb forces overran U.N. safe havens in Zepa and Srebenica in July 1995. News of thousands of men supposedly under U.N. protection being slaughtered horrified international opinion. American public opinion was resolutely behind efforts to get the Clinton administration to act in the face of clear failure by Europe and the United Nations to manage the conflict. A further devastating artillery attack on a Sarajevo marketplace in August proved the final straw. Clinton gave the go-ahead for NATO to begin an air operation to end the war. With Security Council resolutions in place that gave NATO the necessary mandate to intervene, air operations began. Combined with a joint military offensive by the Croatian Army and Bosnian forces, the air operation succeeded in turning the tide of the war. Serb forces were reeling from the combined offensive and rapidly began losing ground. In a panic, Serb leaders decided to support peace efforts they had earlier spurned. In November 1995, with the joint Croatian-Muslim offensive in top gear, Slobodan Milosevic of Serbia signed the Dayton Peace Accord on behalf of Bosnian Serb leaders.

The Bosnian crisis was a vivid demonstration that American inaction in the face of an international crisis was a recipe for catastrophe. The Clinton administration had crossed the return threshold. Rather than wait for an international crisis to unfold, with mounting pressure from the American and international media to act, America would take a far more proactive role.

Master of the Two Worlds

The Kosovo crisis marked an important watershed in American foreign policy. Once more, for the seventh time in its history, American foreign policy was based on a grand synthesis of power and morality. The synthesis was one of using America's resources in three areas essential for a New World Order. First, America would use its military resources for supporting humanitarian intervention in cases of ethnic conflicts that reached genocidal proportions and threatened to destabilize regions. Second, it would use political and diplomatic influence to convince governments to better protect the rights of ethnic minorities. Finally, America would use its economic might to promote the creation of democratic political systems.

The Kosovo crisis unfolded as a consequence of America and Europe overlooking the conflict in Kosovo at Dayton in 1995. In a conspicuous demonstration, Kosovo leaders protested outside the Dayton airbase where the Bosnian conflict was being settled. The protestors' fears that Kosovo would also break out into a destructive war if not settled proved all too real in 1998 as civil war broke out with the emergence of the Kosovo Liberation Army (KLA). Enjoying an overwhelming superiority in weapons and supplies, the Yugoslav army begin a scorched earth policy that served only to increase local support for the KLA. In October 1998, Richard Holbrooke brought about a settlement that would at least stop the conflict during the harsh Balkan winter. In early March 1999, however, Serb forces began what looked like a systematic attempt to cleanse large portions of Kosovo of its Albanian population. The Clinton administration was forced to make a fundamental decision. Due to Russian opposition, there was no explicit U.N. Security Council support for military intervention by NATO. With the support of Britain's Tony Blair, Clinton decided that the authority of NATO as a European security body of nineteen nations that operated on consensus was sufficient legitimacy for military action to begin. NATO authorized military intervention in the form of an air campaign that lasted eleven weeks and ended in early June. The campaign succeeded in bringing Milosevic to accept peace on NATO's terms. Clinton had won a stunning victory that surprised his critics on both the right and left who argued respectively that an air campaign would not be enough to end the crisis and that he had been too quick to commence the air campaign.

Coming toward the end of the Clinton administration, the Kosovo crisis has resulted in American foreign policy taking a decisive shift in support of what has been termed the Clinton Doctrine. Clinton explained this new policy in a speech soon after the crisis:

I think there's an important principle here that I hope will be now upheld in the future. . . . And that is that while there may well be a great deal of ethnic and religious conflict in the world—some of it might break out into wars—that whether within or beyond the borders of a country, if the world community has the power to stop it, we ought to stop genocide and ethnic cleansing.[16]

Through the prestige and authority of NATO, America can play a much more proactive role in responding to international crises. With the prospect of U.N. Security Council support for similar Kosovo-like interventions un-likely, NATO has already taken preliminary steps to fill the breach. At NATO's fiftieth anniversary celebration in Washington, D.C., a new stra-tegic vision for NATO was agreed upon that would enable it to operate in future Kosovo-like crises. America through NATO and other multilateral organizations is therefore ready to fuse power and morality in responding to international crises in the twenty-first century. America, once more, has become "Master of the Two Worlds." How long America can occupy this phase of its hero's journey depends on its leadership and how well it com-mits itself to its seventh grand synthesis of power and morality.

AMERICA'S SEVENTH HERO'S JOURNEY

The four steps of the hero's journey—call to adventure, great remem-bering, the return to international society, and deep forgetting—form a cycle that requires states, just as individuals, to periodically renew the three archetypal encounters at the heart of the hero's journey. These periodic renewals are necessary in order to meet the new challenges that states en-counter with changing global conditions. Hesitation in meeting these chal-lenges and renewing the archetypal encounters is to become mired in the deep forgetting as a psychosocial process in which a state neither draws on its founding ideals nor learns from past mistakes.

The end of the Cold War has coincided with America beginning an active foreign policy era based partly on a booming economy and partly on the shared perception that America has the global vision and capacity to usher in a new world order. The Clinton presidency ushered in a powerful period of renewal that has transformed America from being an exhausted super-power in relative economic decline to a global economic powerhouse that will ensure America's political and cultural hegemony well into the twenty-first century. A set of new challenges and different global circumstances confront America as the globe's preeminent state. America cannot with-draw from the international system and needs to remain committed to the task of shaping and influencing global politics more than it ever has in its entire history. At the same time, it has to avoid a foreign policy shift into a deep forgetting where America does not take up its challenges due to fear, imperialism, or materialism.

The new challenges and the complexity of the post–Cold War world mean that America needs to renew its hero's journey by undergoing once more the three archetypal encounters at the heart of the hero's journey. As the global hero that achieves mastery of the two worlds—political and ethical—America needs to commit itself to a global order based on its national mission. This will require defining and interpreting its national interest increasingly in terms of the global interest. John F. Kennedy's promise that America "shall pay any price, bear any burden, meet any

Table 9.1
America's Seventh Hero's Journey—Human Rights, Humanitarian Intervention, and a
New World Order (1974–   )

Phase of Hero's Journey	Step of Hero's Journey	Key Events
CALL TO ADVENTURE — Human Rights Diplomacy (1974-1981)	Hearing the Call	• Congressional resolution passed linking human rights performance to military/economic assistance (1974) • Bureau of Human Rights created by Congress (1974)
	Refusal of the Call	• America gives tacit support to Indonesian invasion of East Timor (1975) • First State Department Report on Human Rights muted in criticism of American allies (1977)
	Crossing the First threshold	• Jimmy Carter's inaugural speech declares his administration's emphasis on human rights (1977)
GREAT REMEMBERING — Human Rights & the New World Order Cooperation (1981-1993)	Slaying the Dragon	• President Reagan's anti-communist crusade & the Reagan doctrine (1981) • Arming Contra rebels (1981); Invasion of Grenada (1983)
	Sacred Marriage	• Reagan's supply-side economics & rapid economic growth (1983-1987)
	Atonement	• President Bush declares a New World Order based on international cooperation (1990) • US leads international response in Iraq-Kuwait war (1990-1991)
RETURN TO INTERNATIONAL SOCIETY — Humanitarian Intervention & the New World Order (1993 –)	Refusal of the Return	• Killing of 17 American soldiers leads to reevaluation of American commitment to humanitarian intervention • No action taken to stop genocide in Rwanda (1994) • American inaction in Bosnia (1992-1994)
	Cross Return Threshold	• NATO begins air operations against Bosnian Serb military forces (1995)
	Master of the Two Worlds	• Humanitarian intervention in Kosovo (1999) • Clinton Doctrine (1999) • **Seventh Grand Synthesis: humanitarian intervention, human rights & democracy**

hardship" in defeating enemies of America's basic values translates into a commitment to redefine short-term national interests in terms of long-term global interests. America need no longer selectively apply the ethical principles it holds dear for all states in the international system—either friend or foe. Supporting such principles must be done on a more comprehensive basis even if unpopular with major allies.

Chapter 10 examines how America should shape its domestic and international policies in order to meet current post–Cold War challenges and thereby maintain its seventh grand synthesis of power and morality. The archetypal encounters of slaying the dragon, sacred marriage, and atonement are central in identifying how America can meet the forthcoming challenges, because they symbolize national events and processes that can bring about a deepening and strengthening in America's capacity and resolve to maintain the beneficial effects of its seventh hero's journey, which is summarized in Table 9.1.

NOTES

1. Sec. 502B of the *Foreign Assistance Act of 1961*, as amended, 22 U.S.C.A. ∫2304.

2. Sec. 116 of the *Foreign Assistance Act of 1961*, as amended, 22 U.S.C.A. ∫2151n.

3. Quoted in Henry Steiner and Philip Alston, *International Human Rights in Context: Law, Politics, Morals* (Oxford: Clarendon Press, 1996), 818.

4. John Gabriel Hunt, ed., *Inaugural Addresses of the Presidents* (New York: Random House, 1997), 465.

5. Paul Johnson, *A History of the American People* (HarperCollins, 1997), 910.

6. Quoted in John Spanier and Steven Hook, *American Foreign Policy since World War II*, 13th ed. (Washington D.C.: Congressional Quarterly Inc., 1995), 199.

7. Ibid.

8. Henry Kissinger, *Diplomacy* (New York: Simon and Schuster, 1994), 774.

9. Quoted in Kissinger, *Diplomacy*, 774.

10. President George Bush, "The U.N.: World Parliament of Peace," address to the U.N. General Assembly, New York, October 1, 1990, in *Dispatch* (U.S. Department of State), vol. 1, no. 6 (October 8, 1990), 152.

11. Paul Kennedy, *The Rise and Fall of the Great Powers: Economic Change and Military Conflict from 1500 to 2000* (New York: Vintage Books, 1987), 534.

12. President Bill Clinton, "Confronting the Challenges of a Broader World," address to the U.N. General Assembly, New York, September 27, 1993, in *Dispatch*, vol. 4, no. 39 (September 27, 1993), 650.

13. Quoted in Robert Schulzinger, *U.S. Diplomacy since 1900*, 4th ed. (Oxford University Press, 1998), 373.

14. Narren Strobel, "The Media and U.S. Policies toward Intervention," in *Managing Global Chaos: Sources of and Responses to International Conflict*, ed. Ches-

ter Crocker and Fen Hampson (Washington, D.C.: U.S. Institute of Peace, 1996), 373.

15. Mortimer Zuckerman, "A Second American Century," *Foreign Affairs* 77, 3 (1998): 19.

16. Quoted in Ivo Daalder and Michael O'Hanlon, "Unlearning the Lessons of Kosovo," *Foreign Policy* (Fall 1999): 128.

CHAPTER 10

RENEWING AMERICA'S SEVENTH HERO'S JOURNEY FOR THE SECOND AMERICAN CENTURY

America is now in its seventh hero's cycle where the chief moral and political dilemma confronting policymakers is how to deal constructively and effectively in situations where states systematically commit human rights violations against ethnic or religious minorities. In an important study by Ted Robert Gurr at the University of Maryland, he found that in 1998 there were 275 minorities at risk of political and military repression in 116 countries.[1] He argued that two thirds of these "minorities at risk" merely wished to have greater protection of their rights rather than redrawing of national borders. In such cases, these minorities see themselves as members of a broader national community. On the other hand, the other one third of these minorities, roughly 90, seek to redraw boundaries on the basis of self-determination. In these cases, these minorities see themselves as distinct peoples who have a right to their own state. In both cases of minorities seeking greater rights and/or self-determination, the potential for future military conflicts and humanitarian crises will extend well into the twenty-first century.

Under President Clinton, America began its seventh "return to international society" where diplomatic and political efforts to improve the rights of minorities and military intervention in humanitarian crises emerged as a foreign policy imperative. Underlying this moral imperative to intervene to prevent massive loss of human life and material destruction is the principle (and right) of self-determination.[2] Although American policymakers are reluctant to recognize minorities as "peoples" with the right to self-determination, self-determination is nevertheless an underlying principle that resonates deep in the psyche of America's national identity. The boundary line between protecting the rights of minorities and recognition of insurgents battling repressive governments as "peoples" with the right to self-determination may become blurred. The tendency to side with an exploited minority resisting a repressive regime leads to an inclination to extend the right of self-determination. This is inevitable given the importance the principle and right of self-determination has played in American foreign policy. Indeed, scrutiny of the principles underlying all of America's grand syntheses reveals that self-determination consistently appears as a moral principle driving American foreign policy (see Table 10.1).

The key to extending the beneficial aspects of America's seventh hero's journey well into the twenty-first century is to maintain its seventh grand synthesis. There is a need for the American public to support policymakers in addressing massive human rights violations and humanitarian crises wherever they occur. There clearly will be significant political and economic costs in pursuing such a policy depending on the size and nature of the conflict in question. Many states may be offended by America's scrutiny into their treatment of ethnic and religious minorities. Costs are likely to be especially high in cases of humanitarian interventions that involve the use of military forces in cooperation with forces from other countries to prevent genocide, ethnic cleansing, and massive human rights abuses. In order to meet these challenges and avoid entering another deep forgetting, America has to renew the archetypal encounters of the "great remembering." Renewing the great remembering and maintaining the seventh grand synthesis can be achieved by addressing a number of issues in the domestic and foreign policy arenas. This chapter examines some of the domestic and foreign policy issues that need attention for America in responding appropriately to foreign policy challenges involving ethnic/religious minorities.

DOMESTIC POLICY IMPERATIVES

The archetypal encounter of the "sacred marriage" represents for individuals a way of integrating all aspects of their unconscious and conscious lives in order to bring about a united and coherent sense of identity. This has the benefit of empowering the individual in his/her hero's journey. If this is projected onto the national level, then a coherent sense of identity corresponds to a state becoming an integrated political community. This suggests an integration of all components of the state—individuals, groups, and communities—that makes them feel part of a larger political community that shares a national identity. The emphasis then would be on identifying how all citizens and communities in America can develop a sense of national identity that fulfills their own life aspirations and histories. In particular, this concerns immigrant communities, African Americans, and Native Americans.

Table 10.1
Grand Syntheses of Power and Morality in American History

Grand Synthesis	Main Principles	Reasons for Collapse of Grand Synthesis
First 1798-1815	Liberty of Sailors, Free Trade, & Neutrality Rights	• End of Napoleonic Wars meant that America's merchant marine no longer faced threat in conducting free trade.
Second 1845	Self-Determination (American settlers in Texas & Oregon)	• President Polk uses disputed Texas boundary issue to begin an aggressive war for Mexican territory. • Fear of Britain purchasing California prompted Polk's hasty campaign soon after admission of Texas and Oregon to the Federal Union.
Third 1865-1875	State Sovereignty & Self-Determination (Assisting Latin American Republics to determine their own destinies without European interference)	• Isolationism becomes the dominant mood in the American public. • The expense of maintaining Federal troops in the South to ensure the rights of emancipated slaves brought about a reaction to maintaining a high degree of morality in the policy making process.
Fourth 1898-1903	Self-determination (Assisting Cuba in its struggle for independence)	• Perceptions that it was the destiny of Anglo-Saxon nations to rule over and 'civilize' less developed nations. • Fear that an independent Philippines would lead to Imperial Germany intervening & taking a strategic edge over America in Asia.
Fifth 1917-1919	Self-Determination, Democracy & a New World Order (Wilson's 14 points)	• Fear that the harshness of the Treaty of Versailles would inevitably lead to a future European War. • Avoiding possible entanglement in European power politics.
Sixth 1941-1954	Self-determination, democracy & global cooperation	• Anti-communist crusade leads to lack of support for principle of self-determination • Unwillingness to pressure authoritarian allies to implement democratic reforms.
Seventh 1995 -	Humanitarian intervention, human rights & democracy	• Likely to be isolationist mood caused by the political and economic costs of participating in multilateral responses to humanitarian crises.

America and Multiculturalism

States that have directly attempted to impose a dominant sense of national identity have typically failed miserably. The Soviet Union, Yugoslavia, and Czechoslovakia are failed states in which efforts to bring about a dominant sense of national identity were attempted by eliminating sources of social difference among its citizens. The underlying sentiment was that community and ideological differences were inherently destabilizing to the harmonious and smooth running of the state. These differences had to be gradually removed or eliminated as far as possible. This would involve direct social engineering by former socialist states of the Soviet camp, and less direct methods used by Western liberal democracies. The attempt to create a prototype "Soviet man" endowed with working class consciousness was evidence of direct social engineering by the Soviet Union and its socialist allies. As Corinne McLaughlin and Gordon Davidson comment: "The former Soviet Union was an attempt to superimpose a national structure on a collection of cultural and ethnic groups that were never integrated into national life."[3]

The social engineering of former Soviet Bloc countries was duplicated indirectly by liberal democracies that attempted to assimilate migrant communities into the culture of the dominant ethnic community. For Anglo-Celtic nations such as Britain, Canada, America, and Australia, this placed enormous pressure on immigrant communities to conform and assimilate by shedding their distinctive community consciousness for a mode of life that stressed individualism. Liberty was translated to mean the freedom an individual had to exercise his/her lifestyle choices rather than for a community to maintain its cohesiveness and cultural integrity. Being a good Australian citizen, for example, traditionally meant that one should attempt to forget one's cultural history and practices, and uncritically absorb Australian culture. From after World War II when Australia began admitting immigrants from outside the traditional immigration sources in the British Isles up until the election of the Hawke Labor government in 1983, this translated into a consistent dose of discrimination against those who exhibited cultural differences and allegiance to an ethnic community. Derogatory terms such as "wog" and "dago" were directed against those who dressed, ate, spoke, or behaved in ways outside of the dominant Anglo-Celtic cultural norm.

A personal experience helps illustrate this point. When I was at elementary school in Melbourne, Australia, most students were descendants of Anglo-Celtic immigrants or convicts, and I was one of the few with parents from Southern Europe. My mother would give me Italian Vienna bread for lunch, and I vividly remember being ridiculed and criticized for eating "wog food." At one point I remember refusing to take Vienna bread to school any longer and wanting my mother to buy the pre-sliced highly processed bread most students took to school. This is a personal example of how, in general, immigrant communities had to bear pressure by the dominant Anglo-Celtic community to assimilate the latter's cultural practices and become more "Australian." Australia was simply repeating a similar process of assimilation taken by America at the turn of the century to deal with Southern European immigrants. This assimilation process was excellently described by Supreme Court Justice Louis D. Brandeis, who discussed the question "What Is Americanization?" in a speech in 1919:

It manifests itself, in a superficial way, when the immigrant adopts the clothes, the manners, and the customs generally prevailing here. Far more important is the manifestation presented when he substitutes for his mother tongue the English language as the common medium of speech. But the adoption of our language, manners, and customs is only a small part of the process. To become Americanized the change wrought must be fundamental. However great his outward conformity, the immigrant is not Americanized unless his interests and affections have become deeply rooted here. And we properly demand of the immigrant even more than this. He must be brought into complete harmony with our ideals and aspirations, and cooperate with us for their attainment. Only when this has been done will he possess the national consciousness of an American.[4]

According to Arthur Schlesinger, Jr., the American melting pot tradition is merely a gloss on the underlying Anglo-Saxon culture that forms the core of the Americanization process:

The melting pot thus had, unmistakably and inescapably, an Anglocentric flavor. For better or worse, the white Anglo-Saxon Protestant tradition was for two centuries—and in crucial respects still is—the dominant influence on American culture and society. This tradition provided the standard to which other immigrant nationalities were expected to conform, the matrix into which they would be assimilated.[5]

What united the social engineering efforts of former socialist states and the assimilation methods of modern liberal democracies was that differences between communities within the state were seen as potentially destabilizing. The emphasis was firmly on establishing national and political unity through cultural and linguistic assimilation as far as possible as the means to creating a modern state. In modern day Turkey, for example, the Kurdish language was not allowed to be taught in schools until 1999, and Kurds are still socialized by the state to see themselves as Turks.

Diversity in terms of immigrant or ethnic communities retaining their distinctive customs, languages, and norms in a state has therefore been viewed suspiciously by modern states due to the potentially destabilizing effects. The breakdown of multiethnic states such as the Soviet Union, Yugoslavia, Czechoslovakia, have become commonly cited examples of the destabilizing effect of communities maintaining their cultural diversity in a modern state. The noted historian Arthur Schlesinger, Jr., has written of the potentially destabilizing influence of diversity in America:

Watching ethnic conflict tear one nation after another apart, one cannot look with complacency at proposals to divide the United States into distinct and immutable ethnic and racial communities, each taught to cherish its own separateness from the rest. . . . The bonds of national cohesion are sufficiently fragile already. . . . If separatist tendencies go on unchecked, the result can only be the fragmentation, resegregation, and tribalization of American life.[6]

The view that welcoming diversity leads to fragmentation needs to be abandoned if America is to maintain its seventh grand synthesis. The archetypal encounter of the "sacred marriage" brings about an **integration** of all aspects of the individual's unconscious and conscious life. At the national level then, integration suggests allowing various communities to combine their distinctive identities within a larger national political community in a way that enriches both. In the case of America, this is to live up to the symbolic significance of the motto *e pluribus unum* (Out of many, One) on the Great Seal.

The social theorist Adeno Addis commented on both the need and the difficulty of the integration process:

The task of political and legal theory in the late twentieth century must be one of imaging institutions and vocabularies that will affirm multiplicity while cultivating solidarity, a task that seems to demand reconciling seemingly irreconcilable commitments. A society that acknowledges the fact of pluralism (and its normative desirability) without providing the institutional means through which the ethic of reciprocal empathy, respect, and inclusiveness are cultivated is a society which at best allows minorities to be tolerated as the marginal Other or, at worst, lays the ground for an endless and distributive conflict, where in most cases the minority will probably shoulder the greater cost. Emphasis on solidarity without providing the mechanism through which the fact of pluralism (and difference) can be recognized and normatively affirmed is to commit the error of the communitarian, who simply asserts solidarity, with the consequence that minorities will be either forcibly assimilated or forcibly removed. Either option is not, and ought not be, attractive to minorities.[7]

The Indian philosopher Sri Aurobindo makes a similar point concerning reconciling the principles of unity and diversity in a society:

The natural variation of human communities from each other proceeds on the same plan as the variation of individuals; each develops its own character, variant principle, natural law. This variation and fundamental following of its own separate law is necessary to its life, but it is equally necessary to the healthy total life of mankind. . . . Therefore we see that in this harmony between our unity and our diversity lies the secret of life.[8]

To achieve integration, then, a state must work to harmonize the political imperative of national unity with the need for cultural diversity. Cultural diversity must not be understood as **individuals** merely being tolerated in expressing their cultural background, because this is an indirect form of assimilation. The emphasis must be firmly placed on helping communities maintain their cohesion and integrity, because this is the lifeblood of cultural diversity. To gain an idea of this process, Joseph Raz identifies three stages that progressively reconcile the principles of unity and diversity:

Toleration . . . consists of leaving minorities to conduct themselves as they wish without being criminalized, as long as they do not interfere with the culture of the majority. *Nondiscrimination* goes further than toleration and is based on the assertion of the traditional civil and political rights of liberalism, which forbid discrimination against any individual on the grounds of race, religion, ethnicity, gender, or sexual preference. . . . The *affirmation of multiculturalism*, finally, transcends the individualistic approach of nondiscrimination and asserts the value of groups possessing and maintaining their distinct cultures within the larger community; the affirmatively multicultural society not only permits but actively encourages and assists different cultures to preserve their separate identities as best they may.[9]

A state that approaches a level of integration that is analogous to individuals approaching self-actualization may be referred to as a fully integrated political community. Such a state has both achieved national unity while celebrating its cultural diversity.

Australia has gone further than any other state in attempting to harmonize the principles of national unity and diversity through the affirmation of multiculturalism that has been adopted by successive Australian governments since the policy was officially inaugurated in 1973. Australia's policy of multiculturalism is an attempt to recognize and celebrate the diverse cultural communities in Australia as a means of strengthening national unity. This has led to Australian federal government funding of ethnic community radio and television, and other programs aimed at maintaining cultural diversity. This policy is exemplified in the 1978 Galbally Report, which stated: "We are convinced that migrants have the right to maintain their cultural and racial identity and that it is clearly in the best interests of our nation that they should be encouraged and assisted to do so if they wish."[10] Official Australian government support for maintaining cultural diversity has led to firm opposition that questions "the wisdom of giving official endorsement and financial support to the maintenance of a plurality of ethnically specific cultures and identities rather than to a shared Australian identity, and the effect of the possible weakening of our national values and loyalties in the community."[11] Popular opposition to multiculturalism, in general, does not extend significantly beyond some sections of the population who trace their ancestry to the first generations of Anglo-Celtic immigrants who display discriminatory attitudes against newly arrived migrants from Southeast Asia. Despite the sometimes vocal nature of such opposition, Australian government officials are generally correct in referring to Australia as one of the "most successful multicultural societies in the world," and extolling their national attempt to reconcile unity and diversity among the various communities that make up Australian society.[12]

In the case of America and its seventh hero's journey, explicit support for ethnic communities keeping their cultural identity and encouraging cultural diversity needs to be viewed as a means of strengthening national unity. Paradoxically, while America is universally recognized as a haven for immigrants, it continues a powerful effort to assimilate these immigrants. Implementing policies that adequately address immigrant community concerns and promote cultural diversity rather than undermine it will help strengthen American national cohesion. Efforts at promoting group rights, bilingual education, and other policies identified with multiculturalism are important means of integrating ethnic minorities by affirming the value of their cultures for American society generally.

As with the Australian experience, policies of multiculturalism in America have come in for strong criticism. John Miller in a recently published work, *The Unmaking of Americans*, argues against multiculturalism due to its Balkanizing effect. "Today," Miller writes,

we face a significant threat to America's tradition of assimilation. This threat does not come from immigrants, but is best understood by listening to the public debate surrounding them. The vital questions are not about how many foreign-born people to let in or whom they should be, although these tend to dominate political discussions about immigrants. Instead, they are about how to treat immigrants and what we should expect of them once they arrive here. In a remarkably short time, the United States has gone from being a country that could confidently lay out a few principles to which immigrants and the native-born could adhere to being a nation unsure of what it should ask of these newcomers.[13]

Integrating the diverse identities of communal groups in American society rather than contributing to a Balkanization of America, as Miller contends, will lead to a more united sense of national identity. As Marianne Williamson thoughtfully points out:

There are people in America who overemphasize our unity yet fail to appreciate the importance of our diversity, just as there are those who emphasize our diversity yet fail to appreciate the importance of our unity. It is imperative that we honor both. It is our unity *and* our diversity that matter, and their relationship to each other reflects a philosophical and political truth outside of which we cannot thrive.[14]

Affirming America's cultural diversity is therefore indispensable for sustaining America in its seventh hero's journey.

America and Racial Justice

Another neglected area in forging a cohesive national identity is the still palpable race divide that exists in America. African Americans live in poverty at three times the per capita rate as whites, and unemployment is twice as high for African Americans as it is for whites. With a similar educational background, African Americans make 82 to 86 percent of the income enjoyed by whites.[15]

Although significant numbers of Black Americans have moved into middle-class jobs and suburbs, urban centers of American cities are still predominantly black with inferior housing, health, and other services that, combined with poor employment prospects, spawn resentment, crime, alcohol abuse, and violence. Federal and state government efforts to deal with these problems often amount to little more than crime control and building bigger jails, both of which are electorally popular but do little to deal with underlying social inequalities. In an interview for the *New York Times* in April 1997, former president Jimmy Carter said that when he was a young governor of Georgia, he and other governors competed over who had the smallest prison population. "Now it's totally opposite," he added. "Now the governors brag on how many prisons they've built and how many people they can keep in jail and for how long."[16] Attempts to address racial inequalities by local residents lack sufficient government support.

A case that illustrates the problem is the sacking of the Washington, D.C. mayor in May 1995 for financial mismanagement and the subsequent installation of a powerful Financial Control Board that would run Washington, D.C. Given that Mayor Marion Barry and the majority of Washington, D.C. residents are Black Americans, installation of a Control Board, as a result of Congressional action spearheaded by North Carolina Senator Lauch Faircloth, immediately raised accusations of racial discrimination. This was despite the leader of the Control Board, Andrew Brimmer, and the majority of Board members being Black Americans; and despite wide consensus that the services offered by the D.C. government were inferior. As reported in a 1997 *Time* magazine article:

Washington spends more money and has more employees than any other city. Yet the high school dropout rate has passed 50%, crime is up 16% since 1991, and tuberculosis and infant-mortality rates are the highest in the nation. Just last week officials announced that the city's public schools would open three weeks late this fall because building repairs haven't been finished.[17]

Barry's effort to provide employment for the large urban black population with little prospect in the private sector was criticized in the same article: "The mayor has turned the city into a machine that would impress Boss Tweed: jobs for all, and once hired, never fired. Money earmarked for services and repairs often found its way to payroll, to put yet more unskilled workers on the clock."[18]

A further problem lay in Barry's D.C. government awarding contracts to companies that had clear ties or links with the communities being serviced rather than solely awarding contracts on the basis of economic efficiency. For example, if two companies competed for a government contract, one based in the local D.C. area and the other in one of the Washington suburbs in northern Virginia or Maryland, then the ties of the former with the community being serviced would be an important factor in its being awarded a contract. Critics of this policy pioneered by Mayor Barry argued that this led to nepotism, cronyism, and corruption. If a more efficient D.C. government was to be achieved, then this policy had to be curbed if not abandoned altogether.

If integration is to be achieved in a way that meaningfully deals with the painful racial divide in American politics, a price needs to be paid in order for African Americans in inner-city locations to rise to levels of socioeconomic affluence commensurate with the white surrounding suburbs. As President Kennedy said at his inaugural address: "If a free society cannot help the many who are poor, it cannot save the few who are rich."[19] A way of helping the poor of America is to award government contracts to companies whose roots lie in urban areas they service even if these are less economically competitive than companies based outside the areas. Furthermore, urban governments in communities with impoverished Black American populations are a major source of employment and should be supported in providing jobs to their residents. Because it cannot be expected that the economic burden should rest on local ratepayers who desire greater efficiency for their tax dollars, the price needs to be paid by the federal government. This can be done in terms of various incentives awarded to local and state governments that give government contracts to companies based in the designated areas—typically inner-city areas with a large majority of African Americans. Such a program is thought to be unnecessary by some who believe that racial problems no longer need government action. For example, John Miller writes:

Racial preferences rank among the most divisive government policies in the United States. . . . Racial preferences violate the fundamental American principle that rights belong to individuals, not to groups. Perhaps there was a time when black Americans deserved a temporary program of affirmative action. That case is increasingly difficult to sustain in the 1990s.[20]

My own personal experience confirms that racial prejudice and discrimination remain powerful undercurrents in American society. I arrived from a country—Australia—that has a very small Black population drawn largely from the indigenous peoples of Australia rather than Africa, and I therefore had only minimal exposure to individuals with Black African heritage. I had also experienced racial prejudice myself as a descendent of southern Europeans from members of the dominant Anglo-Celtic community, that had me consciously opposed to any form of racial discrimination. Yet, I was surprised at how quickly I absorbed dominant white fears and stereotypes about Black Americans after my arrival in America. Primary sources were the advice of friendly work colleagues who advised me on choosing "safe" areas to live; "good" schools for my children; and the constant barrage of media reports on violent crime that typically involved young Black males. A recently arrived "White" is very quickly socialized to associate safety and quality of life with a low percentage of Black faces in any area. If few White faces are seen in an area, a school, or other venue, then something is wrong and one ought go elsewhere. This has the effect of encouraging racial stereotypes about Black Americans and the urban communities in which they form a large proportion of the population. My personal experience confirms that Miller's views over the inappropriateness of affirmative action and racial preferences are wrong. America needs a massive program similar to the Marshall plan, which helped European postwar recovery, to deal with the poverty and inferior public services that spawn crime and that in turn reinforce a powerful undercurrent of racial prejudice in America. As Marianne Williamson argues: "[nothing] short of a massive investment in America's poor Black population—the true legacy of slavery—is a responsible sign of America's willingness to heal itself racially."[21]

Recognizing the divisive legacy of America's racial history, President Bill Clinton made overcoming all forms of ethnic and racial division in America a centerpiece of his two administrations. In a speech given during the Million-Man March in 1995, Clinton stated:

Abraham Lincoln reminded us that a house divided against itself cannot stand. When divisions have threatened to bring our house down, somehow we have always moved together to shore it up. My fellow Americans, our house is the greatest democracy in all human history. And with all its racial and ethnic diversity, it has beaten the odds of human history. But we know that divisions remain, and we still have work to do. . . . I ask every governor, every mayor, every business leader, every church leader, every civic leader, every union steward, every student leader—most important—every citizen—in every workplace and learning place and meeting place all across America to take personal responsibility for reaching out to people of different races; for taking time to sit down and talk through this issue; to have the courage to speak honestly and frankly; and then to have the discipline to listen quietly with an open mind and an open heart, as others do the same.[22]

Clinton emphasized the themes of reconciliation in a variety of initiatives he undertook to heal racial and ethnic divisions. No other American president was as committed as Clinton to breaking down these divisions as part of his presidential legacy. These domestic initiatives have been important steps in overcoming the racial and ethnic tensions in America. Such initiatives need to be maintained and augmented by Clinton's successors if America is to remain united in its efforts to promote principles at the heart of America's identity onto the world stage.

America and Native Americans

The hope and optimism America brought to its European immigrants had as its flipside nothing but despair and devastation for the Native American population. In 1492, estimates of the number of indigenous people who lived north of Mexico ranged between 10 to 25 million population. Within 150 years this had dropped to fewer than 1 million.[23] America's founding fathers, reflecting the dominant attitude of the age, thought it their duty to "civilize" the native population. Thomas Jefferson's second inaugural address outlined the policy to be taken by America in dealing with a native population driven from its abundant hunting territories into areas that made it almost impossible to maintain their former lifestyles:

[H]umanity enjoins us to teach them agriculture and the domestic arts; to encourage them to that industry which alone can enable them to maintain their place in existence and to prepare them in time for the state of society which to bodily comforts adds the improvement of the mind and morals. . . . But the endeavors to enlighten them on the fate which awaits their present course of life, to induce them to exercise their reason, follow its dictates, and change their pursuits with the change of circumstances have powerful obstacles to encounter; they are combated by the habits of their bodies, prejudices of their minds, ignorance, pride, and the influence of interested and crafty individuals among them who feel themselves something in the present order of things and fear to become nothing in any other. These persons inculcate a sanctimonious reverence for the customs of their ancestors; that whatsoever they did must be done through all time; that reason is a false guide, and to advance under its counsel in their physical, moral, or political condition is perilous innovation.[24]

Jefferson and his peers were children of the European Enlightenment and thought reason the indispensable guide for human emancipation. The life view of the Native American population, on the other hand, was grounded in establishing a relationship with both Mother Earth and the Father Creator. There is therefore a contrast between lifestyles of head and heart, reason and spirit that gives an insight into what needs to be done to integrate Native Americans into American society, as the following passage suggests:

A Hopi Indian legend says that they were to look to the East for the return of their lost white brother, for he was to bring a missing stone tablet to complement the one the Hopis already had. The lost white brother had traveled to the East to develop, record, and invent things. However, when he returned, he did not recognize these Native Americans as his brothers. He killed most of them and pushed those remaining off their sacred lands and onto reservations. The white man had developed the mind, while the Native American had developed the heart—and we see this symbolically as the two halves of the stone tablet that must be reunited if America is to fully express her Soul and her true spiritual destiny.[25]

Responding to concerns of the Native American population is not to find adequate material compensation for the devastation wrought on their communities, though there is a place for this, but to bring together or reconcile two contrasting approaches to life. Integrating Native Americans into American society means therefore to incorporate a view of life essential for America in its hero's journey.

The archetypal encounter of the sacred marriage corresponds to a need to achieve an integrated sense of national identity. Dealing effectively with concerns raised by immigrants over culturally insensitive assimilation policies, concerns of the descendants of African slaves forcibly brought to America who continue to struggle against racial prejudice and intolerance, and the concerns of Native Americans is the way to achieve the type of integrated political community necessary for America to maintain the grand synthesis of power and morality in its seventh hero's journey. America as an integrated political community would be a state where all citizens *do* rather than *can* live their personal American dream. Marianne Williamson reminds us that it is not enough to merely provide opportunities but to remove obstacles to living one's American dream:

The American dream is a dream in process, a not yet fully manifested image of a nation of people with equal access to their own creative powers. Many people in America have lived lives of very limited, even cruelly squelched dreams, not through any fault of their own but through accidents of history and various forms of obstruction and injustice. . . . If any Americans are denied the right to weave their dreams, then America itself isn't weaving hers. It is the job of every generation of Americans to further expand and fulfill the dream of freedom and justice for all.[26]

FOREIGN POLICY IMPERATIVES

An important feature of encountering the Father archetype for individuals is that *atonement* means sacrificing one's personal desires to pursue a calling based on an expanded moral consciousness. For America, this was earlier argued to mean subordinating short-term national interests for the national calling or mission—the promotion of liberty and democracy throughout the globe. It is worth repeating John F. Kennedy's pledge that America would "pay any price, bear any burden, meet any hardship, support any friend, oppose any foe" in order to point out America's awareness of the sacrifice involved in pursuing its sense of mission.

The subordination of the national interest for wider global interests on the basis of America's historic sense of mission has not been achieved. There exists a firm perception that American global leadership translates into little more than a hegemonic pursuit of power rather than supporting freedom through the promotion of universal human rights. The promotion of universal human rights is done on a selective rather than consistent and comprehensive basis. Universal human rights abuses are condemned and followed up with punitive trade sanctions against Cuba, Myanmar (Burma), and Iran but have little more than rhetorical force for countries such as China, India, Indonesia, and Turkey. This is nowhere better demonstrated than in the annual ritual between since 1980 and up to 2000 of granting Most Favored Trading Nation (MFN) status to the government of China despite its gross human rights abuses in Tibet and against its own citizens. While MFN is a nondiscriminatory trade practice that is standard for trading countries, America has in the past denied MFN status to states that have permitted gross human rights abuses—for example, Afghanistan, Albania, Cambodia, Cuba, and North Korea. With the end of the Cold War, Congress has attempted stronger support for promoting and protecting human rights around the world. This led to fierce debates between the Congressional leaders and President Clinton over the wisdom of extending MFN to China in the absence of significant human rights improvement. For example, Congress passed the U.S. China Act of 1992 which denied MFN status to China unless the President could report that

China had taken "appropriate actions" to "begin adhering" to the UDHR in China and Tibet; allowed emigration for reasons of political or religious persecution; accounted for and released political prisoners and prevented export to the U.S. of goods made by prison labor. Moreover, the President's report had to state that China had "made overall significant progress" in other respects including ending unfair trade practices against American business.[27]

President Clinton successfully vetoed the bill, and the Senate was unable to override the veto. The influence of a range of powerful industrial groups has been able to persuade significant numbers of congressmen and senators to support the extension of MFN due to the benefits of trading with China for the American economy. In a 1998 *Foreign Policy* article on China, David Lampton illustrates China's trade importance for America:

According to U.S. Commerce Department figures for 1990–96, China was the fastest-growing major U.S. export market. During that period, American exports grew at a compound rate of more than 19 percent, if one includes U.S. exports initially exported to Hong Kong but then reexported to China. The PRC is now

America's ninth largest export market. By way of comparison, U.S. exports to Japan grew at 6 percent, and those to Brazil by 15 percent, annually.[28]

A powerful supporting argument for not introducing trade sanctions against China is the liberalizing effect of free trade as outlined by Boeing's Vice President for Planning and International Affairs in 1994, Lawrence W. Clarkson:

We believe strongly that U.S. trade is contributing to the rapid decentralization and transformation of China's economy, helping millions of Chinese to obtain greater freedom to choose their work, their employer and their place of residence. . . . As in Taiwan and South Korea, the development of a vigorous middle class will bring the development of social and political freedom for all Chinese more than any other factor.[29]

The same argument was more recently used by President Clinton in June 1998 calling for MFN to be once more extended to China: "Trade is a force for change in China, exposing China to our ideas and our ideals, and integrating China into the global economy."[30] The overall argument for the political consequences of economic liberalization is succinctly explained by the human rights scholar Jack Donnelly:

Markets, it is argued, lead those whom they make prosperous to demand civil and political rights. Economic "freedom" leads to calls for political freedom that repressive governments cannot ultimately resist. Therefore, fostering economic development contributes to fundamental political change. Manipulating selfish economic interests thus becomes a way to realize civil and political rights. Economic support that appears to help stabilize repression actually undermines it.[31]

The implication here is that American policymakers should not allow human rights differences to impact on trade relations with China nor unduly damage relations with the Chinese government. This leads to broad support for the policy of "constructive engagement," which is a policy based on balancing human rights concerns with other interests such as trade and security. Balancing human rights interests therefore translates into rhetorical support for human rights while vigorously pursuing a number of other relationships in the trade and security spheres. This culminated in the ratification of a trade treaty with China in 2000 that approved China's entry into the World Trade Organization. This had the consequence of normalizing trade with China and ending the annual Congressional debates over MFN.

The policy of constructive engagement is to suspend the first pillar of America's national sense of mission—freedom—on the debatable grounds that the marketplace will bring about desired changes in China better than any government policy. Such a laissez-faire approach to human rights makes a virtue out of short-term economic interests. This marginalizes human rights critics who correctly view such an approach as self-serving and dangerously ignores the role the American government can play in promoting human rights. Richard Gephardt, the House Democratic leader, has eloquently argued that "America must stand for more than money," yet has been defeated time and time again when the contentious issue of MFN comes to a vote in Congress.[32] The same argument was again defeated by the ratification of the treaty approving China's entry into the WTO. "Constructive engagement" has been rightly criticized for assuming that economic liberalization will automatically result in the desired political changes essential for respecting universal human rights. Nevertheless, there clearly are some legitimate concerns and perspectives from both sides that in the end make it difficult for consensus to be achieved in policy-making circles over the correct response to human rights abuses.[33]

The point here in the debate over constructive engagement and its optimistic assumption of the effects of economic liberalization is that the latter really pertains only to the civil and political rights of individuals. There is evidence that economic liberalization does indeed bring about broad political reform that improves the civil and political rights of citizens. A number of countries provide examples of this: South Korea, Taiwan, and Russia. However, when it comes to the treatment of ethnic or religious minorities, there is less evidence that economic liberalization and political reform have the desired effect. The treatment of Kurds in Turkey and Kashmiri Muslims in India suggests that political reform and improved civil and political rights for individual citizens do not translate into the recognition of the rights of minorities within a state, or the end of repression against minorities suspected of secessionism. Though democracies may lead to an appreciable improvement in the civil and political rights of individuals, they, in many cases, do little to improve the rights of minorities. This is especially a problem with newly established democracies, as pointed out by Fareed Zakaria:

Mature liberal democracies can usually accommodate ethnic divisions without violence or terror and live in peace with other liberal democracies. But without a background in constitutional liberalism, the introduction of democracy in divided societies has actually fomented nationalism, ethnic conflict, and even war. The spate of elections held immediately after the collapse of communism were won in the Soviet Union and Yugoslavia by nationalist parties and resulted in the breakup of those countries. . . . Elections require that politicians compete for peoples' votes. In societies without strong traditions of multiethnic groups or assimilation, it is easiest to organize support along racial, ethnic, or religious lines. Once an ethnic group is in power, it tends to exclude other ethnic groups.[34]

China does not have a tradition of constitutional liberalism. When, and if, it does undergo a democratization process, it cannot be expected that the rights of minorities such as Tibetans will figure prominently in the minds of pro-democracy forces. The latter are likely to embrace nationalist policies seeking the aggrandizement of Chinese power and prestige. In the case of China, therefore, a clear distinction needs to be drawn between recognizing the civil and political rights of Chinese citizens, and recognizing the minority rights of Tibetans. Economic liberalization may well, in a few decades time, bring about the desired political changes and democratization to improve the former, but is more than likely not to bring about the improvement of the latter. A policy of constructive engagement with China may in the end improve the life of Chinese dissidents, workers, and peasants but may do little to improve the rights of Tibetans and other oppressed minority groups. A more vigorous policy that involves punitive measures as a consequence of not recognizing the rights of minorities such as Tibetans in China, and more generally minorities "at risk" in other countries, is what ought to guide America's foreign policy. The granting of full trading rights to China by Congress in 2000 does not end the moral and political debate over how best to respond to China's atrocious human rights record.

A comprehensive study conducted by Ted Robert Gurr at the University of Maryland's Center for International Development and Conflict Management points out the number of minorities at risk in the international system:

In 1990 more than one-sixth of the global population (17.3 percent, 915 million people) belonged to the 233 groups identified in the Minorities at Risk study. These are groups whose members either have experienced systematic discrimination or have taken political action to assert their collective interests against the states that claim to govern them. Not all people in each group agree about their common identities and interests; most minorities are divided by cross-cutting loyalties to different clans, localities, classes, or political movements. . . . Shared adversity and conflict with dominant groups almost invariably sharpen the sense of common interest and build support for political action.[35]

In an update using figures for 1998, Gurr had increased this to 275 minorities at risk in 116 states, and just over 1 billion people.[36] Over 1 billion people are exposed to state violence because of political, economic, or cultural grievances they have with the central government. Many basic freedoms recognized in the 1992 U.N. General Assembly's Declaration of the Rights of Persons Belonging to National or Ethnic, Religious or Linguistic Minorities are denied these minorities. This makes the plight of many ethnic minorities a focus for America's role in promoting freedom in the post–Cold War world.

The economic cost to America for supporting a firmer human rights stance in the case of China cannot be discounted. Estimates go as high as billions of dollars worth of contracts and hundreds of thousands of American jobs.[37] Bill Clinton, for example, argued in June 1998 that over 170,000 American jobs would be at risk if trade with China came to an end.[38] Such estimates often exaggerate the effect of possible retaliatory measures by the Chinese government. A trade war would seriously damage China's ambitious modernization program—an absolute imperative for China becoming an advanced industrial state in the twenty-first century. Put simply, China desperately needs access to America's vast market in order to fund its modernization program. The current trade deficit with China is being used by the Chinese government to develop China into superpower status by the middle of the twenty-first century.[39] On the other hand, the cost for America of a trade war with China would be felt, but would not be nearly as serious for the American economy as it would for the Chinese.

Despite the final costs of government policies that restricted trade with China on the basis of human rights, the cost would pale into insignificance when compared to the cost involved in containing the Soviet Union throughout the Cold War. President Kennedy was well aware of the cost of opposing the Soviet Union in calling for America to "pay any price" in defending liberty. America needs to commit itself as firmly to the cause of protecting the rights of minorities as it did to containing the Soviet threat to individual liberty. In the absence of a major geopolitical threat to America and its Western allies, America can afford to pay the price in strongly supporting human rights for minorities at risk not only in China, but also for other countries that oppress ethnic minorities. Recognition and protection of minority rights is a policy consistent with America's national sense of mission. Despite the economic costs of such a policy, it is important for America's seventh hero's journey that it pursues its historic mission in a way that is both consistent and comprehensive rather than selective and ad hoc as is presently the case.

This takes me to the second pillar of America's historic national mission, which corresponds to the nature of political governance. Establishing representative political institutions throughout the globe has long been a staple of American foreign policy. It was what underscored Woodrow Wilson's Fourteen Points and his New World Order. Democratization has become such an established feature of the international system in the post–Cold War era that one of Boutros Boutros-Ghali's last acts as U.N. Secretary General was to inaugurate a program for democratization that is indistinguishable from Wilson's view of the role democracy plays in establishing peace among states and freedom for their national citizens.[40] A key component of Wilson's Fourteen Points was the emphasis on a global institution that assume many of the responsibilities entailed in global governance.

Global governance is based on the idea that multilateral intergovernmental organizations such as the United Nations ought to take increasingly upon themselves a host of functions essential for establishing international peace and security. These range from crisis management to alleviating global poverty and underdevelopment. The United Nations as the premier global representative body for global governance has insufficient support from major states. America, as of May 1998, continues to be the largest debtor to the United Nations, making it difficult for the United Nations to fulfill many functions entailed by its mandate.

The important role of the United Nations in establishing international peace is nowhere better illustrated than in the role it can play in intervening in violent internal conflicts. It has been widely recognized that the character of international conflict has changed to the extent that one author claims that the Iraq-Kuwait war may well be the last of the classical interstate aggressions.[41] Violent internal conflicts involving the disintegration of states in cases such as Somalia and Albania, or where the challenge of the state by minorities in cases such as Sri Lanka and the Sudan, are the dominant source of international conflict. Of the twenty-six major armed conflicts occurring in late 1999, all were internal, although some involved external support for some of the protagonists.

America's experience in Somalia led to President Clinton issuing Presidential Decision Directive 25, which listed a number of conditions for American intervention in violent internal conflicts. These conditions include the following:

The possibilities of advancing U.S. and international community interests; the existence of a threat to international peace and security; clear objectives; the means to accomplish the mission; consideration of the consequences of inaction; realistic criteria for ending the operation; and, in the case of a traditional peacekeeping operation, the consent of the parties to the conflict and a cease-fire.[42]

An important further decision was the refusal to support the creation of a rapid reaction force under the direct command of the U.N. Secretariat. This combination of restrictive conditions on possible American intervention with refusal to support a U.N. rapid reaction force will lead to future ethnic conflicts in which international intervention is delayed or nonexistent. This makes it possible for future Rwandas to occur where ethnic conflict spirals into genocidal campaigns that have few limits. In the case of Rwanda nearly 800,000 people lost their lives in an ethnic bloodlust in just over six weeks in April–May 1994 that only ended with the government being driven from power by a rebel movement comprising the ethnic minority Tutsi tribe. It has been argued that a U.N.

military corps of five to fifteen thousand experienced, battle-hardened troops could be deployed by the Security Council into crisis situations without member states anguishing over casualties in their national contingents. Obviously, such a small force could do only so much, but a highly trained and well-equipped one could prove more than a match for many of the ragtag militias and free-lance killers who often spearhead the worst excesses of ethnic violence.[43]

America must support the United Nations in fulfilling its mandate because, despite its limitations, it is the most representative international body for global humanity and is an important part of the yet evolving concept of "global democracy." Supporting the United Nations requires ultimately giving it an independent source of revenue such as taxing international flights, and a simultaneous effort to democratize the United Nations further by making the Security Council more representative.[44] Strengthening the United Nations would require America overcoming the traditional reluctance of states to transfer power to multilateral organizations that involve less state control and sovereignty. As David Callahan points out: "It is, however, a basic fact of life that delegating power of any kind means losing control. A central adjustment in post-cold war foreign policy must be for the United States to accept new limitations on its influence over the management of international problems."[45]

If America does not take the lead in transferring power to the United Nations, other states will be unlikely to act to empower the one representative political institution that enjoys greater legitimacy than any other institution or state in dealing with global problems. A key part of America's hero journey is to fulfil Wilson's vision of empowering representative political institutions at the global level, which today means the United Nations. President Kennedy was well aware of this at his inaugural address when he said:

To that world assembly of sovereign states, the United Nations, our last best hope in an age where the instruments of war have far outpaced the instruments of peace, we renew our pledge of support—to prevent it from becoming merely a forum for invective—to strengthen its shield of the new and the weak—and **to enlarge the area in which its writ may run** [emphasis added].[46]

Despite the undoubted need to strengthen the United Nations, there still may be occasions in which lack of consensus among the five permanent members makes the U.N. Security Council ineffectual. This was vividly demonstrated by the Kosovo crisis in 1998–1999 when Russia's refusal to sanction force to put an end to ethnic cleansing in Kosovo made the Security Council ineffective in adequately dealing with the crisis. Worried that Security Council action against the will of a sovereign state would set an international precedent that could in the future threaten Russian interests, Russia prevented U.N.-authorized military action knowing full well that this would pave the way for NATO to step in to deal with the crisis. Even though the mandate of NATO is less representative of global public opinion, NATO nevertheless carries great legitimacy due to it being a multilateral organization comprising nineteen advanced industrial states that operate on consensus in authorizing military actions. In the Kosovo crisis, NATO demonstrated its capacity for determined military action to deal with an internal conflict in the absence of U.N.-authorized Security Council action.

It is imperative for America's seventh hero's journey that its foreign policy attempts to follow Kennedy's pledge to "enlarge the area in which its [the United Nations] writ may run." This pledge means adopting a clear global interest that transcends limited definitions of what constitutes America's national interest. In the absence of effective U.N. action, multilateral organizations such as NATO should fill a breach created by U.N. Security Council inaction due to a permanent member's veto. Again, NATO action will be based on meeting what is clearly in the global interest. Part of America's mission is to see its national interest anchored firmly in the global interest defined in terms of the three pillars of America's mission: liberty, democracy, and rule of law. This is what constitutes the archetypal experience of atonement that is at the apex of America's hero's journey—making possible in the global arena the New Order of the Ages at the heart of America's national sense of mission. The authors of *Spiritual Politics* make a similar point:

Nations are not going to disappear in the near future. But they can become the building blocks of a true new world order, if we learn how to invoke their Souls and a greater Soul consciousness within their populations. Citizens will have to demand that their countries start realizing that the survival of our planet depends on nations considering their own interest within the context of larger planetary needs.[47]

With the dawn of a new millennium, America stands at a great historical juncture in terms of the fundamental principles upon which it bases its foreign policy. It is imperative that the United States maintains the grand synthesis of power and morality in its seventh hero's journey in order to exert a beneficial impact on global politics. America needs to renew the archetypal encounters that make up its "great remembering." As Marianne Williamson insightfully points out:

The fundamental ideals of American society are just that—ideals. They are transcendent archetypes that stand over and above the material realities of life. . . . We must test our first principles, understand them, and hopefully come to love them. They must remain alive in us if they are to remain alive in the world.[48]

In 1936 President Franklin Roosevelt made a comment that is equally relevant today: "To some generations much is given. From some generations, much is expected. This generation has a rendezvous with destiny."[49] As we begin a new millennium, there is much to expect from this generation of Americans.

NOTES

1. Ted Robert Gurr, *Peoples versus States: Minorities at Risk in the New Century* (Washington, D.C.: U.S. Institute of Peace, 2000), 11.

2. The right of self-determination is recognized in the U.N. Charter and in the first articles of the International Covenant on Civil and Political Rights, and in the International Covenant on Economic, Social, and Cultural Rights.

3. Corrine McLaughlin and Gordon Davidson, *Spiritual Politics: Changing the World from the Inside Out* (New York: Ballantine Books, 1994), 282.

4. Louis D. Brandeis, "True Americanism," in *Immigration and Americanization: Selected Readings*, ed. Philip Davis (Boston: Ginn and Company, 1920), 639–40.

5. Arthur Schlesinger, Jr., *The Disuniting of America: Reflections on a Multicultural Society* (New York: Norton and Co., 1992), 28.

6. Ibid., 17–18.

7. Adeno Addis, "On Human Diversity and the Limits of Toleration," in *Ethnicity and Group Rights*, ed. Ian Shapiro and Will Kymlicka (New York: New York University Press, 1997), 126.

8. Sri Aurobindo, *The Human Cycle, The Ideal of Human Unity, War and Self-Determination* (Pondicherry, India: Sri Aurobindo Ashram Trust, 1977), 402–3.

9. John Kane, "From Ethnic Exclusion to Ethnic Diversity," in *Ethnicity and Group Rights*, ed. Ian Shapiro and Will Kymlicka (New York: New York University Press, 1997), 541–42.

10. Ibid., 550.

11. Andrew Parkin, John Summers, and Dennis Woodward, *Government, Politics, Power and Policy in Australia*, 5th ed. (Melbourne: Longman, 1995), 244.

12. See Kane, "From Ethnic Exclusion to Ethnic Diversity," 561.

13. John Miller, *The Unmaking of Americans: How Multiculturalism Has Undermined the Assimilation Ethic* (New York: The Free Press, 1998), viii–ix.

14. Marianne Williamson, *The Healing of America* (New York: Simon and Schuster, 1997), 72.

15. Ibid., 200.

16. Cited in Williamson, *The Healing of America*, 82–83.

17. Tamala Edwards, "Disaster on the Potomac: How Not to Run a City," *Time* 150, 7 (08/18/97): 22.

18. Ibid.

19. John Gabriel Hunt, ed., *The Inaugural Addresses of the Presidents* (New York: Random House, 1997), 429.

20. Miller, *The Unmaking of Americans*, 240–41.

21. Williamson, *The Healing of America*, 204.

22. Jerome Agel, *Words That Make America Great* (New York: Random House, 1997), 336–37.

23. Figures from Williamson, *The Healing of America*, 196.

24. Hunt, *The Inaugural Addresses of the Presidents*, 32.

25. McLaughlin and Davidson, *Spiritual Politics*, 296.

26. Williamson, *The Healing of America*, 48–49.

27. Henry Steiner and Richard Alston, *International Human Rights in Context: Law, Politics, Morals* (Oxford: Clarendon Press, 1996), 849.

28. David Lampton, "China," *Foreign Policy* 110 (Spring 1998): 21.

29. Quoted in Steiner and Alston, *International Human Rights in Context*, 855.

30. "Clinton Proposes Renewing China's Most-Favored Trade Status," June 3, 1998, CNN Allpolitics. Http://allpolitics.com/1998/06/03/china.trade."

31. Jack Donnelly, *International Human Rights*, 2nd ed. (Boulder, Colo.: Westview Press, 1998), 128.

32. "Clinton Proposes Renewing China's Most-Favored Trade Status."

33. Donnelly, *International Human Rights*, 129.

34. Fareed Zakaria, "The Rise of Illiberal Democracy," *Foreign Affairs* 76 (1997): 35.

35. Ted Robert Gurr, *Minorities at Risk* (Washington, D.C.: U.S. Institute of Peace, 1995), 315.

36. Gurr, *Peoples versus States*, 11.

37. Steiner and Alston, *International Human Rights in Context*, 854–56.

38. "Clinton Proposes Renewing China's Most-Favored Trade Status."

39. For criticism of such a view, see Lampton, "China," 13–16.

40. Boutros Boutros-Ghali, *An Agenda for Democratization* (New York: U.N. Publications, 1996).

41. Kalevi Holsti, *The State, War and the State of War* (Cambridge: Cambridge University Press, 1996).

42. Adam Roberts, "The Crisis in UN Peacekeeping," *Managing Global Chaos: Sources of and Responses to International Conflict*, ed. Chester Crocker and Fen Hampson (Washington, D.C.: U.S. Institute of Peace, 1996), 310.

43. David Callahan, *Unwinnable Wars: American Power and Ethnic Conflict* (New York: Hill and Wang, 1998), 206.

44. For discussion of these and other needed U.N. reforms, see Gareth Evans, *Cooperating for Peace* (Sydney: Allen and Unwin, 1993), 169–81.

45. Callahan, *Unwinnable Wars*, 205.

46. Hunt, *Inaugural Addresses of the Presidents*, 429.

47. McLaughlin and Gordon, *Spiritual Politics*, 285.

48. Quoted in Williamson, *The Healing of America*, 65–66.

49. Ibid., 29–30.

Conclusion—America's Seventh Hero's Journey and the Second American Century

The "hero's journey" is a process of self-discovery for both individuals and political communities. The four steps of the hero's journey—call to adventure, great remembering, return to (international) society, and deep forgetting—form a cyclic process that individuals and political communities undergo in the self-discovery process. America exemplifies how states have the necessary degree of self-consciousness and moral awareness to travel the hero's journey and undergo archetypal encounters similar to the experience of individuals. Analysis of American history and its political traditions reveals a very clear perception of a political community that has achieved some degree of self-consciousness of its national mission. Understanding America as fundamentally engaged in a hero's journey is enormously important for clarifying the policy directions it ought to take in meeting domestic and international challenges in the twenty-first century. The hero's journey represents not so much a morally desirable policy direction but a moral policy imperative. The hero's journey emerges with profound intensity and with increased national consciousness of what makes America distinct, and how it should best use its immense political, military, and economic resources. Individuals seek to achieve self-actualization not because it is a desirable moral norm but because it satisfies unconscious needs that are imperative for individual health. Similarly, America must more seriously engage with the responsibilities of its national mission because it is vital for the health and integrity of America.

Understanding American politics in terms of cycles as I have suggested is not a new idea. As explained earlier, Arthur Schlesinger, Jr., believed that

America moved in generational thirty-year cycles between periods of private interest and public purpose. In the foreign policy sphere, this amounted to cycles of withdrawal and return that correspond to two of the four steps of the hero's journey: call to adventure and return to international society.[1] A similar cyclic theory for American foreign policy that swung between "extroversion" and "introversion" was proposed by Frank Klingberg.[2] A more impressive study of the cyclic nature of American history and foreign policy was described by William Strauss and Neil Howe.[3] All these cycle theories reveal that American politics does undergo periodic fluctuations similar to what I have described for America's hero's journey. The main limitation of Schlesinger's and Klingberg's cycle theories of introversion and extroversion is that little idea is gained of the forces and processes that lead to these conflicting swings other than that of generational change. Similarly, Strauss and Howe based their theory on generational change rather than on an implicit failure of a set of societal norms to deal with domestic and international crises. The two additional steps in the hero's cycle to the introversion and extroversion mentioned by Klingberg—great remembering and the deep forgetting—give an idea of the forces and processes that foreshadow that a new national epoch is underway. The swing in periods from "return to international society" to "call to adventure" is sparked by a deep forgetting in which Americans become focused on gross material values and individual needs due to economic uncertainty and hardship. Similarly, the swing from "call to adventure" to "return to international society" is made possible by a great remembering in which America undergoes, once more, the archetypal encounters.

Another limitation of the cyclic swings pointed out by Schlesinger, and Klingsberg, Strauss and Howe is that they are historically deterministic. It suggests that we need to wait for generational change for new policy directions and emphases to come about. Though cyclic changes in domestic and foreign policy may sometimes correspond to generational changes, generational change is not the basis by which America enters new phases of a cycle—rather, implicit moral principles undergird cyclic changes. Therefore, the hero's cycle can be **indefinitely** maintained in its most beneficial step—return to international society—by maintaining a supportive public mood. Maintaining such a supportive public mood means that individuals and political communities have to constantly renew the three archetypal encounters—slaying the dragon, the sacred marriage, and atonement—described in this book.

In the case of America, the hero's journey as a perennial cycle of national self-discovery helps understand the domestic and foreign policy aspects of American history in terms of unfolding archetypal encounters. The hero's journey helps identify the nuances and directions in American policymaking in terms of America playing a transformative role in the global arena. This transformative role is graphically depicted on America's Great

Seal, showing the Founding Fathers' deepest and most profound global vision of America as the harbinger of a "new order of the ages." Similarly, other states are undergoing their own hero's journey, but what makes America's distinctive is its superpower status in the political, economic, military, and cultural spheres. As we stand on the dawn of the "second American century," America needs to maintain the grand synthesis of power and morality in its seventh hero's journey. Its latest journey represents the culmination of a long historical process in which America has moved gradually closer toward a realization of the global vision of its Founding Fathers. The principles at the heart of the seventh journey thereby represent the culmination of this gradual historical process. The seven hero's journeys of America represent a historical spiral moving upward toward the Founding Fathers' global vision. America must therefore be ready to take up the burden and cost of its seventh hero's journey.

The tendency for the general public and policymakers alike to support the hero's journey undertaken by America is based on the implicit knowledge that they as individuals are also unconsciously engaged in a hero's journey. Therefore a close connection exists between the individual and the nation, between the micro and macro, that influences policy-making at all levels of human interaction. The psychologists David Feinstein and Stanley Krippner make a similar point:

Ideally, political leaders should be those who have undergone a substantial exploration of their own unconscious motivations and have reached an advanced level of emotional maturity. . . . The real problem is to raise the consciousness of the general public so that it is capable of recognizing public figures whose policies mask their own inner conflicts. Policy makers could be educated to find both sides of an ideological conflict within themselves. Even if the process did not change their ideology, it would increase the likelihood of empathy and respect for opponent's position, thus enhancing their capacity for creative collaboration.[4]

The hero's journey alerts us to the powerful unconscious processes that drive foreign policy makers in their "rational" deliberations. The journey describes how an individual moves from a fragmented sense of identity whose psychic powers and energies are dissipated in conflicting desires and actions, to an integrated identity where one's psychic powers and energies become focused. This enables individuals to transform their personal and social environments. In a similar way, states can move from being fragmented entities comprising political communities that conflict with one another, to integrated states where national energies can be focused to transform the national and international environment. This is not a linear process, however, because states, like individuals, can undergo a deep forgetting that results in a state's refusal to recognize and pursue its national mission or life calling.

We all want and need to be heroes because each individual experiences a sense of fragmentation and psychological conflict that leads to a desire to integrate, empower, and find purpose in one's life. States, too, as fragmented political communities experiencing conflict that weakens national capacity and resolve, need similarly to integrate, empower the nation, and discover a sense of national mission. States, then, need to embark on a hero's journey. The hero's journey as an encounter with archetypes of the collective unconscious is an important psychoanalytical insight whose relevance for states, and world politics more generally, needs to be better understood.

The second American century promises to be one in which America once again casts a decisive influence on how people around the world conduct their political, economic, and cultural lives. This places an important responsibility on America to use its influence and leadership in a benevolent way in responding to international conflicts. The most likely source of future international conflict will be internal or ethnic conflicts involving the 275 ethnic and religious minorities that Ted Gurr identified in his study on minorities at risk.[5] The goals of these minorities in their struggles against central governments will range from greater recognition of cultural and social rights to outright campaigns for political independence. Lacking resources, legitimacy, and the political institutions to adequately respond to such goals, many governments will resort to the time honored mix of political bribery and military repression to deal with the goals of such minorities. The predictable failure of such an approach usually drives ethnic and religious minorities into adopting more radical and violent ways of achieving their goals. This in turn increases governmental efforts at repressing such minorities through armed force, thereby leading to a vicious spiral of armed conflict. The potential for massive human rights violations and humanitarian crises will therefore cast an imposing shadow over the minds of policymakers well into the twenty-first century. The information revolution has led to a symbolic shrinking of the planet so that the suffering of ethnic and religious minorities can no longer be ignored. Policymakers will need to respond to the demands of their own populations who see the plight of such minorities on their television screens or read about them on their electronic news services.

Responding to ethnic conflicts involves a number of policy options. Sometimes quiet diplomacy will be sufficient in getting governments to end repressive policies in secessionist territories. The idea is that economic growth and integration into the global marketplace leads to gradual changes in many countries when more liberal leaders eventually come into power. The thinking then is that these liberal leaders will be more responsive to human rights criticism from around the globe and will attempt to deal with the problem through political, rather than military, means. The policy of quiet diplomacy has been remarkably vindicated in the recent case of Indonesia and East Timor, where the Indonesian government under the reformist leaderships of Presidents Habibie and Wahid responded to the quiet diplomacy of Australia and America in settling the East Timor problem. However, for more than twenty years, President Suharto refused to make concessions in response to Western diplomatic pressure and human rights. The lesson is that while quiet diplomacy can work with reformist oriented leaders, it may fail dismally with authoritarian rulers. Quiet diplomacy has been conducted by America in a range of other ethnic conflicts—China/Tibet, India/Kashmir, and Turkey/Kurdistan—all with little progress in settling the chronic problems faced by ethnic and religious minorities in their struggles against central governments. Simply waiting for economic growth and global integration to produce more liberal political leaders who respond positively to human rights criticism is more often a recipe for inaction in the face of massive repression by states. While "quiet diplomacy" cannot and should not be dismissed, it more than often falls far short of what is needed to end an ethnic conflict.

A more radical and controversial policy option is to impose economic sanctions on countries repressing ethnic and religious minorities. This policy raises enormous controversy because this challenges some of the central tenets of quiet diplomacy. Rather than encourage more liberal leaders to rise in the decision-making process in the hope they will deal with the conflict in a more humane and enlightened way, economic sanctions may produce the reverse phenomenon. Sanctions could lead to liberals being purged from the government and the rise of hard-liners who advocate more aggressive policies in dealing with ethnic/religious minorities and responding to international criticism. This suggests that sanctions need to be carefully considered in terms of the political context and processes underway in any country. Nevertheless, it would be a mistake to dismiss economic sanctions as counterproductive, because they can be instrumental in breaking the will of more obdurate political leaders. With the difficulties faced by many developing countries in dealing with the challenges presented by the global market, economic sanctions may be simply devastating for the country's modernization efforts. This is especially the case in the military sector where the different sectors of the armed forces are all too aware of the need to modernize their weaponry and the financial cost in doing so. Sanctions can therefore speed up desired changes with the discrediting of the older generation of political leaders and the promotion of more liberal thinkers capable of making the necessary concessions to settle ethnic/religious conflicts.

The final policy option is that of military intervention in humanitarian crises. The massive scale of death and destruction in ethnic conflicts in which governments are determined to find a quick military solution to a conflict with an ethnic or religious minority raises a moral imperative. Delay typically results in the unnecessary deaths of civilians who are trying to escape the conflict. The political and financial costs of America assuming a responsibility in ending such crises should not be underestimated. Sometimes America will need to assume the leadership role in humanitarian intervention such as in the cases of Bosnia and Kosovo. At other times it can play a supportive role as it did in the Australian-led intervention in East Timor. The benefits of humanitarian intervention are often very easy to see in terms of the relief and gratitude of ethnic minorities who shelter behind heavily armed peacekeepers. The disadvantages, however, are also easy to see in terms of the material destruction and death of security forces on both sides of the conflict who are conducting official government policies. Domestically, the massive use of military force to stop ethnic slaughter appears contradictory to many who advocate more peaceful ways of ending the conflict. Though laudable, such sentiment is often misplaced and ignores the political realities faced by minorities at risk who face governments and security forces often opposed to making even the most minor concessions to end the conflict. Often governments using repression have their hard-liners firmly committed to the belief that a military solution can be achieved for the conflict. The credible threat of American military intervention is unfortunately sometimes necessary to deter governments from pursuing a military solution to an ethnic conflict.

Maintaining America's seventh grand synthesis far into the twenty-first century depends on how well political leaders can respond to the national mood to intervene adequately in ethnic conflicts. A host of domestic and international factors can significantly impact on the national mood presently behind support for American leadership in responding to ethnic conflicts. Domestically, a robust national economy will be important in responding to domestic concerns over the costs of maintaining the military preparedness to intervene in ethnic conflicts. More importantly, issues concerning minority rights, racial reconciliation, poverty relief, and unemployment can all impact on the national mood. Arguments calling for American intervention in far-off places to prevent ethnic genocide and slaughter ring hollow to those Americans suffering from inadequate health, education, employment, and social services.

At the international level, the single most important factor in maintaining public support for America's seventh grand synthesis will be to promote multilateralism in pressuring governments to recognize the rights of their ethnic/religious minorities. Multilateralism is critical for the success of either quiet diplomacy, economic sanctions, or humanitarian interventions in ending ethnic conflicts. The most desirable multilateral forum is the United Nations. In the case of humanitarian intervention, however, NATO needs to be maintained as a suitable alternative due to the real possibility of a veto of U.N. action by Russia and/or China. Similarly, regional bodies such as the Organization of American States or the Organization of African Unity will be desirable fora for the success of quiet diplomacy, initiating multilateral economic sanctions or launching humanitarian interventions. Failure to promote multilateral cooperation in responding to ethnic conflicts may quickly lead to a shift in the national mood against economic or military intervention in such conflicts. This would mark the transition of America into a new deep forgetting with potentially devastating results for the 268 minorities at risk around the planet.

The hero's journey is essentially a means of discovering the political will to put into effect the moral vision that goes to the heart of national identity. The three moral principles that make up the Founding Fathers' vision of America and of a New World Order are liberty, democracy, and rule of law. Extending these principles into the international arena was the implicit faith and hope of America's Founding Fathers who had a broader vision than merely legitimizing the victory of colonial rebels against the mighty British Empire. Each of America's seven grand syntheses reflects the political will of policymakers to put into effect principles based on these three core moral principles. Maintaining America's seventh grand synthesis will only be possible if policymakers apply this broad global vision in responding to ethnic conflicts and the dangers posed by minorities at risk from their own governments. There are ample international resources to both prevent and react appropriately to ethnic conflicts. What is necessary for using these resources is the political will to intervene in the domestic affairs of sovereign states that ruthlessly pursue military solutions in disputes with their ethnic minorities. If policymakers continue to find the political will to put into effect America's moral vision, the beneficial effects of America's seventh hero's journey can be extended far into the Second American Century.

NOTES

1. Arthur Schlesinger, Jr., *The Cycles of American History* (Boston: Houghton Mifflin, 1986), 51.

2. Ibid., 43.

3. William Strauss and Neil Howe, *The Fourth Turning: An American Prophecy: What the Cycles of History Tell Us about America's Next Rendezvous with Destiny* (New York: Broadway Books, 1997).

4. David Feinstein and Stanley Krippner, "Bringing a Mythological Perspective to Social Change," *ReVision* 11, no 1.

5. Ted Robert Gurr, *Peoples versus States: Minorities at Risk in the New Century* (Washington, D.C.: U.S. Institute of Peace, 2000), 11.

SELECTED BIBLIOGRAPHY

Abrams, Jeremiah. "Shadow and Culture." In *The Shadow in America: Reclaiming the Soul of a Nation*, edited by Jeremiah Abrams. Los Angeles: Nataraj, 1994.

Addis, Adeno. "On Human Diversity and the Limits of Toleration." In *Ethnicity and Group Rights*, edited by Ian Shapiro and Will Kymlicka. New York: New York University Press, 1997.

Agel, Jerome. *Words That Make America Great*. New York: Random House, 1997.

Aligheri, Dante. *Monarchy*. Cambridge: Cambridge University Press, 1996.

Anderson, Benedict. *Imagined Communities*. London: Verso, 1991.

Arnold, Sir Edwin. *The Light of Asia*. Wheaton, Ill.: The Theosophical Publishing House, 1969.

Bailey, Thomas. *A Diplomatic History of the American People*. 8th ed. New York: Appleton-Century-Crofts, 1969.

Barber, Benjamin. *Jihad vs. McWorld: How Globalism and Tribalism Are Reshaping the World*. New York: Ballantine Books, 1996.

Bennigsen, Alexandre, and Marie Broxup. *The Islamic Threat to the Soviet State*. London: Croom Helm, 1983.

Beveridge, Albert. "The Star of Empire." In *Selected American Speeches on Basic Issues, 1850–1950*, edited by Carl G. Brandt and Edward M. Shafter, Jr. Boston: Houghton Mifflin, 1960.

Bierlein, J. F. *Parallel Myths*. New York: Ballantine Books, 1994.

Bolen, Jean. *Gods in Everyman: A New Psychology of Men's Lives and Loves*. San Francisco: Harper and Row, 1989.

Borah, William. "Against the League of Nations." In *Selected American Speeches on Basic Issues, 1850–1950*, edited by Carl G. Brandt and Edward M. Shafter, Jr. Boston: Houghton Mifflin, 1960.

Boutros-Ghali, Boutros. *An Agenda for Democratization*. New York: U.N. Publications, 1996.

Brandeis, Louis D. "True Americanism." In *Immigration and Americanization: Selected Readings*, edited by Philip Davis. Boston: Ginn and Company, 1920.

Bryan, William Jennings. "Noboth's Vineyard." In *Great American Speeches 1898–1963*, ed. John Graham. New York: Appleton-Century-Crofts, 1970.

Brzezinski, Zbigniew. "The Cold War and Its Aftermath." *Foreign Affairs* 71 (1992): 45–46.

Bull, Hedley. *The Anarchical Society: A Study of Order in World Politics*. London: Macmillan, 1977.

Burner, David, Virginia Bernhard, and Stanley Kutler. *Firsthand America: A History of the United States*, 4th ed. St. James, N.Y.: Brandywine Press, 1996.

Bush, George. "America—The Last Best Hope for Man on Earth: A World in Which the Rule of Law Prevails." *Vital Speeches of the Day* 59 (1993): 194–95.

———. "The U.N.: World Parliament of Peace." Address to the U.N. General Assembly, New York, October 1, 1990 in *Dispatch* vol. 1, no. 6.

Bush, Robert, and Joseph Folger. *The Promise of Mediation: Responding to Conflict through Empowerment and Recognition*. San Francisco: Jossey Bass Publishers, 1994.

Callahan, David. *Unwinnable Wars: American Power and Ethnic Conflict*. New York: Hill and Wang, 1998.

Calvocoressi, Peter. *World Politics since 1945*, 4th ed. London: Longman, 1982.

Campbell, David. *Writing Security: United States Foreign Policy and the Politics of Identity*. Minneapolis: University of Minnesota Press, 1992.

Campbell, Joseph. *Creative Mythology*. New York: The Viking Press, 1968.

———. *The Hero with a Thousand Faces*. 2nd edition. Princeton, N.J.: Princeton University Press, 1968.

———. *Myths to Live By*. New York: Bantam Books, 1988.

———. *Myth and Reality*. New York: Harper and Row, 1963.

Campbell, Joseph, and Bill Moyers. *The Power of Myth*. New York: Doubleday, 1988.

"Clinton Proposes Renewing China's Most-Favored Trade Status." June 3, 1998, CNN Allpolitics. Http://allpolitics.com/1998/06/03/china.trade.

Clinton, Bill. "Confronting the Challenges of a Broader World." Address to the U.N. General Assembly, New York, September 27, 1993 in *Dispatch* vol. 4, no. 39. Washington, D.C.: U.S. Department of State, 1993.

Daalder, Ivo, and Michael O'Hanlon. "Unlearning the Lessons of Kosovo." *Foreign Policy*, Fall 1999.

Dante. *The Divine Comedy*, English ed., trans. Henry Wadsworth Longfellow. http://www.divinecomedy.org/divine_comedy.html

Donnelly, Jack. *International Human Rights*, 2nd ed. Boulder, Colo.: Westview Press, 1998.

Dozier, Rush. *Fear Itself: The Origin and Nature of the Powerful Emotion That Shapes Our Lives and Our World*. New York: St. Martin's Press, 1998.

Dulles, Foster Rhea. *Prelude to World Power: American Diplomatic History, 1860–1900*. New York, 1965.

Edwards, Tamala. "Disaster on the Potomac: How Not to Run a City." *Time* (18, August 1997): 22.

Erikson, Erik. *Life, History and the Historical Moment*. New York: W.W. Norton and Co., 1975.

Evans, Gareth. *Cooperating for Peace*. Sydney: Allen and Unwin, 1993.

Farley, Lawrence T. *Plebiscites and Sovereignty: The Crisis of Political Illegitimacy*. Boulder, Colo.: Westview Press, 1986.

Freud, Sigmund, *The Complete Psychological Works of Sigmund Freud*. Standard Edition, vol. V.

———. "Civilization and its Discontents." *Civilization, Society and Religion, The Pelican Freud Library*. Vol. 12. New York: Penguin Books, 1985.

———. *A General Introduction to Psychoanalysis*. Garden City, N.Y.: Garden City Publishing Co., 1943.

———. "Letter to Albert Einstein: Why War?" *The Pacifist Conscience*, edited by Peter Mayer. London: Penguin Books, 1966.

———. "The Psychical Apparatus and the Theory of Instincts." *An Outline of Psycho-Analysis*. Standard ed. Vol. 23. New York: W.W. Norton, 1949.

Fromm, Erich. *The Anatomy of Human Destructiveness*. New York: Holt, Rinehart and Winston, 1973.

Fukuyama, Francis. "The End of History?: The New Shape of World Politics: Contending Paradigms in International Relations." *Foreign Affairs* (1997): 1–25; originally published in *National Interest* (Summer 1989): 3–16.

George, Alexander, and Juliette George. *Woodrow Wilson and Colonel House: A Personality Study*. New York: Dover Publications, 1964.

Gilligan, Carol. *In a Different Voice: Psychological Theory and Women's Development*. Cambridge, Mass.: Harvard University Press, 1982.

Green, T. H. "Society as Positive Freedom." In *The Development of the Democratic Idea*. New York: Washington Square Press, 1968.

Gurian, Michael. *Mothers, Sons & Lovers: How a Man's Relationship with His Mother Affects the Rest of His Life*. London: Shambhala, 1994.

———. *The Prince and the King: Healing the Father-Son Wound*. Los Angeles: Tarcher/Putnam, 1992.

Gurr, Ted Robert. *Minorities at Risk*. Washington, D.C.: U.S. Institute of Peace, 1995.

———. "Minorities, Nationalists, and Ethnopolitical Conflict." In *Managing Global Chaos: Sources of and Responses to International Conflict*, edited by Chester Crocker and Fen Hampson. Washington, D.C.: U.S. Institute of Peace, 1996.

———. *Peoples versus States: Minorities at Risk in the New Century*. Washington, D.C.: U.S. Institute of Peace, 2000.

Hegel, Georg. *Lectures on the Philosophy of World History*. Translated by H. B. Nisbet. Cambridge: Cambridge University Press, 1975.

———. *Reason in History: A General Introduction to the Philosophy of History*. New York: The Bobbs-Merrill Co., 1953.

Holsti, K. J. *International Politics: A Framework for Analysis*, 3rd ed. Englewood Cliffs, N.J.: Prentice Hall, 1977.

Holsti, Kalevi. *The State, War and the State of War*. Cambridge: Cambridge University Press, 1996.

Holy Bible. New International Version. London: Hodder and Stoughton, 1984.

Homer. *The Odyssey.* Translated by E.V. Rieu. New York: Penguin Classics, 1992.

Hunt, John Gabriel, ed. *Inaugural Addresses of the Presidents.* New York: Random House, 1997.

Huntington, Samuel. "The Clash of Civilizations." *Foreign Affairs* (Summer 1993): 22–49.

James, Alan. *Sovereign Statehood: The Basis of International Society.* London: Allen and Unwin, 1986.

Johnson, Paul. *A History of the American People.* New York: HarperCollins, 1997.

Jung, C. G. "Aion: Phenomenology of the Self." In *The Portable Jung.* New York: Viking Press, 1971.

———. "The Concept of the Collective Unconscious." In *The Portable Jung.* New York: Penguin Books, 1976.

———. *Man and His Symbols.* New York: Doubleday, 1964.

Kane, John. "From Ethnic Exclusion to Ethnic Diversity." In *Ethnicity and Group Rights,* edited by Ian Shapiro and Will Kymlicka. New York: New York University Press, 1997.

Kant, Immanuel. *The Critique of Pure Reason.* 1781. Translated by Norman Kemp Smith. London: Macmillan, 1986.

Keen, Sam. *Faces of the Enemy: Reflections of the Hostile Imagination.* San Francisco: Harper and Row, 1991.

Kennedy, Paul. *The Rise and Fall of the Great Powers: Economic Change and Military Conflict from 1500 to 2000.* New York: Vintage Books, 1987.

Keohane, Robert, and Joseph Nye. *Power and Interdependence: World Politics in Transition,* 2nd ed. Glenview, Ill.: Scott, Foresman and Co., 1989.

Kissinger, Henry. *Diplomacy.* New York: Simon and Schuster, 1994.

Klingberg, Frank. *Cyclical Trends in American Foreign Policy Moods: The Unfolding of America's World Role.* New York: University Press of America, 1983.

Laing, R. D. *The Divided Self.* New York: Penguin Books, 1979

Lampton, David. "China." *Foreign Policy* 110 (Spring 1998): 13–28.

Locke, John. *An Essay Concerning Human Understanding,* edited by John Yolton. London: Dent, 1961.

———. "Second Treatise of Civil Government." In *The Development of the Democratic Idea,* edited by Charles M. Sherover. New York: Washington Square Press, 1968.

Marx, Karl. *Selected Writings and Social Philosophy,* edited by T. B. Bottomore and Maximilien Rubel. New York: Penguin, 1984.

Mayer, Peter, ed. "Address to the Congress de la Paix held in Paris, 1851." In *The Pacifist Conscience.* London: Penguin Books, 1966.

McLaughlin, Corinne, and Gordon Davidson. *Spiritual Politics: Changing the World from the Inside Out.* New York: Ballantine Books, 1994.

Merk, Frederick. *Manifest Destiny and Mission in American History.* New York: Knopf, 1963; Westport, CT: Greenwood Press, 1983.

Miller, John. *The Unmaking of Americans: How Multiculturalism Has Undermined the Assimilation Ethic.* New York: The Free Press, 1998.

Morgenthau, Hans. *Politics among Nations,* 5th ed. New York: Knopf, 1978.

Morison, Samuel Eliot. *The Oxford History of the American People.* New York: Oxford University Press, 1965.

Mosse, G. L., ed. *Nazi Culture: Intellectual, Cultural, and Social Life in the Third Reich*. New York: Schocken Books, 1966.

Mueller, John E. *Approaches to Measurement in International Relations*. New York: Appleton-Century-Crofts, 1969.

Niebhur, Reinhold. *Moral Man & Immoral Society*. New York: Charles Scribner's Sons, 1960.

Nimmo, Dan, and James Combs. *Subliminal Politics: Myths and Mythmakers in America*. Englewood Cliffs, NJ: Prentice Hall, 1980.

Otto, Rudolph. *The Idea of the Holy*. Oxford: Oxford University Press, 1923; reprint 1958.

Paine, Thomas. *Common Sense*. Oxford: Oxford University Press, 1995.

Parkin, Andrew, John Summers, and Dennis Woodward. *Government, Politics, Power and Policy in Australia*, 5th ed. Melbourne: Longman, 1995.

Pearson, Carol. *The Hero Within*. New York: Harper and Row, 1989.

Pfaltzgraff, James, and Robert Dougherty. *Contending Theories of International Relations: A Comprehensive Survey*. 4th ed. New York: Longman, 1997.

Plato. "Republic." *Plato: The Collected Dialogues*, edited by Edith Hamilton and Huntington Cairns. Princeton: Princeton University Press, 1982.

Pratt, Julius. *A History of United States Foreign Policy*. Newark, N.J.: Prentice Hall, 1955.

Psychologists for Social Responsibility. *Dismantling the Mask of Enmity: Educational Resource Manual*. Washington, D.C.: Psychoanalysts for Social Responsibility, 1991.

Raknerud, Arvid, and Harvard Hegre. "The Hazard of War: Reassessing the Evidence for the Democratic Peace." *Journal of Peace Research* 34 (1997): 385–404.

Redfield, James. *The Celestine Vision: Living the New Spiritual Awareness*. New York: Warner Books, 1997.

Rieber, Robert. Ed. *The Psychology of War and Peace: The Image of the Enemy*. New York: Plenum, 1991.

Roberts, Adam. "The Crisis in UN Peacekeeping." In *Managing Global Chaos: Sources of and Responses to International Conflict*, edited by Chester Crocker and Fen Hampson. Washington, D.C.: U.S. Institute of Peace, 1996.

Rosenau, James, and Michael Fagan. "A New Dynamism in World Politics." *International Studies Quarterly* 41 (1997): 656–86.

Rosenberg, Marshall. *Nonviolent Communication: A Language of Compassion*. Del Mar, CA: Puddle Dancer Press, 1999.

Salla, Michael E. "Political Islam and the West: A New Cold War or Convergence?" *Third World Quarterly* 18 (1997): 729–43.

Schlesinger, Arthur, Jr. *The Cycles of American History*. Boston: Houghton Mifflin Co., 1986.

———. *The Disuniting of America: Reflections on a Multicultural Society*. New York: Norton and Co., 1992.

Schlesinger, Arthur, Sr. *Paths to the Present*. Boston: Houghton Mifflin Company, 1964.

Schulzinger, Robert. *U.S. Diplomacy since 1900*, 4th ed. Oxford University Press, 1998.

Schurmann, Franz. *American Soul*. San Francisco: Mercury House, 1995.

Segal, Robert. *Joseph Campbell: An Introduction*. Rev. ed. New York: Montor, 1990.

Sharp, Gene. *The Politics of Nonviolent Action*. Boston: Porter Sargent, 1973.

Sharpless, Isaac. "Colonial Pennsylvania: The Quest for Non-Violence." In *The Quiet Battle: Writings on the Theory and Practice of Non-Violent Resistance*, edited by Mulford Sibley. Garden City, N.Y.: Doubleday Anchor, 1963.

SIPRI Yearbook 1996. Oxford: Oxford University Press, 1996.

Smith, Philip. "Civil Society and Violence." In *The Web of Violence*, edited by Jennifer Turpin and Lester Kurtz. Chicago: University of Illinois, 1997.

Solomon, Robert, and Kathleen Higgins. *A Short History of Philosophy*. Oxford: Oxford University Press, 1996.

Spangler, David. *Conversations with John*. Elgin, Ill.: Lorian Press, 1980.

John Spanier and Steven Hook. *American Foreign Policy since World War II*, 13th ed. Washington, D.C.: Congressional Quarterly Inc., 1995.

Springborg, Robert. "Selling the War in the Gulf." In *After the Gulf War: For Peace in the Middle East*, edited by StJohn Kettle and Stephanie Dowrick. Leichardt, NSW: Pluto Press Australia, 1991.

Sri Aurobindo. *The Human Cycle, The Ideal of Human Unity, War and Self-Determination*. Pondicherry, India: Sri Aurobindo Trust, 1977.

————. *Letters on Yoga*. Part III. Pondicherry, India: Sri Aurobindo Ashram, 1995.

Steel, Ronald. *Walter Lippman and the American Century*. New York: Vintage Books, 1980.

Stein, Janet Gross. "Image, Identity, and Conflict Resolution." In *Managing Global Chaos: Sources of and Responses to International Conflict*, edited by Chester Crocker and Fen Hampson. Washington, D.C.: U.S. Institute of Peace, 1996.

Steiner, Henry, and Richard Alston. *International Human Rights in Context: Law, Politics, Morals*. Oxford: Clarendon Press, 1996.

Strauss, William and Neil Howe. *The Fourth Turning: An American Prophecy: What the Cycles of History Tell Us about America's Next Rendezvous with Destiny*. New York: Broadway Books, 1997.

Strobel, Warren. "The Media and U.S. Policies toward Intervention." *Managing Global Chaos: Sources of and Responses to International Conflict*, edited by Chester Crocker and Fen Hampson. Washington, D.C.: U.S. Institute of Peace, 1996.

Summy, Ralph, and Michael Salla, eds. "Europe 1989: The Role of Peace Research and the Peace Movement." In *Why the Cold War Ended*. Westport, CT: Greenwood Press, 1995.

Thoreau, Henry David. "On Civil Disobedience." In *The Pacifist Conscience*, edited by Peter Mayer. London: Penguin Books, 1966.

Virgil. *Aeneid*. Translated by W. F. Jackson Knight. London: Penguin, 1958.

Walt, Stephen. "International Relations: One World, Many Theories." *Foreign Policy* (Spring 1998): 29–46.

Waltz, Kenneth. *Man, the State and the State of War: A Theoretical Analysis*. New York: Columbia University Press, 1959.

Weber, Max. *Basic Concepts in Sociology*. Secaucus, N.J.: Citadel Press, 1980.

Williamson, Marianne. *The Healing of America*. New York: Simon and Schuster, 1997.

Woodward, Beverly. "Civil Society in Transition." In *Rethinking Peace*, edited by Robert Elias and Jennifer Turpin. Boulder, Colo.: Lynne Reinner, 1994.

Yogananda, Paramahamsa. *Autobiography of a Yogi*. Los Angeles: Self-Realization Fellowship, 1983.

Zakaria, Fareed. "The Rise of Illiberal Democracy." *Foreign Affairs* 76 (1997): 22–43.

Zuckerman, Mortimer. "A Second American Century." *Foreign Affairs* 77, 3 (1998): 19.

INDEX

Abolitionists, 87, 98, 100
Adams, John, 47
Adams, John Quincy, 73, 82–83
Addis, Adeno, 184
Afghanistan, 168, 192
Africa, 156
African Americans, 180, 187–89
Aidid, Mohammed Farah, 171
Alabama, 83
Albania, 146, 192, 197
Albright, Madeline, 171
Alexander, Tsar, 42
Angola, 168
Antietam, 102
Archetypes. *See* Collective unconscious
Argentina, 166
Arnold, Sir Edwin, 26
Articles of Confederation, 65–66. *See also* United States
Asia, 122, 156
Asoka, King, 2
Athens, 131. *See also* Greece
Aurobindo, Sri, 17, 38, 184
Australia, 60, 155, 182–86, 189, 208
Austria, 73; Hapsburg Empire, 135

Bailey, Thomas, 70, 106
Balkanization, 186
Balkans, 171, 174
Barbary Pirates, 71
Barry, Marion, 187–88
Bayard, Senator, 107
Beveridge, Albert, 118
Bismarck, Otto von, 42
Blaine, Jim, 114
Blair, Tony, 174
Bolen, Jean, 9, 17
Bolivar, Simon, 81
Bosnia, 6, 7, 172–74, 208
Boston, 63
Boston Tea Party, 63
Boutros-Ghali, Boutros, 196
Boxer Rebellion, 120
Brazil, 166, 193
Brezhnev Doctrine, 158, 169
Brimmer, Andrew, 187
British Guiana, 114
Brown, John, 98
Bryant, William Jennings, 92
Buddha, 21, 26–27, 50
Bull, Hedley, 36

Burke, Edmund, 69
Burma, 155, 192
Bush, George, 169–71
Bush, Robert, 49

California, 90–94
Callahan, David, 198
Cambodia, 192
Campbell, Joseph, 2, 16, 18, 19, 23, 26–28
Carranza, Venustiano, 131
Carter, Jimmy, 164–69, 187
Carthage, 131
Cherokee Nation, 83
Chicago Tribune, 115
Chile, 166
China, 92, 120, 124, 144, 207–8; conflict with USSR, 157–58; human rights, 192–96; Japanese imperialism, 139–40
Churchill, Winston, 147, 151, 155
Civil society, 43–45
Civil War, 66, 83, 97–107, 123. *See also* United States
Clarkson, Lawrence, 193
Clay, Henry, 82–83
Cleveland, Grover, 114, 116
Clinton Doctrine, 174
Clinton, William Jefferson, 170–74, 189–93, 196–97
CNN (Cable News Network), 171
Cold War, 151–152, 163, 170, 175
Collective unconscious, 2, 10–12; Archetypes, 4, 10–15, 206. *See also* Hero's Journey; Jung
Colombia, 123, 206
Colonialism, 153, 156
Communism, 151–59, 163–64, 167–68
Containment, 154
Confederate States of America, 99, 103
Constitution, 66, 103, 154. *See also* United States
Constitutional Convention, 66
Constructive engagement, 193, 195
Coolidge, Calvin, 139
Crazy Horse, 109
Cuba, 115–24, 139, 158, 192
Cuban missile crisis, 158

Cultural diversity, 7, 185–86, 208
Custer, George, 109
Czechoslovakia, 146, 158, 182–83

Dante, Alighieri, 21–22
Davidson, Gordon, 18, 48–49, 182
Davis, Jefferson, 99, 103
Dayton Peace Accord, 173
Declaration of Independence, 65, 67, 103, 154
DeJarnette, Daniel, 100
Delaware, 107
Democratic Party, 107, 109, 119, 122, 130, 170
Dickenson, John, 64
Diem, Ngo Dinh, 156
Dollar diplomacy, 124, 132
Dominican Republic, 124–25
Domino theory, 155
Douglas, Frederick (senator), 97–98
Dred Scott decision, 98. *See also* Slavery

East Timor, 158, 165, 207, 208
Economic sanctions, 207, 209
Einstein, Albert, 150
Eisenhower, Dwight D., 154–56, 167
Eliade, Mircia, 28, 30
Emancipation Proclamation, 102–4, 109. *See also* Slavery
Emerson, Ralph Waldo, 98
Era of Good Feeling, 75
Erikson, Erik, 14
Ethiopia, 145, 168
Ethnic cleansing, 174, 180
Ethnic conflict, 1, 7, 179, 197, 206–9
Ethnic minorities, 1–2, 180, 195–97, 206–9
European Union, 170, 172

Faircloth, Lauch, 187
Fascism, 6, 146, 151
Feinstein, David, 205
Florida, 74
Folger, Joseph, 49
Ford, Gerald, 158, 163–65
Fort Sumter, 99, 101. *See also* Civil War; United States

Founding Fathers, 5, 61, 66–67, 205, 209

Fourteen Points, 135, 196. *See also* Wilson, Woodrow

France, 52, 80, 104–6, 133, 138, 156, 172; Napoleonic Wars, 69–72; U.S. War of Independence, 62–65; World War II, 146–47, 152

Franco, Fransisco, 145

French Revolution, 68–69

Freud, Sigmund, 11, 20, 22; Oedipus complex, 16, 20, 22

Fromm, Erich, 14

Fukuyama, Francis, 44

Galbally Report, 185

Gallatin, Albert, 92

Gandhi, Mahatma, 140

Geneva, 156

Genocide, 172, 180, 208; Ethnic cleansing, 174, 180

George, King, 62–65

Gephardt, Richard, 194

Germany, 124, 133–37, 140, 145–50

Gladstone, William, 42

Gorbachev, Mikhail, 154, 169

Grant, Ulysses S., 103–4, 107, 109

Great Britain, 52, 84, 105, 209; Independence War with United States, 60–67; Latin American Independence, 73–75; Mexico Coup, 130–31; Monroe Doctrine, 80–82, 84; Napoleonic Wars, 70–72; Parliament, 62–63; Texas and Oregon, 87–90; Venezuela dispute, 114–15; World War I, 132–35, 139–40; World War II, 146–52

Great Depression, 140

Great Experiment, 65–66

Great Seal, 135–36, 184, 204–5

Greece, 60–61, 100, 152

Green, T. H., 39

Grenada, 168

Gross Stein, Janice, 14

Guam, 118, 122

Guilded Age, 109

Gurian, Michael, 16

Gurr, Ted Robert, 1, 179, 195

Habibie, President Bucharuddin (Indonesia), 207

Haiti, 139, 172

Hamilton, Alexander, 47, 131

Hapsburg Empire, 135; Austria, 73

Harding, Warren, 139

Harper's Ferry, 98; abolitionists, 87, 98, 100. *See also* Civil War

Harrison, William, 113–14

Hawaii, 114

Hay, John, 121

Hayes, Rutherford, 108

Hegel, Georg, 23, 38–41, 45, 50–51

Helsinki Accords, 165

Hero's Journey, 1–4; atonement, 4, 20–23; call to adventure, 2–3, 23–24, 46–47; deep forgetting, 2, 27–30, 53–54; grand synthesis, 1, 4, 27, 53; great remembering, 2–3, 24–26, 47; monomyth, 2, 9; return to society, 2, 4, 26–27, 51–53; sacred marriage, 4, 15–20, 49–50; slaying the dragon 4, 12–15, 48

Herrera, President Jose (Mexico), 90. *See also* Mexico

Hitler, Adolf, 40, 145–49

Holbrooke, Richard, 174

Holy Alliance, 73, 80–81

Homer, 18–20, 24, 31

Hong Kong, 192. *See also* China

Hoover, Herbert, 139

Hopi Indians, 190–91. *See also* Native Americans

Howe, Neil, 59, 204

Huerta, Victoriano, 130–31. *See also* Mexico

Human Rights, 1, 6, 43, 53, 68, 171, 173, 180; China, 192–96; U.S. foreign policy, 166–68, 206–7; Vietnam War, 163–65

Humanitarian intervention, 1, 6–7, 174, 180, 207–8

Illinois, 86

Independence War, 5, 61–65

India, 51, 89, 121, 191, 194, 207

Individuation process, 9–10

Indochina, 150, 155
Indonesia, 37, 155, 158, 165, 192, 207
Industrial Revolution, 39
Inter-American Development Bank, 166
International Monetary Fund, 36, 166
Iran, 152, 192
Iraq, 169–70, 197
Isolationism, 137, 140, 146–48
Italy, 140, 145–46

Jackson, Andrew, 74, 82–84
Japan, 124, 130, 139–40, 144–46, 149–51, 155–57, 170, 172, 193
Jay, John, and Jay Treaty, 70
Jefferson, Thomas, 60, 65, 68, 72, 97, 129, 190
Johnson, Andrew, 102–4
Johnson, Paul, 167
Jung, Carl, 5, 10–15, 20, 22, 25

Kai-shek, Chiang, 144
Kashmir, 207. See also India
Keen, Sam, 13, 49
Kennan, George, 154
Kennedy, John F., 156, 175, 188, 191, 196–99
Kennedy, Paul, 170, 172
Kissinger, Henry, 41, 46, 57, 158–59, 165
Klingberg, Frank, 59, 80
Korea, 124, 152, 166, 192–94
Kosovo, 1, 6–7, 173–75, 198–99, 208; Kosovo Liberation Army, 174
Kuwait, 169–70, 197

Laing, R. D., 19
Lampton, David, 192
Larkin, Thomas, 90
Latin America, 5, 74–75, 80–81, 156, 167. See also Western hemisphere
League of Nations, 6, 52, 136–40, 143–46
Lincoln, Abraham, 98, 101–4, 189
Lindbergh, Charles, 147
Little Big Horn, 109
Locke, John, 43, 65

Lodge, Henry Cabot, 121, 137
Louis XVI, King, 68
Lucas, George, 2

Mahan, Alfred, 121
Maine, 82
Maine, sinking of, 116. See also United States
Malaysia, 155
Manifest Destiny, 86–88, 92, 118, 121
Marcos, Ferdinand, 167
Marshall Plan, 189
Maryland, 65
Massachusetts, 63, 100, 105; Concord, 63; Lexington, 63
Maxmillian, Prince, 104–6
McCarthy, Joseph, 154
McKinley, William, 115, 116, 121
McLaughlin, Corinne, 18, 48–49, 182
Merk, Frederick, 86
Metternich, Prince von, 42
Mexico, 5, 84–87, 90–92, 94, 104–5, 130, 190
Mexico City, 91
Miller, John, 186–89
Milosevic, Slobodan, 173
Minh, Ho Chi, 155–56
Mississippi, 83, 103
Missouri Compromise, 98, 100. See also Slavery
Monroe Doctrine, 6, 79, 81, 104–7, 113–14, 123, 132, 139
Monroe, James, 47, 73–75, 79, 81
Morganthau, Hans, 37–38, 41
Morocco, 124
Morrison, Samuel, 62, 65, 84, 91, 103
Multiculturalism, 7, 185–86, 208
Mussolini, Benito, 145–46, 149

Naples, 80
Napoleon, 2, 72–73; Napoleonic Wars, 68, 75, 134
Napoleon III, 104–6
Native Americans, 74, 83–84, 108–9, 180, 190–91; Indian Removal Act, 83–84
Netherlands, 82
New Haven, 63

New Mexico, 6, 90–91. *See also* Mexico; United States
New World Order, 135–37, 166, 169–75, 190, 205, 209
New York, 62, 119
New Zealand, 155
Nicaragua, 124–25, 132, 139, 166–68
Niebhur, Reinhold, 41–42
Nixon, Richard, 157–58, 163
North Atlantic Treaty Organization (NATO), 2, 173–75, 198–99, 208

Ohio, 99
Oregon, 88, 92, 118. *See also* United States
Organization of African Unity (OAU), 208
Organization of American States (OAS), 208
O'Sullivan, John, 86
Otto, Rudolph, 20–22
Ottoman Empire, 135. *See also* Turkey

Pakistan, 60, 171
Panama, 123
Panama Canal, 123
Panama Congress, 81–82
Paris, 65, 106, 137
Peacekeeping, 171–72
Pearl Harbor, 148–49
Pearson, Carol, 10, 27
Philadelphia, 66, 75
Philippines, 118–23, 130, 140, 145, 166–67
Pinochet, Augusto, 167
Plato, 21, 28
Platt Amendment, 120, 139. *See also* Cuba
Plotinus, 21
Poland, 89
Polk, James, 5, 87–92
Portugal, 158
Pottawotami Massacre, 98
Pratt, Julius, 117, 124, 132
Providence, 5, 66, 86, 100, 105, 133, 136
Prussia, 39
Puerto Rico, 118, 121–22, 130

Racial Justice, 186–89
Radical reconstruction, 103–4, 107, 109. *See also* United States
Reagan Doctrine, 168
Reagan, Ronald, 154, 167–70
Redfield, James, 18, 30
Republican Party, 98, 107, 115, 121, 130, 137, 139, 143
Revenue Act, 62. *See also* Independence War
Rieber, Robert, 14
Rome, 66, 100
Roosevelt Corollary, 123, 125, 132
Roosevelt, Franklin, 143–52, 199
Roosevelt, Theodore, 42, 121–25, 129–31, 138
Rosenberg, Marshall, 15
Russia, 40, 48, 52, 73, 81, 124, 150, 208; Cold War, 151–53, 167–70; ethnic assimilation, 182–83; human rights, 194, 196
Russo-Japanese War, 124
Rwanda, 7, 172, 197

Sandino, Augusto, 139
Santa Anna, General, 85, 91, 94
Santa Cruz, 105
Santo Domingo, 107
Schlessinger, Arthur, Jr., 3, 59, 183–84, 203
Schlessinger, Arthur, Sr., 58, 60
Scruggs, William, 114
Self-determination, 115, 156, 163, 179–80; fascism, 143–45, 150–53; Spanish-American War, 118–22; Woodrow Wilson, 135–36, 140
Sepoy Mutiny, 121. *See also* India
Seward, William Henry, 105, 107
Shultz, George, 168
Slavery, 42, 84, 97–104, 107
Slidell, John, 90
Smith, Phillip, 44
Social Darwinism, 118
Somalia, 171–72, 197
Somoza, Anastasio, 139
Somoza Regime, 166–67
Sons of Liberty, 63–64. *See also* Independence War

Soviet Union. *See* Russia
Spain, 62–65, 73–74, 80–81, 91, 105, 107, 115–19, 122
Spangler, David, 66
Sri Lanka, 197
Stalin, Joseph, 40, 150
Stamp Act, 63. *See also* United States
Star Wars, 24
Strauss, William, 59, 204
Strobel, Warren, 171
Strong, Josiah, 118
Sudan, 197
Supreme Court, 83. *See also* United States

Taft, William, 124–25, 129–30, 138
Taiwan, 158, 193–94
Tardieu, Andre, 124
Taylor, Zachary, 91
Teller, Henry, 116
Texas, 5, 84–92, 102
Thailand, 60, 155
Thoreau, Henry David, 100
Tibet, 192, 195, 207
Townshend Act, 63–64
Treaty of Ghent, 72, 82
Treaty of Versailles, 6, 42, 52, 136–38, 143, 145
Treaty of Westphalia, 81
Truman Doctrine, 152
Truman, Harry, 151–55, 167
Turkey, 152, 183, 192, 194, 207
Tyler, John, 87–88

United Kingdom. *See* Great Britain
United Nations, 52–53, 151–52, 169–73, 196–98, 208; General Assembly, 169, 170; Secretariat, 197 ; Security Council, 152, 158, 169–75, 197–99
United States: African Americans, 180, 187–89; American century, 1, 2, 7; Declaration of Independence, 65, 67, 103, 154; Democratic Party, 107, 109, 119, 122, 130, 170; Era of Good Feeling, 75; Founding Fathers, 5, 61, 66–67, 205, 209; Great Experiment, 65–66; Great Seal, 135–36, 184, 204–5; Guilded Age, 109; Independence War, 5, 61–65; Indian Removal Act, 83–84; isolationism, 137, 140, 146–48; Native Americans, 74, 83–84, 108–9, 180, 190–91; racial justice, 186–89; Republican Party, 98, 107, 115, 121, 130, 137, 139, 143; slavery, 42, 84, 97–104, 107

Venezuela, 114
Vera Cruz, 131
Vermont, 116
Vietnam, 153–58, 163, 170
Virgil, 22, 28, 66
Virgin Mary, 12, 16
Virginia, 62–63

Walker, Francis, 108
Wall Street Crash, 140
Walt, Stephen, 38
Waltz, Kenneth, 42
Washington, D.C., 90
Washington, George, 64, 68–69, 72, 80, 82, 101
Wentworth, John, 86
Western hemisphere, 80, 82, 114, 123–25, 129–33, 138–39. *See also* Latin America
Williamson, Marianne, 10, 67, 186, 189, 191, 199
Wilson, Woodrow, 6, 42, 129–40, 143, 147, 151, 196, 198
Woodward, Beverly, 43–44
World Bank, 166
World Trade Organization (WTO), 193–94
World War I, 6, 132–35, 145–48
World War II, 52, 146–51, 156, 159, 182

Yeardley, Sir George, 62
Ying and Yang, 18
Yogananda, Paramahamsa, 27
Yugoslavia, 174, 182–83, 194

Zakaria, Fareed, 194
Zuckerman, Mortimer, 172

About the Author

Michael E. Salla is currently Researcher in Residence, Center for Global Peace, American University; and was previously Assistant Professor in the School of International Service, American University (1996–2001). He has been involved in non-official peacemaking efforts for ethnic conflicts in East Timor and Kosovo since 1995. He is the author of *Islamic Radicalism, Muslim Nations and the West* (1993); co-editor of *Why the Cold War Ended* (Greenwood Press, 1995); and *Essays on Peace* (1995). He has had over 60 articles and book reviews published in a variety of journals. He has a Ph.D. in Government from the University of Queensland, Australia.